MW01100500

Posthumanism and Educational Research

Focusing on the interdependence between human, animal, and machine, posthumanism redefines the meaning of the human being previously assumed in knowledge production. This movement challenges some of the most foundational concepts in educational theory and has implications within educational research, curriculum design and pedagogical interactions. In this volume, a group of international contributors use posthumanist theory to present new modes of institutional collaboration and pedagogical practice. They position posthumanism as a comprehensive theoretical project with connections to philosophy, animal studies, environmentalism, feminism, biology, queer theory and cognition. Researchers and scholars in curriculum studies and philosophy of education will benefit from the new research agendas presented by posthumanism.

Nathan Snaza is Director of the Bridge to Success Program and member of the English Department at the University of Richmond, USA. His writings have appeared in journals such as *Journal of Curriculum and Pedagogy, Angelaki, Educational Researcher* and *Journal for Critical Animal Studies.*

John A. Weaver is Professor of Curriculum Studies at Georgia Southern University, USA. He is the author of *Educating the Posthuman* (2010), *Popular Culture: A Primer* (2004/8), *Rethinking Academic Politics in Germany and The United States* (2000) and editor of four other books including *(Post) Modern Science (Education)* (2001). He is the author of 30 journal articles and book chapters.

Routledge International Studies in the Philosophy of Education

For a full list of titles in this series, please visit www.routledge.com

Posthumanism and Educational Research

Edited by

Nathan Snaza and John A. Weaver

Routledge
Taylor & Francis Group

NEW YORK   LONDON

First published 2015
by Routledge
711 Third Avenue, New York, NY 10017

and by Routledge
2 Park Square, Milton Park, Abingdon, Oxon OX14 4RN

*Routledge is an imprint of the Taylor & Francis Group,
an informa business*

© 2015 Taylor & Francis

Library of Congress Cataloging-in-Publication Data
A catalog record has been requested for this book.

ISBN13: 978-1-138-78235-8 (hbk)
ISBN13: 978-1-315-76916-5 (ebk)

Typeset in Sabon
by IBT Global.

SUSTAINABLE FORESTRY INITIATIVE

Certified Sourcing
www.sfiprogram.org
SFI-01234
SFI label applies to the text stock

Printed and bound in the United States of America
by IBT Global.

Contents

Foreword

Dennis Carlson

We live in an age in which democratic progressive cultural politics is very much about deconstructing the binary oppositions that have governed the construction of power relations of inequality and "otherness" in the modern era, which define some as fully human and recognized as having "unalienable human rights," while the Others of the modern era are relegated to the status of partially human, subhuman, or nonhuman "animals" who have no rights and therefore may be exploited and oppressed. This certainly is a divide bequeathed to the postmodern world largely by a religious legacy, as humans (at least male humans) were created in God's image and given dominion over the animals and the Earth. Somewhat ironically, the ancient Greeks had a similar mythology, which, as I have argued elsewhere, mapped nicely on the religious humanist mythology, and from there it found its way into Plato's philosophy (Carlson 2002). Humans were highest in the "great chain of being" because they were capable of reason and the contemplation of universal (godly) truths, such as justice, equity, and freedom. The genealogy of Western humanism, as Nathan Snaza indicates in his chapter in this volume, has interwoven these two roots and rhizomes, along with others throughout the centuries, and the result has been to construct a belief system, an epistemology, that is so deeply rooted and taken for granted that it seems the "natural" way things are. That, of course, is hardly the case, as Charles Darwin recognized more than a century and a half ago, which is why his obvious conclusions were treated with disbelief by many then and still are viewed as inconsistent with a literalist, fundamentalist religiosity. Nietzsche in philosophy, like Darwin in biology, tried to articulate a posthumanist philosophy for the coming posthumanist age. Yet he began to believe that most people were not ready for this news and might not be for another century. Consequently, he said, he wrote for future readers, a "philosophy of the future" (Nietzsche 1989, p. 42).

Now the emergence of a posthumanist discourse in the academy, and in curriculum studies more particularly, is a hopeful sign that perhaps people are ready to listen, ready to face the truth (Spanos 1993; Gough 2004). This is more than accepting that humans are indeed animals, but animals who are "the crown of creation" in nature, the most highly evolved. We are more highly evolved in intelligence of a certain sort and communication of a certain sort, but animals cannot neatly be positioned on an evolutionary great chain of being, with humans on the top. That would not really be moving toward posthumanism and would maintain the internal logic of humanism, in a scientific form. The posthumanist challenge is far more transformative and socially reconstructive and calls for forms of democratic education, curriculum, and pedagogy that deconstruct the commonsense, taken-for-granted naturalness of humanism, not from an antihumanist perspective, but as a movement beyond the limits and contradictions of the humanist project while still maintaining the modernist and humanists projects of rights, justice, equity, and freedom. History was and still is a human story, and perhaps that is inevitable.

But as the authors in this important volume argue, at least humanism has become more self-reflective, more able to turn a critical gaze back upon its own commonsense assumptions, its governing binaries and tropes. Posthumanism is a call to move beyond the limits and contradictions of the humanist project, to transcend its regimes of truth, without at the same time setting itself up as the antihuman, the antihumanist. For that would be to deny the important contributions of humanism to democratic and emancipatory projects over the past century and would only offer a politics of negation. Important human rights and social justice battles must continue, and much remains to be done to extend "human" rights to those who have been denied them in the United States and around the world. Instead of articulating an antihumanist politics, posthumanism at its best seeks to carve out a third space of critique and reconstruction where it might be possible to recognize the human as animal and reclaim a natural animality. Darwin ruptured the divide that separated the human and the animal more than 150 years ago. Yet, as the authors in this volume indicate, culturally we are just beginning to realize the momentous implications of that scientific rupturing. Posthumanism is critically important at this historical juncture, for unless we are able to move beyond the human–animal opposition, and with it the human–nature opposition, the future our children and grandchildren inherit is bleak and unsustainable.

Part of what is needed in a posthumanist curriculum is a genealogy of humanism, something Snaza sketches out in his introductory chapter and that other contributors develop in their own ways. A genealogy is a history of the present, in Foucault's terms, that traces back the roots of ideas such as "humanism" and the "human" to show how they have been involved in constituting human subjects along certain lines, and how, in doing so, they have been involved in constituting the "animal" in the mirror of the human, and what the effects of this have been in terms of capitalist modes of production. The devastating effects of a global corporate industry of raising food for animals who are then processed as food for humans, ending up on the shelves at Wal-Mart or at McDonald's, ready for mass consumption, can no longer be ignored. They are part of global environmental changes, associated with the unrestricted exploitation of the natural environment, that now threaten the human species, not just the other species.

A posthuman future is in some ways the logical completion and fulfill-ment of the modern, humanist project—as its utopian promise. It is more than a bit ironic that humanistic utopias have been slightly revised versions of Western culture's myth of origins, the Garden of Eden, when humans supposedly lived as animals in the natural world, nonalienated from other animals and their "species being," as Hegel and Marx said. Derrida (1987) has observed that this humanist mythology of a prehumanist utopic past suggests that progress follows a "path of repetition," but not one in which we actually return to a mythic past. For in "advancing towards the possi-bility of what you think you recognize," you are actually "going to what is quite other than what you think you recognize" (113). That is, the return to the garden that is the promise of posthumanism, like all utopias, provides us with only a general direction for an evolutionary development of culture. It is a pragmatic teleology that provides a promise and vision that must then be translated into pragmatic agendas and movements for change.

Posthumanism is already present, if yet unnamed, in the environmen-tal and animal rights movements, which are (in their most transformative forms) articulated with antiglobal capitalism movements, for the interests of neoliberal, global capitalism are beyond much of the environmental deg-radation and crisis we now witness. These new progressive movements, in turn, will need to articulate their interests with anticolonialist, antiracist, antisexist, and LGBTQ struggles, for all represent struggles by humanism's Others, and all are engaged in critiquing humanism's limitations and con-tradictions while at the same time affirming its democratic and emancipa-tory promise. As Snaza reminds us, "the human is a political category," and the critique of humanism must go beyond "asserting that some people excluded from the category of 'the human' are really human." The broader project must be to destabilize and disrupt "the *structure* of educational humanism" as a hegemonic discourse and rearticulate its promise with a counterhegemonic movement, based on a new "common sense" (in Grams-ci's terms).

Humanism is a great inheritance, in its most radically democratic and revolutionary forms. In *Specters of Marx* (1994), Derrida identified Marx-ism as a great "inheritance," from which much can be learned that has application to contemporary democratic cultural politics. "We are inheri-tors," he proclaimed, but that should not mean we receive something solid, unified, and already formed as an inheritance (94). The unity of an inheri-tance, if there is one, "can only consist in the injunction to reaffirm by choosing." To choose an inheritance is to "filter, select, criticize . . . [and] to sort out among several of the possibilities which inhabit the same injunc-tion" (40). Through such a choosing, an inheritance becomes a living mem-ory, open to being worked and reworked and stitched together with other inheritances. That is the important work of the authors in this volume.

REFERENCES

Carlson, D. (2002). *Leaving Safe Harbors: Toward a New Progressivism in American Education and Public Life.* New York: RoutledgeFalmer.
Derrida, J. (1987). *Of Spirit: Heidegger and the Question.* Trans. Geoffrey Bennington and Rachel Bowlby. Chicago: University of Chicago Press.
Derrida, J. (1994). *Specters of Marx: The State of the Debt, the Work of Mourning, and the New International.* Trans. Peggy Kamuf. New York: Routledge.
Gough, N. (2004). "RhizomANTically Becoming-Cyborg: Performing Posthuman Pedagogies." *Educational Philosophy and Theory* 36 (3): 253–265.
Nietzsche, F. (1989). *Beyond Good and Evil.* Buffalo, NY: Prometheus.
Spanos, W. (1993). *The End of Education: Toward Posthumanism.* Minneapolis: University of Minnesota Press.

Acknowledgments

This book is a radically collective production. Trillions of nonhumans directly (but, for most humanists, invisibly) have a claim to participation. It also emerges from a (supposedly) human community distributed in different institutions, countries, and disciplinary configurations. One of this book's arguments—that posthumanism is an intellectual assemblage connecting diverse expressions of political and affective engagement in rhizomatic ways—is similarly expressed in its facticity. Without this motley group of contributors, there could be no book. We wish to acknowledge here this labor in common.

We wish to think our editors at Routledge—Stacy Noto and Lauren Verity—for their enthusiasm, guidance, and willingness to invest in a text that will have been, we hope, an early drop in a great sea of posthumanist research washing away the humanist sediments of educational thinking. As this future anterior is not yet with us, their foresight deserves special commendation.

We wish also to thank those institutions that have been hospitable to this emergent line of thinking, especially the American Association for the Advancement of Curriculum Studies, the Foundation for Curriculum Theorizing (and their annual Bergamo Conference on Curriculum Theory and Classroom Practice), the Curriculum and Pedagogy Group, the new(ish) subsection of Division B of the American Educational Research Association (AERA) devoted to posthumanism, and the Critical Issues in Curriculum and Cultural Studies Special Interest Group of AERA. In addition to these institutional supports, the individual investments of Robert Helfenbein, Peter Appelbaum, João Paraskeva, Dennis Carlson, Gabriel Huddleston, Jennifer Sandlin, and Will Letts have been invaluable. Erik Malewski's long-standing affirmation of our work cannot go without acknowledgment.

We also wish to offer a few individual thanks.

Nathan: I want to thank my colleagues at the University of Richmond, in the English Department and elsewhere, for their support, encouragement, collegiality, and friendship. Suzanne Jones's support has made all the difference. I also want to thank my students, especially those in my "Feminist and Queer Theories," "Rethinking American Education," and "Democracy and Education" seminars. I would not have come to this project or, indeed, much of my current research in education without the intellectual companionship of Tom Friedrich, Kyle Greenwalt, Christian Haines, Timothy Lensmire, John Mowitt, Shaden Tageldin, and Mark Vagle. Above all, I owe an incalculable debt to Julietta Singh, my closest and most abiding companion, intellectual and otherwise, without whom I would not know how to think about the matters in this book or anything else. She, Isadora, and Cassie daily remind me that there is no difference between ethics and living, and that complexity can instigate extraordinary happiness.

John: I begin with an acknowledgment of the fruitfulness of my colleagues in curriculum studies at Georgia Southern: Marla Morris, Ming Fang He, Dan Chapman, and Sabrina Ross. In spite of the territorial encroachments and myopia of politicians and educational leaders in Georgia and the nation, we have created a vibrant and intellectually challenging program that has made a significant difference in the lives of many teachers, administrators, and professors. I thank my doctoral students who helped me think through many issues surrounding the posthuman and posthumanism, including Jeremy McClain, Sean Fretwell, Dana McCullough, Stacey Brown, Mimi Varquer, John Cook, Tony Young, and John Cato. This book is also for those who live the posthumanist life, such as the people at Hunter Cattle Del and Debra Ferguson, Anthony Ferguson (whose artistry is amazing), and Kristan Fretwell. Their farm is a model for a sustainable posthumanist lifestyle. It is also important for me to acknowledge the energy and intellectual commitment of my coeditor, Nathan Snaza. I was ready to move onto other topics and issues after my book *Educating the Posthuman* appeared in 2010, but Nathan invited me back into the conversation. I am so glad and thankful he did.

Helena Pedersen's "Education Policy Making for Social Change: A Posthumanist Intervention" originally appeared in 2010 in *Policy Futures in Education* 8 (6): 682–696. We wish to thank the editor of that journal, Michael Peters, for assistance in reprinting the essay.

Introduction
Education and the Posthumanist Turn

Nathan Snaza and John A. Weaver

[handwritten annotation: human nature has not changed]

As Donna Haraway (1991) noted almost thirty years ago, biotechnologies, virtual realties, prosthetics, pharmacology, robotics, and genetic manipulation all create a situation in which distinguishing the "ontologically" human from the inhuman or nonhuman is difficult if not impossible. Working from this axiom, N. Katherine Hayles (1999) argues that we have *already become* posthuman. It is not a question of consciousness or recognition or even of a task. The present moment *is* posthuman (without becoming "transhuman"). A posthumanist viewpoint, however, is different (Wolfe 2010). It is about how one relates to that present and to the enormous, almost crushing weight of several millennia of humanist thought. Although posthumanists vary enormously in the specifics of their engagements (and we believe we are nowhere near discovering all the permutations), they share in turning toward the legacies of humanism and using posthumanist reconceptualizations of human/animal/machine/thing relations to diagnose how humanism ignores, obscures, and disavows the *real* relations among beings and things that make up the stuff of the world.

The contributors to this book believe that a growing assemblage of texts that can be understood as "posthumanist" has the potential to reconfigure education. The whole thing: not just pedagogy, not just curricular design, not just educational research, and not just disciplines or even institutions such as schools at different levels (from preschool through doctoral programs). We all engage questions of pedagogy, of disciplinary or subject-area knowledges, of curricular experiences, of schools and their relations to a world within and beyond their walls, but we all approach these concerns with a sense they are implicated in a tectonic shift in the understanding of "the human" that has undergirded virtually all educational thought in the West.

Like so many philosophers of education before us, we ask: What is the aim of education? Virtually every previous answer to this question took for granted that only humans *have* education. Beginning with the posthumanist claim that "the human" is a cultural, historical production (a production involving religion, philosophy, biology, the social sciences, the humanities, agribusiness, etc.), we try to figure out how to ask what education means without presupposing that the answer will always, at least implicitly, take the form: "Education will make the kind of human who can . . ."

Since this book appears at a moment when "posthumanism" has become ubiquitous in humanistic and social scientific fields (and even to a certain extent in the "natural" sciences),[1] but has yet to receive much attention within educational fields, one task of this book is to introduce posthumanism. Indeed, in the second chapter of this book, Brad Petitfils sketches the importance of discussions surrounding the definition of the word *posthumanism* and its morphemes (especially the distinction between "the posthuman" and "posthumanism") within the field.[2] It is far from a settled matter, and rather than attempt any kind of homogenizing gestures, this book will operate from as broad an understanding of "posthumanism" as we can muster from our generally humanist, generally disciplinary vantage points.

It should not go without saying that our aim here is not to make the case for any particular theory or politics of posthumanism. Rather, we want to map a terrain for educational studies that is, almost entirely thus far, unacknowledged by contemporary academic discourse, science, and even common sense. Of course, this terrain is not actually "out there" in some elsewhere; it is, rather, the present, material, somatic, affective, and historical *stuff* of our world. Humanism, through a radical truncation of the definition of the "world" (so much is even suggested by the word's etymology), has made a tiny part of the world (what pertains to "humans") seem as if it were the whole. Humanism is, to combine phrases from classical rhetoric and Giorgio Agamben's (2004) philosophy, a machine that produces the human world as synecdoche. "Man" is *made to be* the measure of all things.

When "man" is the measure, it implies that humans and everything they do is inherently more valuable than any nonhuman animal or any thing (and what they do, although humanism has constructed elaborate frameworks for denying nonhuman actants the ability to "do" anything). As a result a hierarchical structure is invented to justify human actions and dismiss any other perspective that does not take into account or accept the predominance of a human viewpoint.[3]

When humanists wish to make a distinction between humans and other sentient beings, the differences concern not just "species" distinctions but also a drive toward human superiority. Let us take the human–animal distinction (in some ways the most fraught of the human's dialectical distanciations): Humans can think, animals cannot; humans can use language, animals do not; humans have souls, animals do not; humans feel pain and suffer, animals do not; and humans are rational, and animals are instinctual. What emerged from these dichotomies was the separation of humans from other animals to the point where humans were no longer viewed *as* animals. As these humanist mind-sets are challenged and exposed for being more ideology than reality,[4] what is also placed in doubt and questioned is the notion that humans are superior to other animals and, in fact, not "animals" at all. To question "man" as the measure of all things is to join with Matthew Calarco's (2008, 149) in suggesting that "we could simply let the human–animal distinction go or, at the very least, not insist on maintaining it." What would a school curriculum be like that used this subjunctive declaration as a starting point in thinking about the meaning, purpose, and relationship of science, literature, language, history, and mathematics? What would a world be that did not insist on human superiority or dominance and that did not disavow the human's ecological entanglements?

TOWARD AN OPEN DEFINITION OF POSTHUMANISM

What if the human doesn't have to be the measure? We would call "posthumanist" any thinking that responds to *this* question. Rather than jumping headlong into providing specific answers (as readers of "educational research"—at least as that term has come to be defined in an intellectual context almost wholly subsumed by neoliberal, globalized capitalism—might desire), we try to begin by noting how difficult this asking is. The main issue, one that Derrida and legions of deconstructionists, feminists, and postcolonial thinkers devoted considerable attention to, is that it is impossible to think, criticize, and write about a system *except from inside it*. One must always inhabit the discourse one wishes to throw into question. Thus, Jacques Derrida and Jean-Luc Nancy call for "re-treating": to go over a discourse (a tradition, a text, an institution) again, carefully and with absolute textual rigor, in order to detach oneself from it, to move away from it, to retreat from it or enable it to retreat from you. It is to turn toward in order to move away from.

Given our saturation in humanism, it is not even remotely possible at the present moment to conceptually or practically lay out a theory of posthumanist education or outline the contours of a posthumanist pedagogy. In Deleuze and Guattari's (1983) terms, the present moment is one of deterritorialization, when previously "solid" aspects of the world become fluid and things blur together; everything gets mixed up and moved around. If we rush to control the form it takes when it is over (to attempt to *plan* it), we automatically repeat the gesture that, in the end, will have been humanism's greatest repetition compulsion: the desire to plan. Reterritorializations will no doubt occur, but for the moment we want to revel in potential drifts.

The problem of planning and letting go of the desire to do so takes us directly to the ways humans and animals have been understood in relation, for the animal is said to not "have" the future. When you realize that much of our sense of what *will* happen is dependent on our being able to think with "future tense" verbs, this gets even more tricky, as the animal is said to lack language. Since politics means open (however limited) discussion of what to do about securing the future of a *polis*, and since animals cannot take part in the debate (because they lack language) and because they couldn't understand what the debate is about anyway (no language, no sense of "the future"), they have no part in "politics." An animal cannot "plan" for the future, but a human can.

Planning, in a different way, takes us to ways the human understands itself in relation to machiniality. However smart a computer is, we are told, it is no match for the human brain because it is materially limited by what it has been programmed (by a human) to do. What this difference amounts to is saying that computers cannot "plan" beyond what a human has "planned" for them (*Blade Runner*, the *Terminator* movies, etc., are a symptom of our fear that this is not the case). In both cases, we are told that the human—and the human alone—is capable of planning. Moving into the educational context, the thing that the human plans above all else is the desired form an educated human will take. As Rousseau wrote in *Emile* (1979): "remember that before daring to undertake the formation of a man, one must have made oneself a man" (95). Those who are already "human" will control the educations of the young so that they too become "human." The most important "learning outcome" (to use the language of contemporary schooling) is that students become "humans" capable of participating in the global economy as productive workers and consumers. The posthumanist challenge is to give up on planning in order to actualize the kinds of potential indicated in a Spinozist immanent ethics: We don't know yet what a body can do, nor do we know what we beings who are used to thinking of ourselves as "human" are capable of.

If giving up on planning seems too much a stretch at the moment, at the very least posthumanist politics would require us to rethink what a democracy means by extending the parameters of who and what is permitted to participate in and be part of a "public" and "public" debate. According to Jane Bennett (2010, 101), publics do not exist naturally; they are invented, configured, and reconfigured depending on the topic at hand. They are also not solely "human": "Problems give rise to publics, publics are groups of bodies with the capacity to affect and be affected." The newly sworn in mayor of New York City, Bill de Blasio, has proclaimed that the horse-drawn carriages in New York City are examples of animal cruelty. The unionized represented by the Teamsters have fired back, citing all the different ways the horses are treated in humane ways, including, since a 2010 agreement, the horses' entitlement to vacation days. In the middle of this public debate are the horses, who in many paradoxical ways have more "rights" than many who live in New York City or anywhere (most working Americas are not entitled to vacation days or suitable shelter). How the horses are treated, viewed, positioned, and represented demonstrates how animals affect and are affected by public debates, even if this also dramatizes how the animals are systematically excluded from participation. If the mayor succeeds in banning carriages in the city, the futures of the drivers will be placed in doubt, but so will those of the horses. For Bennett (2010, 108), what this kind of debate does is to create what she

[handwritten margin notes: "are bugs good? included... but we still making decision on our categories like stairs"]

calls a "vital materialist theory of democracy" that "seeks to transform the divide between speaking subjects and mute objects into a set of differential tendencies and variable capabilities." A vital materialist theory of democracy requires humans to plan differently, to account not only for the different human constituencies, but also the nonhuman *participants* in public debates. This requirement will not only transform planning in public settings; it will certainly make it more complex and multilayered in a way that goes beyond humanist "democracy."

As these last three paragraphs reveal, one way to begin tracing posthumanist thought is to sketch how it is critically interrogating the relations among the terms in the "cybernetic triangle" of human, animal, and machine. Posthumanism draws from a wide range of academic disciplines, including biology, cybernetics, philosophy, animal studies, political theory, psychology, and literary studies, in order to challenge long-standing ideas about the definition of "the human" and its place in the world (Haraway 2008; Wolfe 2010). Indeed, one of the reasons we are so excited about posthumanism is that it doesn't just require interdisciplinary thought; it calls into question the entirety of the disciplinary structure, its segregations of fields, its methodological provincialism. Posthumanism, therefore, offers unmeasurable potential to stimulate antidisciplinary research that cuts across the natural and social sciences as well as the humanities (since these very divisions are all constructed around the human, even if only as "knowing" subject). It would be very possible, for example, to imagine a curriculum studies project undertaken by a theorist of pedagogy, a horticulturist, an etymologist, a geneticist, an urban planner, a sociologist, and an architect.

Such a research project, radical as it may seem from prevailing disciplinary perspectives, does not address what will turn out to be the greatest difficulty facing a future posthumanist (educational) research: acknowledging the "agency" of knowing in nonhuman subjects. What sorts of research could emerge that might include nonhumans as *subjects*? Although this question is implicit in many of the contributions to this volume, Stephanie Springgay's chapter takes it up directly, pointing to the ways in which affect theory, Deleuze-Guattarian philosophy, and a pragmatics of aesthetics open onto radically in- or ahuman forms of research. As in the posthumanist engagements with ecological action and education in the chapters by jan jagodzinski, Jason Wallin, and Nikki Rotas, embodiment—material, affective, finite—proves to be of greater importance (ontologically) than consciousness. This shift away from consciousness (which is not a move toward psychoanalytic theories of the unconscious) was signaled by Hayles (1999, 2–3): "the posthuman view considers consciousness, regarded as the seat of human identity in the Western tradition long before Descartes thought he was a mind thinking, as an epiphenomenon, as an evolutionary upstart trying to claim that it is the whole show when in actuality it is only a minor sideshow." In this move away from consciousness and toward embodiment, materiality, and affect, posthumanism puts enormous pressure on human-ist research methods that remain stuck in this "sideshow." As Wolfe (2009, 572) puts it, "It is a matter, then, of locating [posthumanism] and its chal-lenge to humanist modes of reading, interpretation, and critical thought not just 'out there,' among birds and beasts, but 'in here' as well, at the heat of this thing we call human." Part of posthumanist thought, then, involves diagnosing the ways that humanism has come to structure our thought, our research, and—perhaps most crucially—our sense of what politics and education could mean in a future not beholden to humanist enclosure.

John Weaver's (2010) *Educating the Posthuman* is an important touch-stone for this collection in that it is—so far as we are aware—the first book-length engagement among curriculum studies, educational philosophy, and posthumanism. The final part of the book contains three essays, all to varying degrees autobiographical, that take Weaver's book (and, in the cases of Noel Gough's and Annette Gough's essays, its engagements with *their* earlier work) as a point of departure. The field has changed so rapidly since the publication of *Educating the Posthuman* that Weaver's chapter in this volume takes up the lacunae in that book, revisiting his arguments in relation to critical animal studies and the emergence of "Object Oriented Ontology" (OOO). This is so because while the term *posthumanism* gained attention in the mid-1990s for its attentions to cybernetics, biosciences, science fiction, and related questions of the human–machine interface, in recent years it has come to include a set of problems and questions associ-ated with the (similarly emergent) field of "critical animal studies." Draw-ing extensively on the work of Haraway (1991), these scholars examine human–animal interactions (companion animals, factory farming, animal experimentation), human–animal hybridization, and the largely disavowed animality of the human (Lemm 2009). In different ways, chapters by Marla Morris, Alyce Miller, and Helena Pedersen in this volume emerge from developments in this stream of research and grapple with its implications for education.

Returning to the human–machine relation, but with a crucial differ-ence, the burgeoning OOO movement asks not about machines but about "things" (beginning with Graham Harman's reinterpretation of Heidegger's writings about a hammer). As Weaver and Jason Wallin explore in this volume, OOO seeks to restore ontological priority to *all* things, without asking about what things mean *for* humans. Although this field is so new that its potential and its problems are not yet entirely clear, it has the signal virtue of demonstrating that when only focusing on the cybernetic triangle, "posthumanism [. . .] is not posthumanist enough" (Bogost 2011, 8). At stake is the production of a *radically* nonanthropocentric account of the world, one that must acknowledge the seeming inescapability of anthro-pocentrism for the human "knower." In other words, OOO pushes us to foreground the necessary *failure* of human knowledge to gain access to the world. While this might sound like a depressing form of resignation, the hope of this field, as Bogost (2011) makes clear, is to return us to "wonder" in the face of the world. *a we*

POSTHUMANIST EDUCATION AND EDUCATIONAL RESEARCH

We think that educational studies could benefit from more wonder. Indeed, in large part due to the neoliberal takeover of schooling at all levels and its attendant shrinking of "educational research" to mean randomized, large-scale quantitative studies of specific pedagogical and curricular interventions, educational studies have become tedious, instrumental, and boring. The present moment's restriction on what counts as "education" and "educational research" have resulted in public debates about schooling that spin in circles, asking again and again the question "what works?" without bothering to ask the far more important question, "works for *what?*" Posthumanism, by virtue of seeming so far outside the realm of what is ordinarily considered relevant to these discussions, may just be able to explode these tired debates, reorienting us toward futures that are far less foreclosed, far less preplanned. *based on humanism*

In precisely this way, posthumanist education is a continuation of the radical, democratic, even utopian projects of the twentieth-century.[5] All the contributors to this volume seek not only schools that are less authoritarian and oppressive, but also a global social formation that is not driven by exploitation, dehumanization, and asymmetrical violence.[6] Thinking about machines, animals, and things is important not (only) because it turns us away from narrowly human political concerns but because the *humanist* relations to these things is shot through with violence and exploitation. Indeed, one of the factors that made dehumanization such a central facet of modernity is the ease with which "humans" feel they can do *anything they want* to all "nonhumans" simply by virtue of these other things and beings' noninclusion in that political category (Snaza, this volume). We believe that contemporary issues like animal rights, the already accomplished ecological catastrophe, bioethics and biotechnology, and the increasing imbrication of human culture with computers and other machines are simply not thinkable within existing humanist frames of thought (Morton 2013). The most glaring problems of our present politics cannot be understood, let alone addressed, within politics or education as we presently understand them (Smith 2011; Wolfe 2012). We need a politics that would recognize animals and things as subjects, and the contributions to this book all explore forms of education that do the same. Given that humanist ideas have installed themselves in literally *every* aspect of "human" thought, the scope of this project is enormous and probably Sisyphean. Although the chapters that follow will all take up some aspect of this task, we want to highlight two issues here that will be of special importance to the educational scholar.

First, the problem of disciplinarity. While we live in a moment when inter-disciplinary work is the watchword of deans, funding agencies, and cutting-edge journals, our institutions are overwhelmingly and often unconsciously disciplinary. Of course, "educational studies" has long been interdisciplinary in the sense that its practitioners mobilize "methods" from a variety of social sciences (psychology, sociology, and anthropology primarily) to understand the "objects" called schools, curricula, and pedagogies. What a broad, post-humanist approach to the history of education and educational institutions reveals is that the most primary divisions in the contemporary academic world—distinctions separating the "human" sciences from the "natural" sciences and the humanities—all *presuppose* "the human" in some form or other and cannot be understood without that "human."

This realization will require us to rethink all the disciplinary divisions that have multiplied at universities in recent decades (many universities now offer more than *one hundred* majors), as well as the divisions among "sub-jects" that prevail in K–12 schools (and we might recall that at one time, those "subjects" were divided in order to prepare students for the disci-plines they would encounter in college). Here, despite an obvious human-ism at the level of their lexicons, the alternative, progressive experiments in education associated with Dewey, Montessori, and Steiner might prove fruitful in novel ways (see Morris, this volume). To give one example that is increasingly visible, the practice of building elementary curricula around gardens opens up not just a thorough integration of different types of disci-plinary knowledge (one needs math, ecology, history, economics, and biol-ogy in order to undertake even the most basic experiments in agriculture) but also a potentially posthumanist viewpoint. While there are no doubt such curricula that are radically humanist, offering students a dominion- or stewardship-based way of understanding the human's relations to plants, soil, animals, wood, water supplies, tools, and so on, these curricula could also produce the awareness of the fundamentally *interconnected*, non-dis-sociable nature of these relations (see Rotas, this volume). "Humans" *are* not without all these Others: These nonhuman Others are not here for us to "use"; they are the condition of possibility for our existence. Although this is one example among myriad possible examples, it gives a quick thumb-nail sketch of how posthumanism might reconfigure classroom practice and curriculum.

The posthumanist challenge to prevailing ideas of disciplinarity also plays out at the level of educational research. The research "methods" that dominate the field—whether quantitative or qualitative—all presume a knowing "human" researcher capable of objectively knowing the stu-dents, teachers, schools, and curricula s/he observes, measures, and seeks to understand. Traditional educational research methods assume a subject/object relationship in the world. The "researcher" is the subject who enters into the "world" or object in order to understand and give meaning to the world. This subject–object hierarchy instinctively and presumptively

What abat hermantus

Introduction 9

alienates the researcher from the world, and as a result from reality, and demotes the world to an object to be analyzed, probed, prodded, tested, manipulated, and silenced. By separating the researcher from the world educational research creates an authorial relationship between humans and nonhumans. In quantitative research this subject–object relationship has created a fantasyland in which databases and correlational numbers have served as substitutes for realities. A language of dominance has emerged in which the researcher hides behind "data" and the researcher proclaims s/he is "just allowing the data to speak." Data, if they had mouths, do not speak; researchers who manipulate, compile, aggregate, and sort data speak through data. In qualitative research, what has emerged from this subject–object invention is a confessional lamentation in which the researcher mourns his or her inability to capture an uncertain, confusing, complex, and always shifting reality and apologizes for speaking for other people and objects. Yet, this is all they can do. This is all anyone can do, even quantitative researchers who would contest and deny their own involvement in inventing data. The current subject–object relationship has created what we call a methodocentrism in which the methodology of a researcher and their faithfulness to a method is the primary concern of most research. Methodocentrism relegates most humans, other sentient beings, and nonsentient objects to a subordinate position in which the role of these beings in their own reality and other realities is removed from the researchers work.

multiple causclin

Hermedrus?

What would happen is the subject–object relationship and methodocentrism were rejected and replaced? What if educational scholars began to look at the world as one in which objects simultaneously interact with one another, shaping their realities through these interactions but, at the same time, always receding from these realities in order to create and shape their own reality? What this means in terms of educational research is that whenever research is conducted in schools there is much more going on than interaction between a teacher and students or teachers and teachers or students and students. There are experiences happening all the time, all over the school, independent of humans. There are always interactions between humans and nonhuman sentient beings and humans and nonsentient objects, such as computers, doors, playgrounds, hallways, utensils, trays, balls, windows, desks, and so on. This is a domain where educational scholars will find it very helpful to consult the recent developments in OOO or Speculative Realism. With some hope and shifts of mind-set, what Michel Serres (2012, 33) argues is happening in the life and earth sciences can emerge in education: "They practice a more sharing, open, connected way of knowing, in which he who knows participates in the things he knows, is even reborn from them, tries to speak their language, listens to their voices, respects their habitat, lives the same evolutionary history, is enchanted by their narratives, limits finally, through them or for them, his power and his politics."

POSTHUMANIST POLITICS

The contributions to this collection strive to situate posthumanist thought in relation to both educational studies—especially educational philosophy and curriculum studies—and politics. The problem is not simply how to produce *more* critiques of prevailing social formations, institutions of learning, disciplinarity, pedagogical practices, and so on. We hope that posthumanism offers something like a self-organizing structure that draws together a variety of politico-theoretical fields that have all been taken up individually by educational scholars: feminist, antiracist, postcolonial, queer, and disability studies; post-structuralism; Nietzschean, Deleuzian, and Foucaultian philosophy; animal studies; media and cultural studies; affect theory; new materialisms; and ecology. Politically, posthumanism offers a way of connecting what have been sadly separable strands of inter-disciplinary political thought and revealing powerful new ways of putting these forces to work in the service of the affirmation of different potential futures (Chen 2012; Grosz 2004). That is, posthumanist politics is not, except contingently, driven by critique of the prevailing order. It is, instead, a radical commitment to experimentation with *new*, unpredictable, perhaps even seemingly impossible forms of relation among animals, plants, objects, machines, and, yes, even those of us who still think of ourselves as "humans." While the *post* in posthumanism will be taken up differently in each chapter that follows, posthumanism's greatest contribution to our thought might not be apparent until we can *get over* humanism and get to work doing something *else*. Education can be so much more than we think. We can be so much more than we think. Just wonder.

ORGANIZATION OF THE BOOK

This book is divided into four parts. The first, "Humanism, Posthumanism, and Educational Research," lays out some of the most crucial directions in which posthumanist educational research is emerging. In one sense, the section has an introductory function, even though only one chapter, Snaza's "Toward a Genealogy of Educational Humanism," is explicitly so, sketching an account of the educational "humanism" against or after which posthumanist education unfurls. Petitfils meditates on terminological complexity within posthumanism and, in the process, reveals technological posthumanism's entanglements with, but divergences from, postmodern theories (of education). Morris situates the anthropocentrism of humanist progressive education in relation to animal bodies and animal "interiority," thus posthumanizing critical curriculum/animal studies. Pedersen uses a posthumanist variety of critical animal studies to address problems of educational policy making in ways that acknowledge the more-than-human inhabitants of schools. Springgay pushes posthumanist (and affective) theories of knowledge into an uneasy, experimental methodology that throws into question the entirety of what "research" would or could entail. These chapters cannot be said to provide an overview of posthumanist thought, but they constellate a series of questions and concepts that will help readers orient themselves through the later parts.

The two chapters in Part II, "Attuning to the More-Than–Human Complexities of the Classroom," emerge out of material and embodied classroom engagements, engaging theory in order to account for the more than human complexities of these engagements. Rotas's chapter turns on an "ugly" class, revealing the insidiousness of "obviousness" in pedagogy and curriculum studies. Miller examines a course on "Animals and Ethics," both in its design and teaching, in relation to a complex set of tensions between animal studies and feminism, animal's and women's bodies, feminine and masculine pedagogies. What these chapters demonstrate is the urgency of locating posthumanist experiments with pedagogy at the most bodily, affective, institutionally captured levels.

Part III, "Ecological Aesthetics," sees jan jagodzinski and Jason Wallin—who recently cowrote *Art-Based Research* (2013)—constellating aesthetics, geophilosophy, and a "dark" approach to the ecological and educational possibilities in the Anthropocene. Both turn to artworks in order to consider forms of pedagogy—not often housed in schools—that attempt to attune viewers to a more-than-human world in which the human's place is radically threatened by an already accomplished ecological catastrophe.

The final part, "What Educational Posthumanism Will Have Been," contains chapters by three of the most well-known posthumanist educational scholars who find occasion to revisit their past research in relation to a very quickly growing and changing field. All three chapters also begin by addressing Weaver's (2010) *Educating the Posthuman*. Noel Gough and Annette Gough, in fact, address Weaver's writing about *their own* work in this book—work that was undertaken at the intersection of environmental education, autobiography, and continental philosophy—and which *subsequently* became "posthumanist." Weaver's chapter closes the book by taking up the significant gaps that now appear in *Educating the Posthuman* given how quickly the field has expanded in just four years. We end the book with this sort of recursive loop in order to spur readers into a future educational philosophy and research that will have made this book, too, seem limited. We hope, before this happens, that readers will find cause to wonder at just how *open* posthumanism makes education—and its theorization—feel.

NOTES

1. The research dealing with posthumanism is abundant in the humanities. Much of it engages the scholarship of Haraway (1989, 1991, 1997, 2008).

For Hayles (1999), the posthuman is an ontological shift, one that calls for a dynamic rethinking of the importance and place of the humanities in the university and society. This work is often referred to as the digital humanities and includes Hayles (2012), Hansen (2004), Kittler (1990, 1999, 2010), and Johnston (1997, 1998, 2008). There are also numerous edited collections on the digital humanities (Hayles and Pressman 2013; Bartscherer and Coover 2011; Gitelman 2013; and Burdick et. al. 2012). When discussing posthumanism as a challenge to the prevalence of humanism in the humanities, one should start with Cary Wolfe (2003, 2008, 2010, 2012). Like Wolfe, other posthumanists take up critical animal studies (Pettman 2012; Calarco 2008; Rowlands 2009; Nagel 1979; Lemm 2009). Carlson (2008) is a major contribution to a theological understanding of posthumanism. The work of Serres (2011, 2012) is indispensible. In the social sciences it is best to begin with Latour (1987, 1993, 1999, 2004, 2009, 2013) or Rabinow (1996, 1999) For an idea of how anthropologists have entered into the fray, see Kohn (2013), Kirksey and Helmreich (2010), and Fischer (2007). In political theory, see Bennett (2010). In sociology, see Pedersen (2010).
2. Cary Wolfe's (2010) *What Is Posthumanism?* sketches the complexity of the field, essentially mapping posthumanist studies on two axes: object of study and method of study. Both axes run from "humanist" to "posthumanist," so that one can find humanist studies of properly humanist objects, but also humanist studies of posthuman objects, and so on.
3. In noting this, posthumanism thus extends a critique of binary oppositions that has emerged in feminist, antiracist, postcolonial, queer, and post-structuralist thought (for example, Cixous and Clement 1986).
4. Which is not to say that "ideology" is not immediately real, material, and corporeal. Rather, we want to foreground that the material, affective becoming of the world is always already misrecognized by the back-formations of conscious thought.
5. But not only the twentieth century, as the writings by people like Charles Darwin, Friedrich Nietzsche, and Baruch Spinoza are proving enormously generative for posthumanist thought, to say nothing of the critiques of property, male supremacy, and racialization that have accompanied modernity's hardening of political divisions masquerading as ontological.
6. Violence is inescapable. The ethical questions are: What forms of violence, in what circumstances, for what purposes?

REFERENCES

Agamben, G. (2004). *The Open: Man and Animal.* Trans. K. Attell. Stanford, CA: Stanford University Press.
Bartscherer, T., and Coover, R., eds. (2011). *Switching Codes: Thinking through Digital Technology in the Humanities and the Arts.* Chicago: University of Chicago Press.
Bennett, J. (2010). *Vibrant Matter: A Political Ecology of Things.* Durham, NC: Duke University Press.
Bogost, I. (2011). *Alien Phenomenology, or What It's Like to Be a Thing.* Minneapolis: University of Minnesota Press.
Burdick, A., Druker, J., Lunenfeld, P., Pressner, T., and Schnapp, J., eds. (2012). *Digital Humanities.* Cambridge, MA: MIT Press.
Caputo, J. (2013). *The Insistence of God: A Theology of Perhaps.* Bloomington: Indiana University Press.

Carlson, T. (2008). *The Indiscrete Image: Infinitude and Creation of the Human.* Chicago: University of Chicago Press.

Chen, M. Y. (2012). *Animacies: Biopolitics, Racial Mattering, and Queer Affect.* Durhuam, NC: Duke University Press.

Cixous, H., and Clement, C. (1986). *The Newly Born Woman.* Trans. B. Wing. Minneapolis: University of Minnesota Press.

Deleuze, G., and Guattari, F. (1983). *Anti-Oedipus.* Trans. R. Hurley, M. Seem, and H. Lane. Minneapolis: University of Minnesota Press.

Fischer, M. (2007). "Four Genealogies for a Recombinant Anthropology of Science and Technology." *Cultural Anthropology* 22 (4): 539–615.

Gitelman, L., ed. (2013). *"Raw Data" Is an Oxymoron.* Cambridge, MA: MIT Press.

Grosz, E. (2004). *The Nick of Time: Politics, Evolution, and the Untimely.* Durham, NC: Duke University Press.

Hansen, M. (2004). *New Philosophy for New Media.* Cambridge, MA: MIT Press.

Haraway, D. (1989). *Primate Visions: Gender, Race, and Nature in the World of Modern Science.* New York: Routledge.

Haraway, D. (1991). *Simians, Cyborgs, and Women.* New York: Routledge.

Haraway, D. (1997). *Modest_Witness@Second_Millennium. FemaleMan©_ Meets_OncoMouse™.* New York: Routledge.

Haraway, D. (2008). *When Species Meet.* Minneapolis: University of Minnesota Press.

Hayles, N.K. (1999). *How We Became Posthuman: Virtual Bodies in Cybernetics, Literature, and Informatics.* Chicago: University of Chicago Press.

Hayles, N.K. (2012). *How We Think: Digital Media and Contemporary Technogensis.* Chicago: University of Chicago Press.

Hayles, N.K., and Pressman, J. (2013). *Comparative Textual Media: Transforming the Humanities in the Postprint Age.* Minneapolis: University of Minnesota Press.

jagodzinski, j., and Wallin, J. (2013). *Arts-Based Research: A Critique and a Proposal.* Rotterdam: Sense Publishers.

Johnston, J., ed. (1997). *Friedrich A. Kittler Essays: Literature Media Information Systems.* Amsterdam: G+B Arts Publishers.

Johnston, J. (1998). *Information Multiplicity: American Fiction in the Age of Media Saturation.* Baltimore, MD: Johns Hopkins University Press.

Johnston, J. (2008). *Allure of Machinic Life: Cybernetics, Artificial Life, and the New AI.* Cambridge, MA: MIT Press.

Kirksey, S.E., and Helmreich, S. (2010). "The Emergence of Multispecies Ethnography." *Cultural Anthropology* 25 (4): 545–576.

Kittler, F. (1990). *Discourse Networks: 1800/1900.* Trans. M. Metteer and C. Cullins. Palo Alto, CA: Stanford University Press.

Kittler, F. (1999). *Gramophone, Film, Typewriter.* Trans. G. Winthrop-Young and M. Wutz. Palo Alto, CA: Stanford University Press.

Kittler, F. (2010). *Optical Media.* Malden, MA: Polity.

Kohn, E. (2013). *How Forests Think: Toward an Anthropology beyond the Human.* Berkeley: University of California Press.

Latour, B. (1987). *Science in Action.* Cambridge, MA: Harvard University Press.

Latour, B. (1993). *We Have Never Been Modern.* Cambridge, MA: Harvard University Press.

Latour, B. (1999). *Pandora's Hope: Essays on the Reality of Science Studies.* Cambridge, MA: Harvard University Press.

Latour, B. (2004). *Politics of Nature: How to Bring the Sciences into Democracy.* Cambridge, MA: Harvard University Press.

Latour, B. (2009). "Will Non-Humans Be Saved? An Argument in Ecotheology." *Journal of the Royal Anthropological Institute* 15:459–475.

Latour, B. (2013). *An Inquiry into Modes of Existence: An Anthropology of the Moderns.* Cambridge, MA: Harvard University Press.

Lemm, V. (2009). *Nietzsche's Animal Philosophy: Culture, Politics, and the Animality of Human Being.* New York: Fordham University Press.

Morton, T. (2013). *Hyperobjects: Philosophy and Ecology after the End of the World.* Minneapolis: University of Minnesota Press.

Nagel, T. (1979). "What Is It Like to Be a Bat?" In *Moral Questions,* 165–180. Cambridge: Cambridge University Press.

Pedersen, H. (2010). *Animals in Schools: Processes and Strategies in Human-Animal Education.* West Lafayette, IN: Purdue University Press.

Pettman, D. (2011). *Human Error: Species-Being and Media Machines.* Minneapolis: University of Minnesota Press.

Rabinow, P. (1996). *Making PCR: A Story of Biotechnology.* Chicago: University of Chicago Press.

Rabinow, P. (1999). *French DNA: Trouble in Purgatory.* Chicago: University of Chicago Press.

Rousseau, J-J. (1979). *Emile; or on Education.* Trans. A. Bloom. New York: Basic Books.

Rowlands, M. (2009). *The Philosopher and the Wolf.* New York: Pegasus' Books.

Serres, M. (2011). *Variations of the Body.* Minneapolis, MN: Univocal Press.

Serres, M. (2012). Biogea. Minneapolis, MN: Univocal Press.

Smith, M. (2011). *Against Ecological Sovereignty: Ethics, Biopolitics, and Saving the Natural World.* Minneapolis: University of Minnesota Press.

Weaver, J. (2010). *Educating the Posthuman: Biosciences, Fiction, and Curriculum Studies.* Rotterdam: Sense Publishers.

Wolfe, C., ed. (2003). *Zootologies: The Question of the Animal.* Minneapolis: University of Minnesota Press.

Wolfe, C., ed. (2008). *Philosophy and Animal Life.* New York: Columbia University Press.

Wolfe, C. (2009). "Human, All Too Human: 'Animal Studies' and the Humanities." *PMLA* 124 (2): 564–575.

Wolfe, C. (2010). *What Is Posthumanism?* Minneapolis: University of Minnesota Press.

Wolfe, C. (2012). *Before the Law: Humans and Other Animals in a Biopolitical Frame.* Chicago: University of Chicago Press.

Part I

Humanism, Posthumanism, and Educational Research

1 Toward a Genealogy of Educational Humanism

Nathan Snaza

> The question as to what it means to be human is also, and perhaps even first of all, an *educational* question. (Biesta 2006, 2)

Progressive and radical educators would do well to engage posthumanist philosophies in order to extend the political projects of feminist, antiracist, anticolonial, queer, and Marxist pedagogies. This is especially important because often these politicized educational praxes are staged around a notion of humanization that ends up reinscribing the same structural mechanism of dehumanization they purportedly critique, one that is firmly lodged within humanism, broadly understood. Thus, I would like to begin this book by asking what "humanism" is, which in turn raises the question of what is "human." I will trace familiar answers to the question "What is humanism?"—answers associated with historical moments or events with (disputed but largely utilized) proper names: Ancient Greece, the Renaissance, the Enlightenment, Modernity.[1] While the general sense of the answers is probably familiar to some readers, what interests me here are a) the ways we have come to think about the continuities and discontinuities that make up this seemingly progressive historical development and b) bringing the familiar history into relation with ideologically disavowed material relations.

GENEALOGY AND HUMANISM

What we should attend to in this evolution of "humanism" and its attendant morphemes (the human, the humanities, humanity, humane) is the fact that every stage of it was beset with anxieties, uncertainties, hegemonic struggles, and a quality of contingency. The transformations "humanism" has undergone in the West should not be understood as the progressive unfolding of history, but as the outcome of a continuous and overlapping series of intensities: moments or nodes where power relations become overdetermined and the outcome or output is unpredictable. What follows is therefore a sketch not of a "history" but a "genealogy" in the Nietzschean sense. As Foucault reads Nietzsche, "The genealogist needs history to dispel the chimeras of the origin [. . .] He must be able to recognize the events of history, its jolts, its surprises, its unsteady victories and unpalatable defeats" (1984, 80). The issue is not some search for the "origin" of humanism nor its teleological development, but the patient tracing of its fraught ascension to the common sense horizon of globalized political philosophy.[2]

Additionally, this project—which can only be schematic in the extreme at this moment—is a direct continuation of the genealogy Nietzsche offers in *On the Genealogy of Morals* (1967), which traces the domestication of "herd" humanity. Nietzsche posits "bad consciousness," "self animal torture," and "the ascetic ideal" as forces that turned the human against its animal self in order to produce the sickness called "humanity." Rather than something that simply exists, Man for Nietzsche is an illness, one that makes civilization as we know it possible (85).[3] Nietzsche's writings not only diagnose the sickness that is humanity; they also proleptically imagine forms of becoming-with that would follow upon getting over this illness (Snaza 2013).

As an experiment in "the critical ontology of ourselves" (Foucault 1984), this genealogy must account both for how we come to think about ourselves as "humans" (a problem of interpolation by and identification with an abstract category of identity) and for how this "human" has come to be thought of and put to work across its career. The first of these problems concerns one's education via curriculum and instruction and any answer cannot ignore the myriad sites of nonschool education that transmit ideas about being human. The second is a question of history, one that should be asked with the long view in mind.[4] A critical ontology of ourselves asks both "How do our schools teach us how to be human?" and "What sorts of struggles, compromises, and inventions produced a situation in which I can identify myself with the category of 'the human' and then use that identification to control the entirety of my system of ethics?"

The human with which we are coerced into identification is nothing simple, bounded, or stable. For Dominic Pettman (2011, 30), "the human [i]s a trope that functions across all sorts of conceptual platforms." To redefine the human as a trope, the result of particular "software" that turns an ontological entity about which we know very little into the "human" as a recognizable, commonsense "being," is to cast the human as, precisely, an "error." Or, more specifically, errors: "our species' systematic deployment of and within technology *creates* the human as an emergent property inside the overlap of the Venn diagram between animal and machine" (99). As it has come to be thought within posthumanist discourse broadly, the human is the construction of particular relational distanciations taking place among the terms in the cybernetic triangle of human/animal/machine. Agamben (2003) has called this production "the anthropological machine." In order to produce "the human" as a being, these other terms must *also* be produced, since their definitions are mutually constitutive and exclusive. Thus, a genealogy of educational humanism must account not just for how "the human" was conceptualized and constructed in particular historical instances and the operations of particular institutions, but also—and as an inescapably linked set of problems—for how it is related to its various constitutive outsides: the animal, the machine, the savage, the slave, nature, the thing.

This posthumanist reconceptualization of "the human" requires a rethinking of "humanism" as a problematic that is considerably wider in scope than prevailing understandings of this term within educational histories such as Herbert Kliebard's *The Struggle for the American Curriculum* (1995), which posits "humanists" as one among several competing interest groups in the ongoing debates about the social function of schooling and, consequently, the problem of curricular design in the United States. As he puts it, referring to Charles Eliot (arguably the most important "humanist" voice in education at the beginning of the twentieth century), "The right selection of subjects along with the right way of teaching them could develop citizens of all classes endowed in accordance with the humanist ideal—with the power to reason, sensitivity to beauty, and high moral character" (10). That is, humanists in this (limited) sense, seek to produce ideal "human" citizens through "the study of ancient Greek and Latin, and of the literature, history, and culture of the peoples who spoke them" (Davies 1997, 9–10). Humanists are those scholars and educators who insist on the study of what have come to be called "The Classics" of Western culture. The aim, for humanists, is to produce responsible, rational citizens according to a model that structures ancient Greek and later Roman philosophy, politics, and aesthetics (we cannot forget that *this* set of languages, texts, and cultures has come to be canonized thus in particular imperialist engagements with non-Western cultures, nonhuman animals, and ecosystems that exceed the merely vital).

While this limited understanding of humanism proves enormously helpful in tracing how this ideal "human" is articulated in ancient Greek and Roman texts and then reconfigured in fraught, uneven, and even disjunctive ways in the intervening centuries, it also obscures some of the most salient features of humanism as I seek to conceptualize it here. As Akeel Bilgrami's "Foreword" to *Humanism and Democratic Criticism* makes clear, Edward Said's definition is more open (Said 2004, x). It has two poles. On the one side, humanism means to be committed to distinguishing the human from its Others in some manner or other, attempting to ontologize this difference under the pretense that the human simply exists. And, on the other, it means to embrace and "show regard for" anything and everything that comes from or is associated with that previously discerned human. The first pole points toward ontology, but often through relations of dialectical negations (the human *is* this *because it is not* that). It would determine who or what is (or counts as) human. The second pole points toward education and a narrative course. One has to *learn* to "yearn [. . .] to show regard for *all* that is human" (x). For Said, the political import of the humanities is that it enables such regard, treating cultures contrapuntally and not as antagonistic, mutually alienated formations (a notion he borrows from Gramsci).

Schreode

This definition has the virtue of making something else very plain: the human is a political category. To be a humanist is to be a partisan. It is to define a group or category and then demonstrate (political) commitment to its members. Schematically, we can say that humanism is then the belief that there exists such a thing as a "human" coupled with the belief that this human should be the center of one's concerns, a belief we may also call "anthropocentrism." This widened definition of humanism includes not only those educators who are partisans of a classical education in the manner of a Charles Eliot, but also virtually every educator and educational thinker within the Western tradition (including, obviously, Said). A genealogy of educational humanism, therefore, will therefore have to account for how humanism has come to structure *the entirety of Western education*, its institutions, its concepts, its practices.

HUMANIZING EDUCATION'S STRUCTURAL DOUBLING OF THE HUMAN

Reframing humanism by removing it from a progressive, teleological narrativization calls into question humanism's own self-understanding and its particular educational modes—its institutions, divisions of intellectual work, pedagogical and curricular practices. This is because humanism has *always already* presupposed a particular view of education, one that is structurally unthinkable without the progressive, teleological narrative. Put most simply, humanizing takes "the human" to be two related, but *structurally* different things. It refers to a particular being said to merely "exist" (*Anthropos*, the rational animal, the talking animal, *homo sapiens sapiens*), and to a being who cannot come into being except through an educational regimen of "humanization." That is, one is not "fully" human until one has been educated. It is not something one is, but something one becomes. The human is both the protagonist of a story and the *result* of that story's unfolding, a being who could only come into being by running the course of the narrative (something the *Bildungsroman* makes apparent).

This structural doubling of "the human" makes it so that the teacher (always in relation to a school and its infrastructure, its hierarchies of authority, its "culture") has to address the students as *both* presently human beings—which they discern through dialectical negation—and as beings who are *not yet* human. They both *are* and *are not* human. We have tended to believe that education would do what it is meant to do if all humans "we" recognize as humans were given access and they all come out being "fully human," something guaranteed in the Universal Declaration of Human Rights and called for in Freire's *Pedagogy of the Oppressed* (2000).

The importance of this structural doubling in the anthropological machine of educational humanism is perhaps most clear in relation to practices of what we have come to call "dehumanization," practices many educators have theorized in relation to Freire's writings. Schematically, this refers to when someone or some institution (broadly understood) treats a person who *is really human* "as if" s/he were an animal, a machine, a cog in the assembly line or the social wheel, and so on. Innumerable critics of life within industrial and postindustrial capitalism have pointed out how cities, modern modes of bureaucracy, capitalist modes of production and distribution, and even statistical demography (and/or sociology, or social psychology, etc.) "dehumanize" everyone (Horkheimer and Adorno 2002). Yet it is crucial for educators to connect this to the dehumanizations of women, slaves, and the colonized: dehumanizations that were so integral to the emergence of modernity that no modern project, including the modern school, is untouched by them.[5] As Chela Sandoval (2000) reminds us, the experience of the marginalized with the most violent, oppressive, and damaging aspects of modernity often *precedes* the experience of the less marginalized with similar phenomena. The political and educational project she calls "the methodology of the oppressed" takes the critiques associated with "postmodern" or "post-structuralist" theory to say, mutatis mutandis, what marginalized groups had to figure out earlier and without feeling the burden of two thousand years of Western philosophy almost breaking their backs (their burdens were differently backbreaking). Although Sandoval does not position it this way, a posthumanist perspective may be the most promising way to create such linkages. This matters because politically speaking, the task is to forge ways of being together that can resist and disrupt the global system that fucks us all over without forgetting that it happens in different ways to each singularity—human and nonhuman—and that these differences always matter.

We might say that what we need is to push Said's political commitments to contrapuntal relations beyond his anthropocentrism. Our present moment is beset by problems—biotechnology, bioethics, biopolitics, computer programming and hacking, surveillance, factory farming and agribusiness, GMOs, extinction, pollution, climate change—that evade and elude our present (humanist) forms of politics and community. Delinking education from the structures of *humanizing* education, detaching it from the anthropological machine, requires radical educators to connect the dehumanizations enabled by state–administered compulsory educational institutions (segregated in so many, many ways) to the ways in which "we" humans pass over in silence the extraordinary violence "humans" do to animals, to ecosystems, to whole species, and, of course, to each other. These violences are inextricably linked.

EDUCATIONAL HUMANISM FROM ANCIENT GREECE THROUGH THE RENAISSANCE

The basic structure of humanist, humanizing education is articulated in Plato's *Republic* (1955). Here, the human is figured as first a kind of raw, ontological input to the educational machine and second as the "fully human" outcome of a particular, civilizing educational practice, a practice Socrates and his interlocutors describe across a series of dialogues. Indeed, Plato's text takes *both* humans as products of state intervention. In this first instance, there is the question of breeding, of state control over the reproduction of humans as the raw form of future citizens: "We must . . . mate the best of our men with the best of our women as often as possible, and the inferior men with the inferior women as seldom as possible" (181). This is so because formal, institutionalized education must begin with the recognition that "we have different natural aptitudes, which fit us for different jobs" (59). And yet this "naturalness" is always already subject to state intervention and control. After taking control of the (bio)political production of "ontologically" human beings, these would-be humans are inserted into a regimen of study designed to produce human subjects. Through constant reflection on the Forms, students of *Republic*'s system are to learn how to reflect on their actions in terms of The Good. This Good is concretized in reflection on "foul and fair," and in this discussion Socrates explains the importance of this reflection in a way that ties it directly to humanization: "Does not one subject the beast in us to our human, or perhaps I should say our divine, element, while the other enslaves our humaner nature to the beast?" (355). That is, education is the process of splitting the human from itself, of structurally doubling it, in order to cultivate the "humaner" nature (based on an identification with Forms) in opposition to the "bestial" part of the human that is the latter's material ground of possibility. The "fully" human being is produced by negating and taming the animality of the human that enters into the educational apparatus. This entails a suppression of embodiment, of bodily desire and passion, and of worldly appetites in favor of the disinterested, rational, philosophical reflection on the extraworldly "Forms."

This suppression and its social imaginaries were directly implicated in the continuation of patriarchal or male supremacist structures of gendering bodies and distributing labor in gendered ways (Rubin 1997). Indeed, a genealogy of educational humanism could learn much from the Marxist-feminist genealogy of the fraught but generally effective working relationship between capitalism and male supremacy, tracing how these were both linked to particular institutionalized forms of domestication of and violence toward nonhuman animals.[6] Animal sacrifice and meat eating were absolutely central to human life for the Greeks (Detienne and Vernant 1998), as was the domestication of animals for labor (as is clear from Socrates's reference to breeding). The structure that emerges positions the human as "above" the animal in the sense that the human can (and should) kill and use the animal for its properly "human" reasons, and "below" the divine in the sense that the human is "fallen" into embodiment and worldliness. Indeed, a great deal of what was at stake in ancient religion had to do with articulating these boundaries separating human, animal, and god (Bataille 1992).[7] Plato's humanizing education is "carnophallogocentric"

(Derrida 1988) in the sense that it positions the masculine, the logical, and the human over and above the feminine, the irrational, and the animal.

Plato's educational philosophy and the institutions it proposes cannot be understood except in relation to a wider confluence of social shifts and struggles attending the emergence of print culture (Havelock 1963). Noting the polemical attack on poetry and Book X's ban on poets in the republic, Havelock reminds us that poetry was a pneumonic, oral repository for cultural knowledge and Plato's educational system jettisons this in favor of the rational reflection on Forms in relation to *written* documents and formalized mathematical symbolization. Thus, the inauguration of Western educational philosophy is always already caught up in a politics of educational *reform* in which education is redrawn in the service of a cultural, political, and economic shift following technological change.

As Martin Heidegger (1998) argues, "We encounter the first humanism in Rome: it therefore remains in essence a specifically Roman phenomenon, which emerges from the encounter of Roman civilization with the culture of late Greek civilization" (244). The Romans extended the Platonic conception of education through an increase in politicization in the sense that it made education a precondition of effective *political* life (with the oration as the hegemonic political form in the empire) and thus performed a gatekeeping function with respect to political participation. Paradoxically, this also set the school further and further afield from "real life" outside since formal schooling intensifies the institutional division of thought, thus privileging discrete forms of rationality and reason detached from the daily affairs of material and political life.

The Medieval Trivium and later the Quadrivium—often considered the first "liberal arts" curriculum—were articulated from the fallen Roman Empire's transformation, reinscription, and recontextualization of Greek thought. Grammar, rhetoric, and logic are the formal, abstract, rational ways of thinking—ways of thinking that are applicable via mechanisms of prescription—that form the condition of possibility for human political and social interaction. To the Platonic idea(l) of education, this medieval articulation adds properly disciplinary divisions among types of thought. To become a fully human citizen, one requires a humanizing education that divides thought from itself, segregating different types of knowledge from each other and from their necessarily combined application in the world of (human) life. This cleaving of world and educational institutions, which both separates and joins, is continued by the *uministi* of the early "Renaissance." These scholars promoted *studia humanitatis* through, again, arguing that a backward-looking education in classical Greek thought would prove beneficial for the production of the first "modern" citizens.

Beginning around the fifteenth century in Europe, this further elaboration of a "liberal arts" idea(l) of education took shape in relation to the emergence of the university in the modern sense (Delblanco 2012) and to a cluster of events signaling the emergence "early modernity." These events include the Western European exploration of the New World and its attendant colonial and imperial ambitions, ambitions that produced mutations in the prevailing notion of the state apparatus; the invention of modern sciences, including physics and comparative anatomy; the emergence of liberal, individualist philosophies; and the earliest experiments in proto-capitalist markets. What a genealogy needs to account for here is how the institutional production of these *studia humanitatis* was materially linked to and (in a certain sense) determined by changes in the (Western) human's relation to environments, the land, bodies both animal and "human," and processes of production and exchange. That is, this reauthorization of a past idea(l) of human being was necessarily implicated in its contemporary moment's material, political, and ecological intensities.

ENLIGHTENMENT HUMANISM

As these "Renaissance" experiments continued into the Enlightenment, the humanizing mission of education became linked to the view that nature is "for" humans and can thus be unconditionally exploited; colonialism and slavery; the sea change in literacy produced by the invention of the printing press; and the state's growing investments in public, compulsory education of its citizens. As Lynn Hunt (2007) has argued, the invention of the novel as a literary form in the eighteenth century was bound up with the invention of human rights as a global political framework through a *shared* and mutually constitutive reconceptualization of what it means to be a "human." Building on the early modern changes in philosophy, hygiene, culture and manners, and social formations increasingly stratified by gender, class, and race in terms approaching how we conceptualize those today, eighteenth-century philosophers, political theorists, and novelists proposed that every "human" *qua human* has an "interiority" that is distinct from every other interiority in such a way that what is common across *all humans* is this particular "form" of interiority. The recognition of this sameness that appears across diverse singularities is what makes the "human" of the early novel and human rights discourse possible. It is abstract, general, and universal. We might add (although Hunt does not) that this formal, abstract conception of the human assumes every human "has" a race, a class, and a gender, thus naturalizing the categories through which stratification operates (Butler 1993; Omi and Winant 1986).

There are two largely disavowed conditions of possibility for these developments linking literacy (and therefore formal education) and politics (human rights law): an approach to nature as standing reserve (Heidegger 1977) and the material realities of colonialism, slavery, class stratification, and sexist exclusions. At issue here is a "will that, with the rise of the Renaissance and the Enlightenment of a humanism grounded in empirical reason and science, becomes an obsession to *dominate* nature, to force 'her' to yield in every sense of the word to 'Man's' desire" (Spanos 1993, 6). The abstract rationality associated with being "human" since Platonic philosophy is pressed into the service of global domination of both natural and "human" resources for the accumulation of private wealth.

When "human rights" assumes predominance as the global political form, the only way to continue to justify sexist exclusions, racially motivated colonization and slavery, and capitalist exploitation on a global scale is to produce systems of thought that regard the oppressed as less than human, as beings who are not afforded the "inalienable" rights of humans. As even the most cursory glance through histories of modernity will reveal, states have had no difficulty in denying the humanity of women, slaves, the poor, and colonized natives.

Taking up and reconfiguring humanizing education's practices of dialectically distinguishing the human from animals and machines, Enlightenment thought produced *intermediate* categories of humanness. Women, slaves, the poor, and colonized natives were conceptualized as *potentially but not yet* human. With the rise of compulsory schooling, this educational form, which is more or less the one within which we operate today, takes the structural doubling of the human and puts it to work in the creation of a properly global, (de)humanizing politics. Gauri Viswanathan's (1989) genealogy of English as a field of study reveals that the justification for colonialism as the coercive instillation of "civilization" foregrounded the *educational* project: the natives were, on their own, not yet civilized, not yet fully human, and a Western educational apparatus was required in order to *humanize* them. As Bhabha (1991, 92) has demonstrated, this project was always, at least unconsciously, configured to fail, producing natives who were almost but "not quite" human (racialized as "not white"), for if the natives were to actually *become* humanized, the justification for colonialism would disappear. Thus, the anthropological machine is put to work training the natives to acquire all the skills and habits of the fully human *telos* of its machinations, and yet no matter how much the native may appear and behave like a European, s/he cannot "really" be European. In officially foregrounding the human as a *telos* of educational humanism (Kant 1960; Rousseau 1979), the founding distinction of humanness proves decisive. No matter how "human" the native appears, s/he will always be in need of more humanization.

The peculiarity of educational humanism in this moment is that it takes its own production of the intermediate humans (women, slaves, natives) as the *raison d'être* of further regimes of humanizing education. I mean this in two distinct ways. First, humanizing education creates a structural loop, *producing* dehumanized people who must, in turn, be humanized. And second, a "counter-discourse" (Foucault 1978) emerges that takes humanizing education's justifications *at their word*, calling for humanizing education as an *antidote* to the dehumanizing effects of modernity (Fanon 1963; Freire 2000). The difficulty, from a posthumanist perspective, is that both of these positions—the oppressor's and the oppressed, respectively—are structurally homologous. Feminist, anticolonial, antiracist, and communist critique thus ends up circumscribing its own horizon of possibility by reinscribing the very same tradition of educational humanism as its declared enemies. That is, for all the debates that have raged since Plato's *Republic* about how precisely education is related to "politics," what has always been taken for granted is that politics is a "human" affair. This has been the case even for those thinkers (again, mostly feminist, antiracist, and anticolonialist) who have articulated an explicit critique of Western humanism and its political investments in dehumanization.

Critiquing dehumanization by asserting that some people excluded from the category of "the human" are really human does nothing to disrupt the *structure* of educational humanism. It does not challenge the possibility and necessity of making a determination of whom or what will count as a proper subject of politics. As long as that determination is merely altered (however progressive and universalist its motivations), the structural possibility of dehumanization is always already present. What is at stake in educational humanism and its peculiar doubling of the human is the defense of the borders of "politics" itself. For this "human," all nonhuman objects are potential "resources" to be extracted, refined, exchanged, and used.

By the nineteenth century, the extraction of fossil fuels (in ways that didn't even bother to raise ecological consequences as a concern) led to an extraordinary takeoff of industrial capitalism, speeding up everything through a standardization of global time and the mechanization of previously "manual" labor. It is this plugging in of a capitalist mode of production (and circulation) and the petroliumization of prehistoric creatures that enabled "the human" to become a geological actor, ushering in an entirely new epoch in geological history: the Anthropocene (Chakrabarty 2009; Morton 2013). The extraction and circulation of these "resources" was only possible on the basis of particular ideas about the political capture of planetary space, ideas concretized in the twin notions of national and ecological sovereignty (Smith 2011): A nation-state may do whatever it wishes with "its" territory (including colonial territories) and "its" resources.

The factory and its attendant divisions of labor becomes the dominant productive apparatus, destroying millennia-long relations between craftspersons and their materials and creating a global working class having nothing to sell but their own labor. This concentration and deskilling of labor is directly linked to urbanization: In order to enable the fabrications necessary to transform extracted "raw" resources into commodities, the human populations of the world began to contract into urban, high-density environments. This required and enabled the emergence of larger-scale forms of farming, heralding a shift from agriculture to agribusiness—a particular mode of production that would quickly cathect on monocultural production and "factory farming" of animals.

In this nexus, where global industrial capitalism based on the exploitation of natural and human resources attains an increasingly dominant role in even geological events, the model of the factory is used to recon-figure schools (Foucault 1977). The school becomes a factory producing "humans" capable of working in factories and/or managing factories: The apparatus is highly stratified. The research university as we know it is also a product of this moment, where the goal of the scholar is to "produce" and circulate knowledge. As Foucault (1970) has famously shown with respect to economics, biology, and linguistics, the transition between the classic and modern periods, a transition concretized in the university, produced the modern disciplines of the "human sciences" as we know them around a particular conception of "Man." This concept of Man, the one that "is still deeply engrained in contemporary self-consciousness and everyday com-mon sense" is a "nineteenth century anachronism" (Davies 1997, 25). At every moment, the past is reauthorized even as it is reconfigured and a contemporary "human" is projected backward as the obvious *telos* of the humanizing project. What is constant, though, is the structure of doubling the human in the anthropological machinery of education.

CONCLUSION: GENEALOGY, POLITICS, AND FUTURITY

All of this to say that contemporary debates about the politics, form, and success of schooling all fail to account for how extraordinarily new the K–12 school and the university are as technologies of education. These debates also completely fail to situate educational institutions in ecological networks that include humans, animals, an enormous number of inanimate objects, and the myriad political relations obtaining among all of these.

Progressive and radical educators often ground their labor in a politics of humanization. And, yet, the only way to stop once and for all the dehu-manization produced by humanizing education is to remove politics and education from their enclosure within humanism. If our politics were not precisely limited to human beings and human concerns, then it would not have *any* meaning to treat someone "as if" they are not human. Without this "as if," we would also lose the ability to engage animals, computers, plants, genetics, ecosystems as "objects" of properly human politics.

As posthumanist thought carries us toward a future politics not reducible to anthropocentric institutions and practices, we need a genealogy of our present that foregrounds how the commonsense "human" of modernity— a common sense that is called into question by modern physics, ecology, posthumanist philosophy, and a wide range of political movements—came to be regarded as self-evident. The human is not something we "are"; it is an error superimposed on complex and mobile relations among a wide variety of bodies, life-forms, objects, and material singularities. Until edu-cation is decoupled from this human, we will continue to face the future with a mixture of dread and paralysis, our "debates" about education (and politics, economics, sustainability, etc.) spinning in place. Until we reject the idea that the human is separate (and separable) from everything else on the planet, we have no traction to move toward different futures, futures explored in the following chapters.

NOTES

1. Since other chapters in this volume address how the posthumanist turn differs from the postmodern one, I don't up take that difference here.
2. There are some notable genealogies of humanism (Spanos 1993), but they tend toward the anthropocentric even as they reveal how "different and clearly incompatible versions of the 'human' are circulating [. . .] within the orbit of a single concept" (Davies 1997, 19).
3. As Freud (2005) reveals, the human's turning against its own animality makes civilization both possible and impossible.
4. Our institutions (the compulsory school, the research university) are a few hundred years old. The notion of "the human" put to work in humanizing education is probably about three thousand years old. The human as a species in the biological sense is slightly less than two hundred thousand years old. In these nested, differently scaled narratives, we catch a glimpse of how restricted the usual temporal framing of the "crisis of education" is.
5. Today, dehumanization is visited upon immigrants, stateless refugees, GLBTQ persons, international workers at the mercies of unrestrained neo-liberal capitalism, and those people nation-states deem unqualified to participate in "liberal" government.
6. Shukin (2009) provides an incredibly important point of departure for this genealogy in her study of twentieth-century and twenty-first-century forms of "animal capital."
7. Thus, Mick Smith (2011) opens his study of dominion as the dominant mode of geopolitics by working through Bataille's interpretation of the paintings as Lascaux. For Bataille and for Smith, the paintings present the "origin" of human difference from other animals in an uncertain, ambivalent, and self-consciously anxious manner, a manner we have lost in the course of "civilization."

REFERENCES

Agamben, G. (2003). *The Open: Man and Animal*. Trans. K. Attell. Stanford, CA: Stanfordn University Press.
Bataille, G. (1992). *Theory of Religion*. New York: Zone.
Bhabha, H. (1991). *The Location of Culture*. New York: Routledge.
Biesta, G.J.J. (2006). *Beyond Learning: Democratic Education for a Human Future*. Boulder, CO: Paradigm.
Butler, J. (1993). *Bodies That Matter*. New York: Routledge.
Chakrabarty, D. (2009). "The Climate of History: Four Theses." *Critical Inquiry* 35:197–222.
Davies, T. (1997). *Humanism*. New York: Routledge.
Delblanco, A. (2012). *College: What It Was, Is, and Should Be*. Princeton, NJ: Princeton University Press.
Derrida, J. (1988). "On Eating Well: An Interview with Jean-Luc Nancy." Trans. P.T. Connor. *Topoi* 7:113–121.
Detienne, M., and Vernant, J-P. (1998). *The Cuisine of Sacrifice among the Greeks*. Trans. P. Wissing. Chicago: University of Chicago Press.

Fanon, F. (1963). *The Wretched of the Earth*. Trans. C. Farrington. New York: Grove.

Foucault, M. (1970). *The Order of Things: An Archaeology of the Human Sciences*. New York: Vintage.

Foucault, M. (1977). *Discipline and Punish: The Birth of the Prison*. Trans. A. Sheridan. New York: Vintage.

Foucault, M. (1978). *The History of Sexuality Vol. 1: An Introduction*. Trans. R. Hurley. New York: Vintage.

Foucault, M. (1984). *The Foucault Reader*. Ed. P. Rabinow. New York: Pantheon.

Freire, P. (2000). *Pedagogy of the Oppressed*. Trans. M.B. Ramos. New York: Continuum.

Freud, S. (2005). *Civilization and Its Discontents*. Trans. J. Strachey. New York: Norton.

Havelock, E. (1963). *Preface to Plato*. Cambridge, MA: Harvard University Press.

Heidegger, M. (1977). *The Question Concerning Technology and Other Essays*. Trans. W. Lovitt. New York: HarperPerennial.

Heidegger, M. (1998). "Letter on 'Humanism.'" Trans. F.A. Capuzzi. In *Pathmarks*, ed. W. McNeil, 239–276. Cambridge: Cambridge University Press.

Horkheimer, M., and Adorno, T.W. (2002). *Dialectic of Enlightenment*. Trans. E. Jephcott. Stanford, CA: Stanford University Press.

Hunt, L. (2007). *Inventing Human Rights*. New York: Norton.

Kant, I. (1960). *On Education*. Trans. A. Churton. Ann Arbor: University of Michigan Press.

Kliebard, H. (1995). *The Struggle for the American Curriculum 1893–1958*. New York: Routledge.

Morton, T. (2013). *Hyperobjects: Philosophy and Ecology after the End of the World*. Minneapolis: University of Minnesota Press.

Nietzsche, F. (1967). *On the Genealogy of Morals and Ecce homo*. Trans. W. Kaufmann and R.J. Hollingdale. New York: Vintage.

Omi, M., and Winant, H. (1986). *Racial Formation in the United States*. New York: Routledge.

Pettman, D. (2011). *Human Error: Species-Being and Media Machines*. Minneapolis: University of Minnesota Press.

Plato. (1955). *The Republic*. Trans. D. Lee. New York: Penguin.

Rousseau, J.J. (1979). *Emile; Or, on Education*. Trans. A. Bloom. New York: Basic Books.

Rubin, G. (1997). "The Traffic in Women." In *The Second Wave: A Reader in Feminist Theory*, ed. L. Nicholson, 27–62. New York: Routledge.

Said, E. (2004). *Humanism and Democratic Criticism*. New York: Palgrave Macmillan.

Sandoval, C. (2000). *Methodology of the Oppressed*. Minneapolis: University of Minnesota Press.

Shukin, N. (2009). *Animal Capital: Rendering Life in Biopolitical Times*. Minneapolis: University of Minnesota Press.

Smith, M. (2011). *Against Ecological Sovereignty: Ethics, Biopolitics, and Saving the Natural World*. Minneapolis: University of Minnesota Press.

Snaza, N. (2013). "The Human Animal *nach* Nietzsche: Re-Reading *Zarathustra*'s Interspecies Community." *Angelaki* 18 (4): 81–100.

Spanos, W.V. (1993). *The End of Education: Toward Posthumanism*. Minneapolis: University of Minnesota Press.

Viswanathan, G. (1989). *Masks of Conquest: Literary Studies and British Rule in India*. Oxford: Oxford University Press.

2 Researching the Posthuman

The "Subject" as Curricular Lens

Brad Petitfils

In his 2000 work, *The Vital Illusion*, French theorist Jean Baudrillard claimed, "The linear tension of modernity and progress has been broken, the thread of history has become tangled" (39). Baudrillard spent the majority of his academic career writing about the fractured nature of the human subject, beginning in the 1960s with his Marxist critique of consumer culture through his 1980s work on simulation culture and hyperreality. He died in 2008, having had the opportunity to witness and reflect on decades of rapid technological innovations. These innovations informed his theorizing, and the quote above is merely one sentence from a tradition of theory with which he and many other authors have engaged in the past quarter century: the idea that we are at the beginning of something radically new. Our digital possibilities allow us to rethink nearly every aspect of our daily lived experiences, from the way we learn to the way we shop, pay bills, fall in love, visit the doctor, travel, and even the way we die. In a broader sense, these possibilities also allow us to rethink our positions in the world, and how our actions and reactions are part of the larger fabric of our complex ecological situatedness.

Baudrillard's "tangle" is an appropriate image for us as we seek to engage with research in the "posthuman" era. He reminds us that we are not quite sure what history will say about our lives in the early twenty-first century, only that we have moved into an age where our assumptions about the past, about our histories—indeed about ourselves—may not be as certain as we once thought. These "tensions of modernity" are comprehensive; the tangle of history exposes the myth of progress.

These tensions and tangles are at the center of discourse about the assumptions that surround the "posthuman era." As we look around us and theorize about the future, we can only presume that—years from now—the present will be seen as a time when we began the work of examining this tangle of a web of new subjectivities. Appropriately, our research methods should reflect this fluidity as these posthuman subjectivities come into more focus. In this chapter, I first engage with what I call the "language of posthumanities," and come to an operational definition of the term as I understand it. I then discuss the various ways in which we might "locate the posthumanist subject," and argue not simply for the "decentering" of the human in light of posthumanity, but also for "recentering" the human so that we might not forget the work of our humanist histories. From there, I engage with some possible ways that we might create a posthuman research agenda, which I place at the nexus of historical (the backward glance) and philosophical (the forward glance) inquiry, but that also seeks to understand some of the complexities of our present situatedness. Finally, I end with some concluding thoughts on the posthumanist subject as a curricular lens through which we might explore current problems facing the academy and classroom discourse.

THE LANGUAGE OF "POSTHUMANITIES"

As an undergraduate student, I once took a philosophy seminar called, "The Philosophy of God." It was taught by a priest who was rather popular with the student body for his unconventional teaching methods (he was fond of tossing around playful threats at students, particularly those who were late to class), his sheer presence (at nearly seven feet tall, he towered above everyone in the room), and, when it came to the subject matter, his gravitas. He shocked many in the room by starting the course with an announcement that, as we began the work of "defining God," we would spend the first half of the course on atheism. He went on to explain why this exercise was necessary: In order to understand what "God" *is*, we must first understand what "God" is *not*. And so, we began in earnest, reading the work of Feuerbach (God = projection), Freud (God = illusion), and Marx (God = opiate). It was a provocative way to teach, and, for an underclassman, an exciting way to learn. Similarly, I find it useful to explore the nature of what is meant by "posthuman" by starting with what it is *not*. Before moving forward, then, I want to be clear in my approach: At least in terms of educational research, the "posthuman" should not be considered solely as the "nonhuman" or "cyborg." Rather, we should engage more critically with the "post" in "posthuman." Weaver (2010) suggested that the "post" in posthuman refers to "the end of the humanist definition of western man . . . The lines between 'Western man,' or now any type of man, no longer exist with nature or technology . . . humans return to nature and technology now enhances or enters into the human body" (193). In my mind, the educational response to posthuman possibilities is a curricular space that explores new humanist definitions of subjectivities on a global scale. The "cyborg" provides us with one possible identity, but the posthuman project is a more complex matter, where subjective multiplicities exist, and where the human role in larger ecological contexts is always in flux.

Obviously, the noun forms of "posthuman" and "posthumanism" ultimately inform the derivative adjectives "posthumanist" and "posthumanistic" (and I consider these terms to all be interchangeable), so we should begin our journey with a foundational definition of the simple form, "post-human." Dow and Wright (2010) looked back to the 1970s and the genea-logical birth of the term "posthuman," and claimed that, at least initially, the term itself seemed to offer an admittedly imperfect "discursive solu-tion to a crisis pertaining to embodiment, desire and representation, to which humanism's vocabulary and ways of knowing seemed increasingly inadequate" (299). This is not surprising, of course, when considered in terms of the global theorizing that marked the tense emergence of postmod-ern thought in the 1970s and the "increasingly inadequate" boundaries of humanistic vocabulary and epistemological frames. In this sense, the birth of the "posthuman" can trace itself back to the death of modernism and reconceptualization of narratives and ontologies. By the 1980s, once West-ern theorists had mourned the death of the metanarrative and embraced the muddy waters of subjectivity (a subjectivity that was, in part, made fractal by the nascent appearance of now-primitive digital technologies), atten-tion began to turn toward the discursive threads of simulation culture. The foundational work of posthuman theorizing was, of course, Donna Har-away's 1991 "A Cyborg Manifesto." It is important to note that Haraway's essay was part of a larger collection that she called *Simians, Cyborgs, and Women: The Reinvention of Nature*. In writing her manifesto, then, Har-away was "reinventing" (at a semiotic level) our ontological situatedness. Particularly important in that piece was the revelation that along with the creation of the cyborg came an inherent problematic: Cyborgs "are the ille-gitimate offspring of militarism and patriarchal capitalism, not to mention state socialism" (151). Here, Haraway reminds us that we should have no celebratory notion of evolution or forward movement with the arrival of the possibility of cybernetic organisms. After all, these organisms are born of traditional systems of oppression and domination. This is particularly evi-dent in terms of our capitalistic consumer culture in the United States and the *horror vacui* that comes with not having the "latest" gadget or techno-logical innovation. As we purchase more technology, and as we spend more time with that technology, we become more cybernetic. Cyborgs carry the promise of innovation that comes along with technological progress, but it is "progress" in name only. As we become cyborgs, we have become the products of the assembly line; the moniker "cyborg" is a veil—old wine in new skins—that masks a larger reality: Our human work to control our environments and our lives actually exposes the myth of progress.

Still, Haraway's work paved the way for others, and as the 1990s ticked by, notions of the "posthuman" were complicated by the emergence of the "transhuman," a developmental detour that deserves a moment's attention, but make no mistake: "Posthuman" is not entirely analogous with "trans-human." Transhumans are biologically enhanced humans that take on more cybernetic characteristics. These entities (cyborgs) "operate" through nanotechnologies and altered biology—they might have bionic limbs, arti-ficial organs, synthetic blood, and so on—and can (theoretically) live to be more than five hundred years old. Bostrom (2005) compared transhumanists with what he called "bioconservatives," and claimed that, while transhumanists laud "human enhancement technologies [that] will offer enormous potential for deeply valuable and humanly beneficial uses . . . [the bioconservative camp] argues against the use of technology to modify human nature . . . [and worry that] these technologies might undermine our human dignity" (203). Largely, these "beneficial uses" of "enhancement technologies" seek to create a cyborg-esque entity, a "posthuman" with central modifications at the level of body systems—cellular, biological systems—under the assumption that these non-biological (or enhanced) "transhumans" will be able to live for extremely extended periods of time when compared with biological (unenhanced) humans. The opposing view—in the "bioconservative" camp—seeks to maintain notions of human dignity in a world that is becoming more "enhanced." This point of view is important to the posthuman definition with which I engage: If there are "dignified" notions of humanity, how might we carry those notions over into the posthuman future as new humanist definitions of subjectivities emerge on a global scale?

Of course, it is arguable that resistance to this transhumanist vision (reality?) is futile. We have already seen the accelerated completion of the Human Genome Project and continue to see the researchers involved still discovering new ways of manipulating biological systems based on the genomic assumptions therein; furthermore, occasionally, stories emerge from research laboratories that read like science fiction. For instance, one recent eye-opening headline read, "We Have Achieved Mind Control."[1] In this case, researchers at the University of Washington have created a noninvasive human-to-human system that uses the Internet as a medium to connect the brain signals of two people, and, using their interface, the researchers were able to successfully have one participant control the hand motions of another participant. Another recent headline from *Nature* was perhaps more shocking: "Stem Cells Mimic Human Brain."[2] Here, researchers at UCLA and the Austrian Academy of Science's Institute of Molecular Biotechnology celebrated the first living model of a human brain that was created in a lab. Dubbed "minibrains" or "organoids," each of these masses was created in a lab from scratch using human stem cells and actually developed a cerebral cortex with the functionality of a nine-week-old fetal brain. The researchers in charge did lament that the minibrains were not capable of consciousness or higher cognitive functions. In either case, it is obvious that we are evolving quickly and our ability to innovate is accelerating. Transhumanists embrace these evolutionary innovations wholeheartedly with a keen eye to the future where our social divides will no longer be constructed within the twentieth-century limitations of race, gender, sexuality, or socioeconomic status; instead, transhumanists are excited about a future where social divides are constructed between the biological human and the enhanced human. Of course, these theories have existed for nearly a century, and these notions can be seen in the works of Aldous Huxley (*Brave New World*), James Cameron (*The Terminator*), and Ridley Scott (*Blade Runner*); the difference here is that today, what was once science fiction is now becoming a technological reality.

DECENTERING AND RECENTERING: LOCATING THE POSTHUMANIST SUBJECT

Transhumanism, then, is not the same as posthumanism, and the construct of posthuman solely as cyborg is insufficient. To locate the posthumanist subject is to engage with the significance of the prefix "post." Back to Weaver's notion of the "end of the humanist definition of western man," the posthumanist subject should be explored beyond the traditions of Western humanism, where we seek out new humanist definitions and subjectivities that are informed by global ecologies. Remember that, in posthuman times, we live in an era of liminal selves. In theorizing about what she called "mestiza consciousness," Gloria Anzaldúa (1987) supposed a "state of psychic unrest . . . a Borderland . . . [a space that] makes poets write and artists create" (73). There are at least two possibilities for locating the posthumanist subject in our current state of psychic unrest. The first is the *de*centered human, which seeks an end to traditional human domination of nonhuman subjects (particularly in nature) and the reconsideration of the human in relation to nature (this is a common thread of posthumanistic theory). The second is the *re*centered human, which seeks to engage with past notions of classical/religious/secular humanism, and which is inspired by Anzaldúa's call to poets and artists. After all, the rapid innovations that have ushered us into the posthuman age are the results of our human creativity; technology *is* a humanism, and the recentered human is necessary for one reason in particular: Especially in an age of exponential innovation, how are young people supposed to understand their "decentered" selves if they cannot first have a reasonable understanding of themselves in relation to the posthumanist world in which they live?

In terms of decentering, consider the provocative questions asked by Lather and St. Pierre (2013) regarding the role of posthuman voices in the conversations of "new" methods of inquiry in the twenty-first century: "Where/how do voices from post-humanist humans fit into the new inquiry? Are they *voices* after all? (Does that word work?)" (630). As we decenter our posthuman selves and explore our digital lives, the notion of "posthuman voices" is poignant. The voices of modernity—of an entire generation of young people—are actually simulated voices: ephemeral and viral. Status updates, Tweets, Instagrams, Vines, and so on, are all indicators of the *vox populi*. Of course, ironically, this digital cacophony also complicates the formation of the posthuman subject (when everything is social, suddenly nothing is). The *vox populi*, then, may be reconsidered in terms of *vox clamantis in deserto*. This exposes an additional layer of complexity of the language of posthumanities: solitude. Our posthuman selves are overwhelmed with the infinite possibilities of the quantum age and we largely remain ignorant of our posthuman relationship to the natural world. In the classroom, the work of posthumanistic education would be to help students decenter themselves and understand the implications of their digital and virtual lives as these formative years of posthumanity emerge. Some guiding questions in this process might include: *Where are my gadgets made? What are the working conditions like in those factories? What happens to my gadgets when I get rid of them? How do we imagine quantum computing? What are the tensions between enhanced humans and biological humans? When might nature begin assaulting us? (Or, has it already?)*

In terms of recentering, I turn back to the work of Jean Baudrillard (2001). If nothing else, he was often a provocateur in his writing, and the following passage from *Impossible Exchange* is one of my personal favorites, particularly in terms of recentering the posthumanist subject:

> Identity is a dream that is pathetically absurd. You dream of being yourself when you have nothing better to do . . . Now, all energies—the energies of minorities and entire peoples, the energies of individuals—are concentrated today on that derisory affirmation, that prideless assertion: I am! I exist! I'm alive, I'm called so-and-so, I'm European! A hopeless affirmation, in fact, since when you need to prove the obvious, it is by no means obvious. (52)

Here, Baudrillard shocks us into the realization that we are delusional if we claim to assert any notion of identity. We live in the era of the hyperreal, where everything we own is mass-produced from mechanisms of domination that are built upon functions of meticulous reduplication. Our commodities define who we are as individuals (I am an iPhone. I am a Galaxy. I am a pair of Google Glasses—and you don't have a pair!); by default, we have become decentered subjects as a result of our consumerist tendencies. It is likely that, from here on into the posthumanist future, individuals will identify themselves through their digital identities before their embodied identities, hence the need for "recentering" the posthumanist subject.

Consider the recent case of Manti Te'o, the Notre Dame football player who was notoriously embroiled in an Internet dating scandal during his senior year. Te'o was involved in an online relationship with a young woman he had never met in person, and whom he publically acknowledged "losing" to a car accident and leukemia in 2012. Despite never having met the woman, Te'o regularly communicated with "her," who actually turned out to be a young man who was a family friend. The colloquial term for this phenomenon—someone that you are "dating" online who you later find to have been lying about their identity—is a "catfish." Te'o, then, was the victim of what we might call "catfish culture." However, what is important to recognize here is that our digital experiences provide us with entirely anonymous platforms through which we are able to construct pluralistic identities that are not bound by our embodied selves. In 1993, a now-famous cartoon from the *New Yorker* depicted a dog sitting at a desktop computer with the caption, "On the Internet, nobody knows you're a dog." The possibilities are endless: For the first time in human history, our bodies do not bind us. Identity, Baudrillard claims, is a pathetically absurd dream; today, embodied identity is merely one possibility from endless options. In the classroom, the work of posthumanistic education would be to help students recenter themselves and understand their own primordial essence as these formative years of posthumanity emerge. Some guiding questions in this process might include: *What do my virtual identities suggest about myself? What image am I trying to create on my social networks? Why do I choose to post the status updates/images/quotes/etc. that I post? Why do I choose not to post about certain things that happen to me each day? Who am I trying to become?*

For now, the fate of the language of posthumanities remains unresolved. This is, after all, the *beginning* of theorizing. It is no easy task to build upon a foundation of sand, but for posthumanist researchers, just like those of us in my undergraduate seminar on the philosophy of God, the work begins in earnest. If nothing else, our paradigmatic genealogical history would ask us not to privilege one thread over another and to seek multiplicities in our theorizing. With that said, shouldn't the posthumanist subject be positioned at the interstices of tradition (back to Baudrillard's image of the "tangle"—the constructs of our embodied selves) with an eye to the future, what Borg (2012) referred to as "reality's inaugural moments . . . *conditions of possibility*" (176)? In the liminal spaces that we currently inhabit, our role as educators should be to help students engage with the posthumanist subject in light of these "conditions of possibility." This tension between the decentering and recentering of the human subject should be central to the future of classroom discourse and educational research, and it requires a critical glance both backward to histories and forward to possibilities.

RESEARCHING THE POSTHUMAN: THE NEXUS OF HISTORY AND PHILOSOPHY

As we set out to engage with posthumanistic classroom discourse and educational research, we should seek to understand some of the dominant forces at play that have shaped notions of subjectivity in the past, with an eye to the ways we are currently being constituted as "educated" posthuman subjects in the twenty-first century. With that said, one of the first concessions that we make as posthumanist educators is that we knowingly theorize at the fringe of society. Hendry (2011) rightly noted, "Scholars in education who train as philosophers, historians, and curriculum theorists are marginalized as not 'scientific,' as too 'political,' and not 'practical' enough. The deintellectualization and ahistorical nature of education make the future devoid of a past" (209). Perhaps we should consider this reality as a badge of honor; after all, might it simply be that posthumanist theorizing begins *after* the admission of the limitations of positivism and the dehumanization that comes along with the objectification of students through the mechanisms of standardization and high-stakes testing? Also, in the nascent twenty-first century, we still seem to be entangled in Thorndike's legacy, where Hendry's second point is confirmed. In mainstream educational discourse, there does not seem to be any role for histories to play. As if the postmodern era never happened, at least in terms of current educational practice, we seem firmly entrenched in the metanarrative of twentieth-century American educational systems: *Dewey is dead . . . all we know is that which we can measure . . . our accrediting agencies will do the "good work" of ensuring compliance with regulations . . . students will demonstrate mastery of measurable learning outcomes . . . they will "become educated" . . . they will earn degrees . . . and Americans will be the most highly intelligent citizens in a global community.* In our posthuman age of exponential innovation and rapid creativity, this metanarrative will not stand for much longer. We have already begun to see some possible systemic changes on the horizon, with the rise of for-profit, online behemoths such as Phoenix; more recently, Massive Online Open Courses (MOOCs) have obliterated the "need" for bricks-and-mortar classrooms. This, of course, does not speak to the *experiences* people have in these spaces (*Is an online degree really comparable to a traditional degree? What happens when the purveyors of the biggest MOOCs—namely, Harvard, MIT, Stanford, etc.—begin charging the fifty-thousand-plus students who enroll in each one? How will small/regional liberal arts universities survive the transition into this "brave new world" of technological change in higher education? What effect will virtual experiments like the Khan Academy have on the future of the classroom?*) But it does introduce some of the more troubling threads that are unraveling before our eyes.

Egéa-Kuehne (2005) compared the tension between past and present with the current separation of the humanities and the sciences in the academy, and labeled this dichotomy as being between the:

> "obsolete past" and "rational present" . . . [where] reason is removed from the humanities as well as from the past, and both are relegated to irrationality. Fewer and fewer seem interested in the humanities and their references to an assumed ancient and archaic knowledge. (134–135)

Of course, this dismissal of the "obsolete" past is one of the reasons for the recentering of the posthuman subject. The "rational" present may provide statistical data that packages our educational institutions in lovely boxes with satin bows, but there are important reminders in the "irrational" and "archaic" past about how we might envision and structure our systems, not the least of which is how Thorndike's theory has led us to a very complicated and frustrating moment in curricular discourse. Historical inquiry, then, enables us to engage with the backward glance as we grapple with the decentering and recentering of the posthuman subject. Baker (2009) considered curriculum histories "as the 'cultural studies of education' with research into *overt* (formal or written content), *hidden* (incidental or implied learnings), and *null* (what could have been taught but was not) curricula taken-for-granted" (x, original emphasis). There is much to learn from these episodes from our past, and, for that reason, we should remember to listen to those silenced voices from yesterday.

Along with the arrival of the posthuman era, we are also headed into a period of radical change in higher education. A century from now, what might be said about "overt" curricula (more positivist "measures" of student success?), "hidden" curricula (which corporate entities are embedding themselves in—and, ultimately, controlling—classrooms?), and/or "null" curricula (moving forward, will we ignore the ecological realm?). This tripartite structure helps us to "keep the past alive" when engaging in educational (and curricular) research. Particularly as we continue to navigate the waters of posthuman subjectivities, we should be mindful of these lessons from the past.

With the past in view (and in mind), philosophical inquiry might better allow us to theorize about the future of the posthumanist classroom. Ruitenberg (2009) constructed "philosophy as research" where the methods refer to "the various ways and modes in which philosophers of education think, read, write, speak and listen, that make their work systematic, purposeful and responsive to past and present philosophical and educational concerns and conversations" (316). For instance, in the summer of 2013, a special issue of the *International Journal of Qualitative Studies in Education* appeared that was called, "Post-Qualitative Research," in which authors engaged with what Lather and St. Pierre (2013) called "rethinking humanist ontology" (629). In this case, Ruitenberg's method of philosophy as research comes to life in Lather and St. Pierre's search for new humanist ontologies (incidentally, the edited volume that you are reading now is an example of educational researchers engaging with various *posthumanist* ontologies).

A larger question, however, looms above: Why are educational researchers so fascinated with engaged work in the "posts"? Post-Marxist, postmodern, post-positivist, post-qualitative, postcapitalist, posthuman . . . Each of these labels suggests a movement beyond the past, a dissatisfaction with the status quo, or perhaps even just a melancholy malaise about the "way things are." In exploring these post-tensions, Taguchi (2013) suggested that such analysis focuses on the "co-constitutive relation between matter and discourse where it is impossible to pull apart the knower from the known"

(715). The impossibility of separating the knower from the known is an important foundational reality for posthumanist research methodology. "The knower" is ontological; "the known" is epistemological. In terms of Ruitenberg's "philosophy as method," the ways in which we think, read, write, speak, and listen in the posthuman era are informed by an ontology that is rooted in fluidity (rapid innovation, confusion about enhanced and biological bodies, etc.) and an epistemology that glows with refracted multiplicities (decentered humanness, recentered humanness, the natural world and ecological systems re-privileged as we "return to the garden").

Historical inquiry helps us to recenter the subject based on the backward glance, and philosophical inquiry helps us to project decentered (and recentered) versions of the subject based on fluid ontologies and refracted epistemologies. There is still something missing from this equation, however: theorizing about the present. On any given day, how might we best understand the interrelations between various forms of knowledge and power in the posthuman era? Mazzei (2013) reminds us that posthumanist subjects exist "in a complex network of human and nonhuman forces" (734); ergo, being cognizant of these complex networks is a requisite for understanding the tangle of posthuman modernity. Michel Foucault's (1988) "technologies of the self" offer the clearest framework for untangling in our midst, as each of those technologies engage the dominant forces at play in the power-knowledge fabric of posthumanity:

> (1) technologies of production, which permit us to produce, transform, or manipulate things; (2) technologies of sign systems, which permit us to use signs, meanings, symbols, or signification; (3) technologies of power, which determine the conduct of individuals and submit them to certain ends or domination, an objectivizing of the subject; (4) technologies of the self, which permit individuals to effect by their own means or with the help of others a certain number of operations on their own bodies and souls, thoughts, conduct, and ways of being, so as to transform themselves in order to attain a certain state of happiness, purity, wisdom, perfection, or immortality. (18)

In terms of technologies of production, we might consider the ways in which our students are limited by their experiences of objectivity; that is, in many classrooms, students are not empowered to "produce" anything that is outside the confines of the objective measures demanded by governmental agencies (at least, they are not able to produce anything that "matters" in the eyes of the school systems). Next, what is the dominant sign system in terms of educational or curricular discourse? Certainly in the K–12 classroom, the sign systems that carry the most meaning seem to stem from the Common Core. After all, it is within the Common Core that "ways of knowing" are defined and delineated: these are the expectations that qualify what it means to "be" an educated fourth grade student, eighth grade student, or twelfth grade student.

Of course, sign systems operate within the larger contexts of technologies of power, which, at least for the time being, might best be seen in the structures of No Child Left Behind and Race to the Top. These are the governmental frameworks that have colonized the intellectual development of an entire generation of young people for the past decade. But, as one acquaintance recently told me during a rather heated argument about these very systems: *Public education in the United States is not about learning; it is about tax dollars.* Finally, there are the technologies of the self, which are not so cynically bound, but instead seek to awaken our minds. Perhaps we might consider technologies of the self as our creative outlets of innovation that can provide us with individual and collective spaces of resistance to the otherwise oppressive structures of institutionalized schooling. In the end, in terms of theorizing about the present state of educational discourse, those of us in the undergraduate classroom wonder why first-year students often appear to be so alienated, unprepared, and disillusioned with the process of learning. It is a miracle that they even arrive at the thresholds of colleges and universities at all. What *should* be the beginning of their own personal development of agency is marred by more than a decade of dehumanization and uncritical thought. If there is any hope moving forward, let us have the courage to anticipate that it will come through the posthumanist exercises of decentering and recentering subjectivities.

THE POSTHUMANIST SUBJECT AS CURRICULAR LENS

To respond to these problems, let us consider a posthumanist praxis for classroom discourse. The work of decentering and recentering of our students—which allows us to engage with the posthumanist subject as a curricular lens—begins in the undergraduate classroom; after all, the objective reductionism of the K–12 experience is, at this point, beyond our control. The work of untangling the subjective experiences of our students provides us with a curricular lens for our complex modernity: This is a posthumanist praxis. Gough (1995) reminded us, "As adults, our fractured postmodernist identities are not constituted by the same kinds of stories as those of the young people we teach" (73). For this reason, traditional teaching methods—particularly, the medieval method of lecture—should be dead, especially because the students we are teaching have such radically different expectations than students of the past. Indeed, as we move into the posthuman era, we will be engaging in new methods of teaching and learning, mindful of the process of decentering and recentering, considering our past histories, philosophically inquiring about possible futures, and unpacking the complications of our present. This will be an exercise in *creation of the self* (it should be an exciting few decades in the academy).

In the end, one would hope that the time our students spend with us might help them first understand the complexities of their posthuman selves before beginning the work of agential development and how their planned career tracks might be affected by and have influence on the convergence of some of the issues explored in this chapter. Of course, in the context of history, Bostrom (2005) reminds us, "In the eyes of a hunter-gatherer, we might already appear 'posthuman'" (213). This is a critically important footnote for our conversations. To move forward with the supposition that we are, in fact, at the "beginning" of the posthuman era is also to recognize the relative milieu: As of this writing, Facebook itself is merely a decade old. Think of how very quickly things are changing today, and how radically different things have already become when compared with just twenty-five years ago, not to mention how the present compares with the Enlightenment, the Renaissance, or the medieval period: Our students need to understand this very fundamental truth (we are always a species in flux), and if we are successful in acting as posthumanist educators, we will live up to Hendry's (2011) claim—"When curriculum is our lived experience, history is always in our midst" (xi). It is nearly inevitable that the future will continue to evolve in terms of rapid innovation. In fact, Garreau (2005) suggested, "There are only four limits to computer evolution: quantum physics, human ingenuity, the market and our will" (52). In theorizing a bit about the future, we can guess that we will make new discoveries in the field of quantum physics, that human ingenuity will continue to lead to new inventions, which will—in turn—drive market demand and will also likely affect our will to engage with the unknown, and the cycle begins anew. Whether this Promethean project will lead us to the fate of Daedalus or that of Icarus remains to be seen, but one thing is for certain: We are headed into a phenomenally different future. With any luck, we will neither continue to exploit nature in the ways we have up to this point nor will we lose sight of our humanness in the process. We have a great balancing act ahead of us, but hopefully, with the help of our students and each other, we might spend these formative years together shaping posthumanist subjects that work to achieve positive change in the world . . . and that is a curricular project worth all of our efforts.

NOTES

1. See http://www.washington.edu/news/2013/08/27/researcher-controls-colleagues-motions-in-1st-human-brain-to-brain-interface/.
2. See http://www.nature.com/news/stem-cells-mimic-human-brain-1.13617.

REFERENCES

Anzaldúa, G. (1987). *Borderlands/la frontera: The New Mestiza*. San Francisco, CA: Spinsters/Aunt Lute Book Company.
Baker, B. (2009). "Borders, Belonging, Beyond: New Curriculum History." In *New Curriculum History*, ed. B. Baker, ix–xxxv. Boston, MA: Sense Publishers.

Baudrillard, J. (2000). *The Vital Illusion.* New York: Columbia University Press.
Baudrillard, J. (2001). *Impossible Exchange.* Trans. C. Turner. New York: Verso.
Borg, R. (2012). "Putting the Impossible to Work: Beckettian Afterlife and the Post-human Future of Humanity." *Journal of Modern Literature* 35 (4): 163–180.
Bostrom, N. (2005). "In Defense of Posthuman Dignity." *Bioethics* 19 (3): 202–214.
Dow, S., and Wright, C. (2010). "Introduction: Toward a Psychoanalytic Reading of the Posthuman." *Paragraph* 33 (3): 299–317.
Egéa-Kuehne, D. (2005). "The Humanities and Serres's 'New Organization of Knowledge.'" *International Journal of Humanities* 3 (3): 131–137.
Foucault, M. (1988). "Technologies of the Self." In *Technologies of the Self: A Seminar with Michel Foucault*, ed. L.H. Martin, H. Gutman, and P.H. Hutton, 16–49. Amherst: University of Massachusetts Press.
Garreau, J. (2005). *Radical Evolution: The Promise and Peril of Enhancing Our Minds, Our Bodies—and What It Means to Be Human.* New York: Broadway Books.
Gough, N. (1995). "Manifesting Cyborgs in Curriculum Inquiry." *Melbourne Studies in Education* 36 (1): 71–83.
Haraway, D.J. (1991). *Simians, Cyborgs, and Women: The Reinvention of Nature.* New York: Routledge.
Hendry, P.M. (2011). *Engendering Curriculum History.* New York: Routledge.
Lather, P., and St. Pierre, E.A. (2013). "Post-Qualitative Research." *International Journal of Qualitative Studies in Education* 26 (6): 629–633.
Mazzei, L.A. (2013). "A Voice without Organs: Interviewing in Posthumanist Research." *International Journal of Qualitative Studies in Education* 26 (6): 732–740.
Ruitenberg, C. (2009). "Introduction: The Question of Method in Philosophy of Education." *Journal of Philosophy of Education* 43 (3): 315–323.
Taguchi, H.L. (2013). "Images of Thinking in Feminist Materialisms: Ontologi-cal Divergences and the Production of Researcher Subjectivities." *International Journal of Qualitative Studies in Education* 26 (6): 706–716.
Weaver, J.A. (2010). "The Posthuman Condition: A Complicated Conversation." In *Curriculum Studies Handbook: The Next Moment*, ed. E. Malewski, 190–200. New York: Routledge.

3 Posthuman Education and Animal Interiority

Marla Morris

A posthumanist education goes beyond a humanist (or modernist) education by thinking through the complex relations between humans, nonhuman animals, and machines. This chapter focuses on our complex relations with animals and animal interiority, briefly defining posthumanism and then pointing out problems with a humanist (or modernist) education. We shall argue that a posthuman education must go beyond the humanist project and examine our relations with animals and our understanding of animal interiority.

A BRIEF EXPLANATION OF POSTHUMANISM

Cary Wolfe (2010) argues that posthumanism deals with "the problem of anthropocentrism and speciesism" (xix). Anthropocentrism is a position that suggests that human beings are the central topic of conversation. Speciesism is the assumption that human beings are better than any other species based on the fallacy that we have reason and other nonhuman animals do not. Interestingly, Kari Weil (2012) comments that "feminists such as Carol Adams and Josephine Donovan have illustrated and theorized how oppressions of gender, race, and species are interlock[ed]" (xviii). A classical liberal humanist education is one where the center of discussion turns on white males and erases notions of "gender, race, and species." In current multicultural literature, gender, sexuality, class, race, and ability are treated, but curiously any other species other than human are ignored (Alan Jones, personal communication). A posthumanist education, however, does not erase the study of nonhuman species, nor does it place humans at the center of the discussion. Rather, posthumanist education places all creatures, both human and nonhuman animals, in a nonhierarchical web. Pramod K. Nayar (2014) claims that posthumanism "is the *radical decentering of the traditional sovereign, coherent, and autonomous human*" (2, original emphasis). Human beings are not the only creatures on the Earth. All we need to do is look around to see that nonhuman animals are everywhere. Nayar (2014) writes that posthumanism "calls for a more inclusive definition of life, and a greater moral-ethical response, and responsibility, to non-human life forms in the age of species blurring and species mixing" (8). An example of species blurring is a hybrid nonhuman animal wolf-dog. Dogs are not wolves and wolves are not dogs, but a wolf-dog is a hybrid wild animal and domestic animal at once. If one adopts a wolf-dog, one does so at one's peril since the wolf half of the wolf-dog is still a wild animal. Wild animals are unpredictable and can be dangerous. But Mark Rowlands (2009) would call this common sense into question as he lived with a wolf for many years and had a loving relationship with Brenin (the wolf). Marc Bekoff and Jessica Pierce (2009) go so far as to argue that wild animals have a sense of morality and goodness. These scholars call this "wild justice" (xi).

Donna Haraway (2008) claims that human animals and nonhuman animals are "entangled, coshaping species of the earth" (5). We are enmeshed in a complicated unfolding drama. We are not alone—ever. Haraway (2008) says that "when species meet [. . .] how to get on together is at stake. Because I become with dogs, I am drawn into the multispecies knot" (35). Haraway is right to suggest that we are all wrapped up in a knot; we are tangled up with all sorts of creatures, not just dogs. A pointed question that Haraway (2008) asks is: "who 'we' will become when species meet" (5). The question can also be asked as: Who will nonhuman animals become when species meet? This goes back to Nayar's (2014) question about "response and responsibility" (8) when it comes to our interrelations with animals. For readers who are familiar with the work of the great humanist ethicist Emmanuel Levinas (1985), the words "response" and "responsibility" (88)— toward other human beings—form a dominant theme in his writings. But can we not extend response and responsibility toward animals?

Posthumanism goes beyond the discourse of animal rights because it takes into consideration the interiority of animals—as hard as that is to imagine. Haraway (2008) takes a very broad view of what posthumanism is when she claims that we are "entangle[ed] [with] a motley crowd of differentially situated species, including landscapes, animals, plants, microorganisms, people, and technologies" (41). Again, in this chapter, we will narrow our inquiry to investigate human animals' relations with nonhuman animals and the interiority of nonhuman animals. We will also examine the ways in which humanist education erases animals. Certainly Haraway (2008) is one of the best writers on the posthuman. Haraway (2003) is especially good at collapsing dualisms between humans, nonhumans, and machines as she suggests that these are all interrelated things. She states, for example, that "cyborgs and companion species—each bring together the human and non-human, the organic and technological, carbon and silicon, freedom and structure, history and myth . . . modernity and postmodernity" (4).

Most humanist (or modernist) scholars drive a wedge between animals and humans—with the exception of Nietzsche and Darwin. But posthumanist scholars insist that this wedge is wrong. Kari Weil (2012) states that "many animal species possess the basic capabilities deemed necessary for subjectivity: self-consciousness, rational agency, the capacity to learn and to transmit language" (4). Human animals and nonhuman animals are on a continuum. There is no radical wedge between them. Why does this finding make some anxious? Is it hard to admit to our own animal-ness? Weil (2012) contends that "the human–animal divide is untenable" (4). W.J.T. Mitchell (2003) states that "perhaps we need a new term to designate the hybrid creatures that we must learn to think of, a 'humanimal' form predicated on the refusal of the human/animal binary" (xiii). A humanist education is built on binaries; a posthumanist education is built on hybridities. Cary Wolfe (2003) points out that:

> the humanities [and I would add the discipline of education] are, in my view, now struggling to catch up with a radical revaluation of the status of nonhuman animals. . . . A veritable explosion of work in areas such as cognitive ethology [see the work of Marc Bekoff, for example] and field ecology has called into question our ability to use the old saws of anthropocentrism . . . to separate ourselves once and for all from animals. (xi)

But we are not "separate . . . once and for all from animals." We are animals! Scholars in the discipline of education have done little or no work on animals. Education tends to lag behind both the humanities and the sciences in this area. Scholars in education who focus on ecology might mention animals in passing but mostly focus on the environment—as we will point out later in this chapter.

That we are not wholly other to animals is a point driven home by Barbara Natterson-Horowitz and Kathryn Bowers (2013) as they explain that "a century or two ago, in many communities, animals and humans were cared for by the same [medical] practitioner. . . . A leading physician of that era named Rudolph Virchow . . . put it this way, 'Between animal and human medicine there is no dividing line—nor should there be'" (8–9). To a layperson, this claim might sound ludicrous, but it is not. Hariet Ritvo (1995) teaches that:

> The distinctive scientific developments of our own time have similarly emphasized the continuity between humans and our anthropoid relatives. DNA analyses have suggested that chimpanzees are more closely related to human beings than they are to gorillas. (73)

This is what Ritvo terms "Border Trouble" as these findings trouble the borders between nonhuman animals and human animals. As we study these relations the borders become more and more slippery and it is this that makes for anxiety. Who are we, or what are we? These basic ontological questions get convoluted against the backdrop of the findings of ethologists and ecologists, and humanist education is troubled or is in trouble because there is little to divide nonhuman animals and human animals.

Many of the premises of humanist education are troubling when we study posthumanism. Many humanist assumptions seem to be simply wrong. Human beings are not better because they have rationality; many nonhuman animals have rationality. Human beings are not better because they have language; many nonhuman animals have language. Human beings are not better because they mourn the dead; many nonhuman animals mourn the dead too. We will discuss more of these later on, but it is enough to say now that the line between human animals and nonhuman animals is fuzzy. Ritvo (2010) asks: "Why do we have to keep reiterating this point again and again, over the decades and even the centuries?" (3). There seems to be some kind of fear of the notion of the animal or of animality. Animality is associated with instincts, wildness, irrationality, emotionality, being uncivilized. But animals are also gracious, elegant, thoughtful, moral, kind, generous, giving (Bekoff and Pierce 2009). Adrian Franklin (1999) puts it this way: "the boundary (or the significant difference) between humans and animals is challenged by the fluidity and the interchangeability of humans and animals in friendships, companionships and love" (5). Rowlands (2009) writes about his love for his wolf, Brenin, and he even calls Brenin his brother. Many people who take care of companion animals think of them as their children or as being part of their family.

PROBLEMATIZING AND BUILDING ON HUMANIST EDUCATION

We are still children of the Enlightenment; we are still children of humanist sentiment. The term "posthumanist" means that we might be post the human but still we are steeped in the humanist tradition, especially in the discipline of education. Posthumanism is not a clean break from humanism, but rather it builds on humanism and goes beyond it. Humanist education has things to offer yet it is problematic. As we mentioned earlier, the main issue of contention scholars take with humanist positions is that the human being is seen as the center of conversation (anthropocentrism) and that because we are in the center, we are better than or superior to other species (speciesism). Posthuman scholars are attempting to move humans out of the center of conversation and into a weblike formation among other creatures. Humans are not better or superior to other creatures but are on an equal playing field with other species. With this in mind, we will take a brief look into claims made by humanist educators to see how we can build on them and go beyond them.

John Dewey (1938/1997) was a humanist educator and the father of the progressive tradition of education. Curriculum theorists are indebted to Dewey and attempt to carry on his progressive project (Pinar et al. 1995).

Social justice, democracy, rigor, experience, dignity, and relationship are all ideas that spring from Dewey's project. One might argue that these are all humanist ideas. They are humanist when they point toward human beings only. Dewey (1938/1997) states, for instance, that "basing education upon personal experience may mean more multiplied and intimate contacts" (21). The upshot of this claim is that relationships—between people—are paramount to building a good educational system. At bottom, for Dewey, relationships—between people—are the bedrock of educational experience. But from a posthumanist perspective, these relationships must also include the nonhuman animal. Think of children for a moment. Many children who grow up with companion animals learn important things about building relationships not only with humans, but with animals. We live on this Earth with animals and can no longer erase their presence—especially in the lives of children. Dewey (1938/1997) goes on to say that "all human experience is ultimately social" (38). From the posthumanist position, experience that is social must include our relationships with nonhuman animals. How we treat our companion animals tells a lot about how we move about in the world. A socially just world is one where animals are respected, taken care of, and loved. Dewey (1938/1997) states "that individuals live in a world means, in the concrete, that they live in a series of situations" (43). These "situations" include not only human encounters, but also animal encounters. How we encounter animals tells a lot about who we are as humans. Haraway (2008) again raises the most poignant question that relates to this discussion as she asks "who 'we' will become when species meet" (5). People who are abusive to animals are usually also abusive to humans (Lockwood and Ascione 1998). Children and animals are the most helpless creatures in our care. We must take care of those who have no power. This too is what we learn in social justice education (Ayers 2010).

Like Dewey, Jim Garrison (2002) is another humanist educator and adds significantly to the literature on progressive education. Garrison (2002) states that "education raises the most profound questions about human beings and their relationships" (41). From a posthumanist perspective, we can build on Garrison's insights by adding to the conversation that education should also "raise the most profound questions" about human beings in relation to not only other human beings, but also to nonhuman animals. We do not live in a vacuum; animals are everywhere around us. And we too must remember that we are animals. What are profound questions about our relationships with companion animals? These profound questions might turn on issues of love, respect, responsibility, and ethicality. Companion animals and animals who live in the wild are our concern. Disturbingly, Patricia Reis (2010) reminds us that, "Scientists concur that we are currently in the midst of the most rapid extinction of plants and animals the world has ever known. Many predict that one-fifth of our planet's species could disappear within the next thirty years" (101). Reis's claim should alarm, if not horrify. Posthumanists must take up the fight to stop the extinction of animals. But there is more to it than being involved in animal rights activism. We must study animals and take the time to understand what makes them healthy and free of harm. In order to understand animals better scholars must make the time to study such disciplines as ethology, biology, and ecology and relate them to the way in which we educate the young.

Educators who write from an ecological perspective push the conversation a little further toward understanding animals and humans' relations with animals. But still for the most part ecological educators seem more concerned about the broader environment than in animals per se. If they do discuss animals, it is usually in passing. Some ecological educators are beginning to take the animal turn but do not go far enough. David Jardine (2006) is an ecological educator who has done much to shift the topic of education away from anthropocentrism toward nature and the landscape. Jardine (2006) writes that "understanding curriculum in abundance requires thinking and experiencing that is substantive, material, bodily, earthly, located, specific" (xxiv). A key term here is the word "earthly." This term moves us away from anthropocentric concerns. But who inhabits the Earth? Jardine does not write much if at all about animals but more on landscapes and our complicated relationships to the Earth. What we would add to this conversation is discussion about the creatures of the Earth. Jardine (2000) writes in his book on what he calls "egopedagogy" that his work is "an attempt to find ways in which ecologically rich images of ancestry, sustainability, interrelatedness, interdependency, kinship, and topography" (3) can help us better understand the educational project at a large. The question here is interrelatedness to whom? Kinship with whom? We must push this conversation further and suggest that we begin thinking seriously about our interrelatedness with other creatures, with other sentient beings, with wild animals and companion animals.

Elaine Riley-Taylor (2002) writes about what she calls "relational knowing" (3). Like Jardine, Riley-Taylor suggests that we should attempt to get children to understand that they live in a larger landscape and that we should be stewards of the land. She goes on to state that "critical, then, is educator's task to help children understand their *interdependence* within the ecological habitat from which humans draw their life and sustenance" (5). We would add to this statement once again that the "ecological habitat" is full of creatures both wild and domesticated. Nonhuman animals live in these habitats, and we must take care to make sure they are taken care of if suffering when threatened by poachers and puppy mills.

David Orr (2002, 2004) is one of the few ecological educators who mentions animals in his work. Although his contribution to this cause cannot be overstated, he still does not go far enough. Two quotes are in order here. Orr (2004) claims:

> We experience nature mostly as sights, sounds, smells, touch, and tastes—as a medley of sensations that play upon us in complex ways.

But we do not organize education the way we sense the world. If we did, we would have Departments of Sky, Landscape, Water, Wind, Sounds, Time, Seashores, Swamps, Rivers, Dirt, Trees, Animals, and perhaps one of Ecstasy. (94)

Toward the end of this most eloquent quote, Orr mentions animals. This is the first step toward taking that turn toward animals and the educative experience. Clearly Orr is more interested in the larger picture of our place in the landscape and he is disappointed that most education is so wrong-headed. Orr (2002) makes a most poignant argument about the relationships between children and animals as he states that "emotionally damaged children, unable to establish close and loving relationships with people, sometimes can be reached by carefully supervised contact with animals" (25). Companion animals can help abused children cope with horrific circumstances. The love for the animal helps the child to survive unthinkable conditions. This is not a new idea, of course, but one well worth stating here. James Serpell (1996) tells us:

The early years of the twentieth century saw the appearance of the first scholarly papers on the potential psychological value of pet animals. In 1903, W. Fowler Bucke published a long and rather extraordinary analysis of 1,200 essays written by children about their pet dogs. In it, he noted the value of dogs as sources of affection when children feel isolated or unwell. (93)

Children's relationships with companion animals become vital when they live in unhealthy environments and are sufferers of abuse. Animals serve as lifelines to horrific situations at home. The survival of the child is because of her or his relation to the companion animal.

ANIMAL INTERIORITY

Posthuman education goes beyond the study of what is human to the study of what is nonhuman, and it goes beyond the animal rights movement by exploring animal interiority. The question is, how can we get inside the mind of an animal? Can we? How can we get inside the mind of another human being? Can we? These questions have opaque answers. Some postmodern theorists argue that we can never really know anybody else because the mind is too complex. But that does not mean we give up the attempt at trying to understand someone else. The same goes for nonhuman animals. We try to find out what they want, how they feel, what they think. Impossible and yet possible. How do we know when a companion animal is sick? If a dog is acting strangely or out of the ordinary, we know something might be wrong. Some dogs vocalize; other dogs will change behavior in sometimes bizarre ways. An attentive person will know when her dog is ill. How do we know this? Because animals have minds much like ours. Most ethologists (scientists who study animal behaviors) will tell you that animals—whether wild or domesticated—think, feel, make plans, use language, mourn. Virginia Morell (2013) tells us:

> Hardly a week goes by that doesn't see a study announcing a new discovery about animal minds: "Whales Have Accents and Regional Dialects," "Fish Use Tools," Squirrels Adopt Orphans," "Honeybees Make Plans," Sheep Don't Forget a Face," "Rats Feel Each Other's Pain," "Elephants See Themselves in Mirrors," "Crows Able to Invent Tools," and . . . "Dog Has Vocabulary of 1,022 Words." (1–2)

One must admit that these studies are rather remarkable. Animals have interiorities; they are not dumb, and they certainly are not machines, as Descartes once suggested. Posthuman scholars must take these studies seriously and include animals in our discussions. Animals are not things to be dominated or abused. Animals are intelligent, sentient creatures with their own unique ways of getting on in the world. Wild animals coevolve with other wild animals; domesticated animals coevolve with human animals. Animals are not inferior things. They are smart creatures living complicated lives. Jodey Castricano (2008) claims that "what is at stake not only involves the ethical treatment of nonhuman animals but also the question of nonhuman subjectivity" (6). Some might doubt that there is such a thing as "nonhuman subjectivity." Some might doubt that animals have complex interiorities. But today scientists—mostly ethologists—agree that nonhuman animals have feelings, thoughts, anxieties, and so forth. When Jane Goodall—years ago—was out in the field studying primates, her colleagues did not take her seriously. Scientists did not give nonhuman animals names and did not think that nonhuman animals were as smart as they were. There is little argument today, though, that nonhuman animals are highly intelligent. Natterson-Horowitz and Bowers (2013) drive this point home as they tell us that:

> Interest in the mental life of animals, dismissed for many years as too speculative and an exercise in anthropomorphizing, has gained greater acceptance, too. Books by Temple Grandin (*Animals Make Us Human* and *Animals in Translation*), Jeffrey Moussaieff Masson (*When Elephants Weep*), Marc Bekoff (*The Emotional Lives of Animals*), and Alexandra Horowitz (*Inside of a Dog)* have demonstrated animal cognition and behavior that resemble what we might call foresight, regret, shame, guilt, revenge, and love. (20–21)

Human animals are not the only creatures who express emotions and think. Animals clearly have an interior world where decisions are made and feelings are felt, where thoughts are generated and knowledge produced. Nonhuman animals have complex epistemologies and make their way in the world via complex ontologies. Animals produce knowledge and have a sense of being and time. Some animals sense that they are going to die; some animals know who their enemies are. They take care of their young and grieve if their young die. All of these ideas fly in the face of humanist education because during the heyday of humanism (again with the exceptions of Darwin and Nietzsche) people thought that animals were for the most part dumb beasts. Some people still think that animals are things and are stupid. Castricano (2008) cites Wolfe, who asks: "Why has it taken so long for the academy to get it?" (7). Even scholars don't "get it." These ideas we are talking about here are not new.

Barbara King (2013) carries on the work of Darwin by arguing that "wild birds, dolphins, whales, monkeys, buffalos, and bears—even turtles—mourn their losses. . . . cats, dogs, rabbits, goats, and horses—experience grief" (2). It used to be thought that only humans grieved. But this is clearly not the case. Grief is a sign of intelligence, and its workings are highly complex. Some of these claims might come as a surprise to our readers, and hopefully these findings will help educators better understand why the lives of animals are important to take into account while teaching children. Children should learn early on that animals are our relatives and we must treat them with the utmost respect. We do not want children learning from adults that animals are dumb and do not matter because these children will carry these attitudes into adulthood and perpetuate indifference and even intolerance toward animals. David Alderton (2011) claims that "emotions in animals remain a controversial subject" (4).

In order to fight for socially just practices, the study of animal interiority must come first. When we study animal interiority, we find out some interesting things, such as: "crocodilians . . . have emerged as devoted parents, rather than mechanistic killers. Elephants can keep in touch with each other across long distances by using ultrasound . . . The song of whales reverberates through the oceans for the same purpose" (4). For some these are shocking revelations, but Darwin—long ago—knew these things. Joe Cain (2009) points out:

> In *Descent*, Darwin quickly turned his attention to mental, intellectual and moral faculties. He complained how frequently observers underrated the faculties of animals, then gave accounts of a myriad of supposedly human qualities found in some form in animals: foresight, memory, reason, imagination, love, jealousy, the ability to learn from mistakes, wonder, curiosity, attention, tool use, inarticulate language, a sense of beauty, and aesthetics. (xx)

People still "underrate" animal emotions and the fact that animals have an interior sense of being at all. And, because of this, ignorance abuse occurs.

This is not to say that mostly everyone ignores animals and ignores animal well-being. The United States is a dog-loving country. Those who live with companion animals might be more sympathetic to animals than those who do not. People who live with companion animals spend more money at the vet than they do at their own doctors. But still there are too many people who are unsympathetic to animals and care little for their well-being. A posthuman education is one where we educate youngsters about companion animals and wild animals. At the college level, a good text to start out with is Darwin's (1872/2009) *The Expression of the Emotions in Man and Animal.* In this text, Darwin says that some animals express "rage" (86), "astonishment" (88), "terror" (91), "joy" (119), "grief" (127), and "jealous[y]" (131). Darwin goes into great detail about animal interiority in this text, and one wonders why this text still seems to be ignored or forgotten when talking about animals. The findings of modern-day ethologists are not new. Even though Darwin knew these things in the 1800s, his findings got lost in all the battles on evolution.

Jacques Derrida (2008) writes that "no one can deny the suffering, fear, or panic, the terror or fright that can seize certain animals and that we humans can witness" (28). The heartbreak of living with companion animals is watching them get older and watching them get ill and watching them suffer. Terrible decisions have to be made when the death of an animal is imminent. Rowlands (2009) writes about the death of his wolf. Rowlands's book is a raw account of Brenin's death from cancer. Rowlands (2009) tells us that after Brenin died, he was "diminished" (4). Rowlands (2009) writes that "Brenin taught me something that my protracted education did not and could not teach me" (4). Animals are our teachers. Sometimes they are our best teachers. They teach us about pain, suffering, and, as Rowlands (2009) points out, they teach us about "love, death, and happiness." Animals teach us about the gamut of emotions. When they suffer, so do we. Euthanasia is the kinder road toward death; it alleviates suffering. Still it is a hard choice we have to make when death calls.

G.A. Bradshaw and Mary Watkins (2007) stress that animals have psyches. Because they have psyches, they experience pain. Bradshaw and Watkins (2007) suggest that many do not think that animals have psyches— but how else can we explain the fact that they feel pain and that they suffer? The seat of suffering is the psyche. Bradshaw and Watkins (2007) write:

> Conventionally, psyche has been restricted to humans and bounded by the paradigm of individualism. A new range of writers stress the need to release psyche from identification with solely human subjectivity. Archetypal psychologist James Hillman returned to Platonism to emphasize that each being—human, plant, animal, and man-made has a soul-spark. (70)

"Psyche" and "soul" are interchangeable terms. Some might argue that animals do not have souls. But we argue that they do have souls/psyches. How else do they negotiate the world? How else do they feel the world? When humans bond with companion species, they bond with other souls. Sharon L. Cromwell-Davis and Thomas Murray (2006) tell us that "the term *psychopharmacology* derives from three Greek words. *Psyche* means soul or mind. *Pharmacon* means drug. Finally, the term *logos* means to study" (3). Vets treat suffering animals (creatures with souls or minds) with drugs. Some of these drugs treat psychological issues that companion animals share with humans. Vets treat "anxiety, fears and phobias" (16). Vets treat animals suffering from "compulsive disorder" (19), posttraumatic stress disorder (21), hallucinations (20), and attention deficit disorder (21). It is made clear here that companion animals suffer from psychological trauma similar to what humans suffer. Why is it so hard to think that we are like animals in many ways?

People who do not live with companion animals might not understand the strong bonds we share with them. When we lose an animal, it is as devastating as losing a child. Natalie Corinne Hansen (2012) writes about this "queer" love we have for animals. She states that queer love "opens possibilities for cross-species affections and partnerships" (118). Haraway (2003) writes about this "queer family of companion species" (11). Some might think it queer to love a dog—for instance—with such intensity. In the case of Rowlands (2009), some might think it queer to love a wolf. Interestingly, Adrian Franklin (1999) states that "in the 1960s a close relationship with a pet was widely considered dissocial and the cause for some concern" (5). There are probably still people who feel this way today. If you take your dog everywhere with you—including on airplanes—some people might think you are crazy. If you feel closer to your dog than you do to your mother, some might think there is definitely something wrong with you. This queer love that some of us have for companion animals goes beyond language or even understanding.

In sum, a posthumanist education builds upon and goes beyond a humanist education. Building ethical relationships with people is important, of course, but we must also build ethical relationships with nonhuman animals—whether they are wild or domesticated. Animals are everywhere around us, and we need to treat them with respect. Posthuman education also means that we remember our own animality, but we must move beyond this too in order to embrace and even love nonhuman animals. We must move out of an anthropocentric mind frame and begin to understand that we are in the middle of nature's web. All creatures are equal. We are not superior in any way to other animals. Speciesism is an immoral position. Animal rights activists are doing good work, but they need also to study animal interiority to better understand the psyches/souls of animals. Although animal interiority may be out of reach, we can still attempt—by careful observation and care—to understand the souls of animals. Sometimes children understand this better than adults. So let us turn to our children because they just might educate us better than we can educate ourselves.

REFERENCES

Alderton, D. (2011). *Animal Grief: How Animals Mourn*. Dorchester: Voloce Publishing.

Ayers, W. (2010). *To Teach: The Journey of a Teacher*. New York: Teachers College Press.

Bekoff, M., and Pierce, J. (2009). *Wild Justice: The Moral Lives of Animals*. Chicago: University of Chicago Press.

Bradshaw, G.A., and Watkins, M. (2007). "Trans-Species Psychology: Theory and Praxis." *Spring Journal* 75:69–94.

Cain, J. (2009). "Introduction." In *The Expression of the Emotions in Man and Animal*, ed. Charles Darwin, xi–xxxiv. New York: Penguin.

Castricano, J. (2008). "Introduction: Animal Subjects in a Posthuman World." In *Animal Subjects: An Ethical Reader in a Posthuman World*, ed. Jodey Castricano, 1–32. Ontario: Wilfrid Laurier University Press.

Cromwell-Davis, S., and Murray, T. (2006). *Veterinary Psychopharmacology*. Ames, IA: Blackwell Publishing.

Darwin, C. (1872/2009). *The Expression of the Emotions in Man and Animal*. New York: Penguin.

Derrida, J. (2008). *The Animal That Therefore I Am*. Trans. David Wills. New York: Fordham University Press.

Dewey, J. (1938/1997). *Experience & Education*. New York: Touchstone.

Franklin, A. (1999). *Animals & Modern Culture: A Sociology of Human–Animal Relations in Modernity*. London: Sage.

Garrison, J. (2002). "James's Metaphysical Pluralism, Spirituality, and Overcoming Blindness to Diversity in Education." In *William James & Education*, ed. Jim Garrison, Ronald Podeschi, and Eric Bredo, 27–41. New York: Teachers College Press.

Hansen, N.C. (2012). "Horse-Crazy Girls: Alternative Embodiments and Socialities." In *Beyond Human: From Animality to Transhumanism*, ed. Charlie Blake, Claire Molloy, and Steven Shakespeare, 97–121. New York: Continuum.

Haraway, D. (2003). *The Companion Species Manifest: Dogs, People, and Significant Otherness*. Chicago: Prickly Paradigm Press.

Haraway, D. (2008). *When Species Meet*. Minneapolis: University of Minnesota Press.

Jardine, D. (2000). *"Under the Tough Old Stars": Ecopedagogical Essays*. Brandon, VT: Foundation for Educational Renewal.

Jardine, D. (2006). "Preface: What Happens to Us over and above Our Wanting and Doing." In *Curriculum in Abundance*, ed. D. Jardine, S. Friesen, and P. Clifford, xxiii–xxviii. Mahwah, NJ: Lawrence Erlbaum Associates.

King, B. (2013). *How Animals Grieve*. Chicago: University of Chicago Press.

Levinas, E. (1985). *Ethics and Infinity*. Pittsburgh, PA: Duquesne University Press.

Lockwood, R., and Ascione, F. (1998). "Introduction." In *Cruelty to Animals and Interpersonal Violence: Readings and Research and Application*, ed. Randall Lockwood and Frank Ascione, 1–4. West Lafayette, IN: Purdue University Press.

Mitchell, W.J.T. (2003). "Foreword." In *Animal Rites: American Culture, the Discourse of Species, and Posthumanist Theory*, ed. Cary Wolfe, ix–xiv. Chicago: University of Chicago Press.

Morell, V. (2013). *Animal Wise: The Thoughts and Emotions of Our Fellow Creatures*. New York: Crown.

Natterson-Horowitz, B., and Bowers, K. (2013). *Zoobiquity: The Astonishing Connection between Human and Animal Health*. New York: Vintage.

Nayar, P. (2014). *Posthumanism*. Malden, MA: Polity.

Orr, D. (2002). *The Nature of Design: Ecology, Culture, and Human Intention*. New York: Oxford University Press.

Orr, D. (2004). *Earth in Mind: On Education, Environment and the Human Prospect*. Washington, DC: Island Press.

Pinar, W.F., Reynolds, W.M., Slattery, P., and Taubman, P.M. (1995). *Understanding Curriculum*. New York: Peter Lang.

Reis, P. (2010). "Where the Wild Things Are: Dreaming the Bioregion." *Spring* 83:99–118.

Riley-Taylor, E. (2002). *Ecology, Spirituality, & Education*. New York: Peter Lang.

Ritvo, H. (1995). "Border Trouble: Shifting the Line between People and Other Animals." In *Humans and Other Animals*, ed. Arien Mack, 67–86. Columbus: Ohio State University Press.

Ritvo, H. (2010). *Noble Cows & Hybrid Zebras: Essays on Animals & History*. Charlottesville: University of Virginia Press.

Rowlands, M. (2009). *The Philosopher and the Wolf: Lessons from the Wild on Love, Death, and Happiness*. New York: Pegasus Books.

Serpell, J. (1996). *In the Company of Animals: A Study of Human–Animal Relationships*. New York: Cambridge University Press.

Weil, K. (2012). *Thinking Animals: Why Animal Studies Now?* New York: Columbia University Press.

Wolfe, C. (2003). "Introduction." In *Zoontologies: The Question of the Animal*, ed. Cary Wolfe, ix–xxiii. Minneapolis: University of Minnesota Press.

Wolfe, C. (2010). *What Is Posthumanism?* Minneapolis: University of Minnesota Press.

4 Education Policy Making for Social Change

A Posthumanist Intervention

Helena Pedersen

One of the most basic purposes with the (Western) formal education system—the economic, social, and cultural reproduction of society—requires education to develop strategies for dealing with transformations and change originating outside the education establishment itself. At the level of educational policy making, these efforts become particularly visible by certain futures-oriented components that are worked into rationales, plans, and statements of purpose of education. An example of an international document where such components are clearly articulated is the so-called *Delors Report* of the mid-1990s (Delors et al. 1996). A more recent document, a draft progress report on the Education and Training 2010 work program from the Council of the European Union (2008), is introduced by the statement: "Education and training are crucial to economic and social change" (2). In post-Delors politics, the instrumental objective of education to bring forth a certain desired future society is ever present but increasingly tangled up with a messy web of relationships emerging from the socioeconomic embeddedness of education in late modernity.

The present chapter addresses tensions between education for social change, as formulated in international policy documents, and education for economic, social, and cultural reproduction in the light of posthumanist theorizing. I explore how futures-oriented instrumental dimensions of educational policy making, ostensibly in service of "the common good," generate particular closures rather than open up for visionary social change. Specifically, I attend to how these closures privilege the formation of certain subject positions and disable others by restricting conceptual space and regulating conditions for subjects to emerge, or, in Biesta's (2006) words, to "come into the world" (ix). I do this by bringing the fields of education theory and animal studies together in dialogue on "posthumanist" education policy, a dialogue whose philosophical directions I have previously sketched (Pedersen 2010b). This is not primarily a refutation of educational instrumentality as such, but rather an attempt to create a few cracks and fissures; to squeeze a little bit of posthumanist "noise" into certain sociopolitical particularities of the education apparatus as they have emerged under modernity.

I have elsewhere pointed to the importance of opening up education theory to debates on posthumanism, particularly as informed by animal studies, to bridge a conceptual "gap" between the two (reflected, for instance, by education's fetishizing of "becoming human" and related forms of species performativity[1]). I have suggested that posthumanism, addressing fundamental questions relating to the problematic project of defining an essential "human nature" (Wolfe 2008), links education theory and animal studies by spaces of ontological/epistemological imperfection, by "radical" intersubjectivities, by open-ended ways of "coming into the world" (cf. Biesta 1998a, 1998b, 1999, 2006; Braun 2004) and by a decentering of the human subject as imagined by Enlightenment humanist thought (Pedersen 2010b). The present chapter, positioned in the interface between critical education theory and animal studies, asks what this theoretical/philosophical account might mean at the level of education policy. Taking departure from five pervasive ideas about the relationship between education and social change that are frequently appearing in contemporary rhetoric of education policymaking—"the knowledge society," "the democratic society," "the multicultural society," "the globalized society," and "the sustainable society"—the chapter identifies a number of posthumanist-inflected challenges to conventional assumptions about the institutionalized production, mediation, and development of knowledge as a catalyst for social progress.

ANALYTICAL APPROACH

My empirical material consists of education policy documents published online and accessed from the websites of five major actors of international policy making in education: UNESCO, the Organisation for Economic Cooperation and Development (OECD), the World Bank, the European Commission, and the Nordic Council of Ministers. I have read presentations of their education policy-making strategies on their websites, but have also downloaded materials that identify, report, and contextualize these strategies in more detail (nine documents in total[2]).

The formal education system is embedded in and is also a cocreator of the forms of species performativity that are the basis of posthumanist critique (Pedersen 2010a). This situation shapes conditions and delimitations for the different notions of social change; the "societies" that education is frequently viewed as an instrument to achieve on local, national, and transnational levels. Inspired by critical pedagogy and critical discourse analysis, I have analyzed the policy documents in order to clarify how the five actors above describe the purposes of education with a view toward desired future societies. I have then explored how posthumanist theory can be used as a critical analytic tool to rework different roles ascribed to formal education in a wider societal context, and to examine preconceived ideas about the relation between education and social development.

When reading the documents, I have been looking for recurring key words and concepts that can be interpreted as descriptors of social changes that education should contribute to bring about. I have distinguished between trends and forces in society that are described as *drivers* of change (that education must consider and address in one way or the other), and societal objectives that are *desirable to work for* by education. For my purposes here, it is primarily the latter concepts that are of interest (although they occasionally become entangled with the former category). It is thus the normative dimensions of the policy documents that are in focus in the present chapter. My reading strategy has furthermore been to note key words that are not only reiterated throughout a particular document, but that recur also in a cross-comparative analysis between the different documents of the five actors. In this manner I have singled out nine normative concepts related to education as a tool for social change: "economic growth," "competitiveness," "social cohesion," "intercultural understanding," "democracy," "knowledge society," "equity," "health," and "poverty reduction." Six of these I have combined to formulate four of the overarching ideas that I will analyze in this chapter, that is, "the knowledge society," "the democratic society," "the multicultural society," and "the globalized society." To these, I have added a fifth, "the sustainable society," which did not appear in the documents to the extent that I had expected.[3] However, as it is the focus of the UN Decade of Education for Sustainable Development 2005–2014, I have included it as a significant priority of the UN and UNESCO's Education Sector.

The most common of these terms in the policy documents, reports, and presentations was "(national) economic growth/prosperity," which appeared in documents of all five actors (UNESCO, the World Bank, the European Commission, OECD, and the Nordic Council of Ministers). I have combined it with "competitiveness" (found in three actors' documents) to form the overarching concept of "the globalized society." "Social cohesion" appeared in the documents of four actors and was combined with "intercultural understanding"/"tolerance"/"communication" (four actors) to form the notion of "the multicultural society."[4] "Democracy/democratic values" appeared in the documents of four actors and formed its own category. "Knowledge society/(economy)" appeared in two actors' documents and similarly formed its own category.[5] There are a few other terms that I have omitted that appeared in the documents of three out of five actors, such as "equity" (cf. note 4), "health," and "poverty reduction."

Thus, these five overarching ideas—"the knowledge society," "the democratic society," "the multicultural society," "the globalized society," and "the sustainable society"—do not cover all objectives of education as articulated in the documents analyzed, nor do they constitute coherent, discrete, unifying concepts. Although they are not arbitrarily constructed, they are charged with a range of different meanings, some of which may be traced in the formulations of the different documents. For instance, dimensions and implications of "the multicultural society" and "the globalized society" are not really described as desirable objectives or conditions to be *achieved* with the help of education, but rather as forces external to education, as "matters-of-facts" that education must address or *adjust* to. The meanings and implications of the ideas will be further discussed in subsequent sections.

"THE KNOWLEDGE SOCIETY": FLEXIBILITY, EMPLOYABILITY, AND "A SUCCESSFUL LIFE"

"The knowledge society" is a concept commonly used to describe the growing importance of knowledge, research, innovation, and the training of experts that is currently changing the role of education (European Science Foundation 2008). There is a widespread assumption that the production, circulation, and cross-fertilization of different forms of knowledge is increasing in both intensity and complexity and that educational institutions need to be equipped to meet such challenges. Knowledge is also acknowledged as a major determining factor for global competitiveness on the levels of the nation-state and the corporation, as well as the individual, turning knowledge into more or less a commodity that can be traded on the world market (much like labor and other forms of resources). These conditions put constraints on what forms of knowledge are considered valid, effective, and legitimate to disseminate in any given context. In the international policy documents, "the knowledge society" is commonly associated with a flexible, employable, and productive workforce, and its assumed benefits for individual human lives are expected results of "employability."

The rationales of "the knowledge society" also indicate a need to integrate different areas of knowledge and science (UNESCO 2005c). Nevertheless, education curricula and organizations are still to a large extent structured by conventional epistemological paradigms, separating knowledge into realms of "natural science" and "social science," and, hence, between "nature" and "society." This demarcation is clearly inadequate to understand and explain complex relations of nature, technology, and society in late modernity, and is also interrogated by posthumanist analysis. By viewing nature as a "topic of public discourse" rather than as a physical place, resource or essence, Haraway (2004) points to an understanding of "nature" as a co-construction among human and nonhuman actors and as a site on which to consider common themes. This understanding largely invalidates the society–nature boundary underpinning conventional organizations and presentations of knowledge in formal education. However, the human–nonhuman interaction processes that Haraway discusses are often taking place within spheres of institutionalized power relations, governed by the production and accumulation of economic profit that relies on the continuous exploitation of animal bodies, their labor, and their reproductive capacities.

This has significant implications for the idea of "the knowledge society." What forms of knowledge emerge from the forces that shape the life conditions shared by humans and animals? In what ways does posthumanism destabilize the epistemological paradigm separating the knowledge areas of "natural science" and "social science," and what are the educational implications?

"THE KNOWLEDGE SOCIETY": ZOONTOLOGIES AND ZOÖEPISTEMOLOGIES

Nonhuman animals enter systems of knowledge production in multiple ways, and on several levels. They may interrupt and disrupt "our" familiar formations of knowledge and alert us to knowledge forms for which we (as yet) have no name. They may challenge preconceived boundaries between subjectivity–objectivity, inside–outside, and center–periphery in knowledge production, and they may, literally and figuratively, eat away at the artifacts that are simultaneously products and signifiers of knowledge (on the agency of "laboratory rats," see, for instance, Birke, Bryld, and Lykke 2004).

Zoontology—a term denoting that "ontology" not only concerns the ontology of the human (Wolfe 2003; Rossini 2006)—points to the fact that there are many ways of relating to the world, of which "human" ways only constitute a small subset. The nongeneric nature of animals and animal agency has potentially unsettling implications for the internal structure of any discipline (Wolfe 2009). Likewise, *zoöepistemology* (Miller 1992) offers an alternative outlook toward forms of knowledge and knowledge creation that not only include nonhuman animals, but bring them center stage as key actors in the innumerable different modes of being in, and making sense of, the world. Similarly, in Pickering's (2005) understanding of a posthumanist approach to knowledge creation, situated human–nonhuman relationalities are in focus. Here, a "mutual becoming" of the human and the nonhuman requires a shift in the unit of analysis. This posthumanist shift opens up a different and distinctive space of inquiry—the study of intertwinings and coupled becomings of the human and the nonhuman. To Pickering (drawing on Deleuze and Guattari), posthumanism is a tool to transcend traditional disciplinary boundaries between natural sciences and social/humanist sciences and study the "evolving dialectic" between human and nonhuman agencies.

From the perspective of his own pedagogical practice as a science educator, Gough (2004) draws on Latour and Haraway to rework humanist discourses in formal education and explains how he has approached "posthumanist pedagogies":

Making these connections between material bodies and discursive formations helped me to question aspects of my practice that were occluded by the epistemological and ontological categories and dualisms that frame and permeate the humanist discourses of contemporary schooling and higher education, especially those that divide humans from others, such as human/animal and human/machine. (255)

In this process, Gough imagines teaching and learning as "material-semiotic assemblages of sociotechnical relations embedded in and performed by shifting connections and interactions among a variety of organic, technical, 'natural,' and textual materials" (255).

If animals, in a certain sense, are coproducers of knowledge, it is more often than not a forced participation since knowledge that objectifies, tyrannizes, harms, and exterminates the animal routinely permeates most dimensions and institutions of human society. Under present conditions, with animal bodies as significant units of production and as accumulation sites of meat, labor, and capital (Watts 2000), this knowledge operates in more sophisticated ways by mass-producing, streamlining, (re)configuring, commodifying, and quality-assuring the animal. UNESCO (2005c) sketches a future scenario of powerful management systems and surveillance techniques where "most products, including plants and domestic animals, will probably be tagged with microchips which will supply, in real time, information as to their state . . . their localization . . . and movements" (48) (on radio-telemetry as a form of biopower in wildlife management, cf. Bergman 2005). Thus, the ideal of a "flexible, employable and productive workforce" finds its own specific meanings in relation to the animal industrial complex in late modernity (Noske 1997).

While any account of "the knowledge society" must necessarily be partial, incomplete, and in a state of flux, interspecies choreographies, performativities, and configurations within the production and use of hegemonic and counterhegemonic forms of knowledge require a radical rethinking of the meanings and implications of the knowledge society. As Fudge (2009) has pointed out, anthropocentrism in knowledge production and dissemination is a *choice*, not an inherent essence. Moreover, it is a choice that effectively exposes the deficiencies, shortcomings, and delimitations of prevalent thought patterns and structures.

"THE DEMOCRATIC SOCIETY": ACTIVE CITIZENSHIP, SOLIDARITY, AND "VOICE"

Formal education is frequently viewed as an important arena for the dissemination of democratic values and the nurturing of competence to participate in and contribute to a democratic society. In Swedish education research, for instance, the democratic "mission" of the education system is rarely questioned or problematized (Arnot, Hopmann, and Molander 2007). Education for democracy generally includes ideas such as tolerance and equality, especially with regard to gender and ethnicity as well as to certain other disadvantaged social groups. The World Bank (1999) further identifies education's contribution to democracy in terms of "helping citizenries develop the capabilities to be well informed, understand difficult issues, make wise choices, and hold elected officials accountable for delivering on their promises" (1). For the European Commission, schools should help ensure open and democratic societies by training people to be "informed and concerned about their society and active in it" (2007, 1) and by training in citizenship, solidarity, and participative democracy (2008b). Another central issue in democracy education, as well as in critical pedagogy, is the notion of "voice" (cf. World Bank 2009). In critical education theory, "voice" refers to the cultural grammar and background knowledge that individuals use to interpret and articulate experience, and denotes the means that students have at their disposal to make themselves "heard" and to define themselves as active participants in the world (McLaren 1998).

Posthumanist theory complicates many assumptions surrounding the relations between education and democracy and provides new perspectives on the notion of "voice" in a context where individual and collective voices of disadvantaged or subordinate groups (human or animal) are marginalized or silenced. What would it mean for democracy education to respond to the "voices" and lived experiences of nonhuman animals?

"THE DEMOCRATIC SOCIETY": BIO-RELATIONAL POLITICAL PRESENCES

The notion of "democracy" structures the relation between the individual and the collective. Drawing on a model by Conradt and Roper, List (2004) has argued that also animal groups may engage in "democratic" decision making about starting or stopping a synchronous activity (by using body postures, movements, and vocalizations) under conditions that contain some dimension of uncertainty, such as when a predator could be nearby, when food could exist at some site, and when a decision needs to be made as to what travel route could be optimal. According to List, a "democratic" decision is more likely to be correct than a despotic decision by one individual. Acknowledging, however, the many complexities embedded in the notion of "democracy" from the vantage point of the social and educational sciences, whose meanings of democracy stretch far beyond the idea of "group decision making," I want to approach the issue from a different angle: What possibilities do animals have to make themselves heard in human society, where anthropocentrism and the exclusion of nonhumans are fundamental to the understandings and practices of democracy as we have inherited it (Bingham 2006)? How can they become politically audible in a society characterized by Clark (1997) as allowing animals into the neighborhood (always, however, under the threat of deportation) as long as they remain quiet, speechless, mute?

Jones (2000) addresses the relation between the individual and the collective as a primary problem in human–(wild) animal interaction. Animals are largely subsumed within the abstract social construction of the group, the species, the population, having severe implications for their life situation as individual, embodied beings who make up these populations: If animal populations are not affected in any statistical way by a particular human action, individual animal suffering and death are considered unproblematic. This argument totally misses the point from the perspective of animal agribusiness and biotechnology, where animals are not threatened by extinction but rather mass-produced and often patented as any other artifactual innovation. Jones suggests that in order to make animals politically present, we need to create ripples in the exploited spaces of the collectives, disrupt the spatialities of oppression, and lift them from the tyranny of the "common." I would like to develop Jones's argument and suggest the articulation of a bio-relational, situated idea of democracy, emerging from interactions among specific constellations or assemblages of mixed non/human individuals and groups. In this understanding, democracy would be a site for human and nonhuman material and discursive realms to be interactively reconfigured (cf. Wilbert 2000). As Sanders and Arluke (1993) put it:

> Rather than a world separated into subjects (scientists, men, the powerful) and objects (women, animals, "savages"), the image of the world ultimately offered is one composed of subjects-in-interaction, human and nonhuman actors cooperating and struggling with the historical, political, cultural forces in which their activities are embedded. (386)

Following this line of argument, a central question in situations of decision making would be: Is the conventional interpretation of democracy appropriate and sufficient to cater for the well-being and interests of every body affected by this decision or action? What is envisioned here is perhaps not a "parliament of things"—even if, in Latour's (1993) words, "things are not things either" (138)—but at least democratic processes where nonhumans are politically present. From education, it would ask for a similarly reconstituted response-ability (cf. Biesta 2006, 70) equipped to address gender/postcolonial/posthuman intersectionalities.[6]

"THE MULTICULTURAL SOCIETY": INCLUSION, COMMUNICATION, AND "SHARED VALUES"

From an educational viewpoint, the ideas of a democratic society and a multicultural society are closely interlinked. Both concepts imply nonrepressive modes of interaction, where, ideally, everybody possesses equal value and opportunities. A multicultural society is, in addition, expected to be open to a diversity of identities, expressions, and lifestyles. Cultural hegemony is, from this perspective, problematic, and in the policy documents, respect for cultural and linguistic diversity is one key competence education should impart (e.g., European Commission 2007). Still, the notions of social inclusion and cohesion that recur in the documents either seem to implicate a "master narrative" of cultural identity (such as "the European identity") or emphasize the promotion of "shared values" (OECD 2009).

Regardless of any ambivalences in these documents, it should be clear that a multicultural society requires a variety of communication forms, not only restricted to rule-bound knowledge in the canonical, standardized national language (Cope and Kalantzis 2000). This opens up possibilities for an expanded notion of "literacy." Furthermore, a posthumanist perspective on "the multicultural society" (and its accompanying multimodal literacy definitions) would argue that such a society needs to consider and accommodate not only a variety of lifestyles, but a variety of life-*forms*. As Armstrong and Simmons (2007) remark, the perceived authority of human modes of self-expression relies on our ignoring "the many languages, crafts, cultures, intelligences, intentions and agencies of nonhuman animals" (20). How can animal alterity be addressed, and human–animal communication and meaning making become part of education for a multicultural society? How can the diversity of animal cultures inform, and be informed by, developments in multiliteracy education?

"THE MULTICULTURAL SOCIETY": ZOOLITERACY AND TRANS-SPECIES EFFORTS TO "BRING FORTH A WORLD"

To begin with the notion of "literacy," Sloterdijk (2009) claims that humanism as such can be viewed as a consequence of literacy:

> Thus we can trace the communitarian fantasy that lies at the root of all humanism back to the model of a literary society, in which participation through reading the canon reveals a common love of inspiring messages. At the heart of humanism so understood we discover a cult or club fantasy: the dream of the portentous solidarity of those who have been chosen to be allowed to read. (13)

According to Sloterdijk, literacy has had a sharply selective sorting effect between "the literate" and "the illiterate," almost comparable to a species differentiation. Sloterdijk further argues that the coexistence of people in present societies has been established on new, posthumanistic foundations, and that modern humanism (and its accompanying literary, humanistic media) no longer serves as a model for schooling and education since political and economic structures can no longer be organized on the model of literary societies. In Sloterdijk's view, "reading" is really a disguise for "breeding," and the purpose of both education and literacy has traditionally been to improve, tame, and de-bestialize humans by exposing them to the proper kinds of influences. Sloterdijk poses the question: "What can tame man, when the role of humanism as the school for humanity has collapsed?" (20). The answer he points to is new biopolitical, or "anthropotechnological," breeding programs, leading to a "human zoo" in which the characteristics of the species can be optimized.

So much for "multiculturalism." I believe that there are spaces for thinking about posthumanist challenges to notions of multicultural and multiliteracy education (and its human–animal connections) in a slightly less deterministic way. I agree with Sloterdijk that orthodox ideas of the prominence of script-based (and logocentric) modes of communication are no longer sufficient. What is needed, however, is not new anthropotechnological breeding programs, but a radically different understanding of "bestialization" in meaning making. In Bartkowski's (2008) view, we must acquire new forms of literacy to know how to "read our way through the rapids of bioethical, biopolitical, and biosocial changes as swiftly as they emerge" (19). I would add that it requires the formation of a new kind of "zooliteracy" that recognizes nonhuman animal influences on "our" (presumably) human linguistic behavior, but also how traditional notions of literacy silence and subsume the animal and how a reworking of these notions can be used for trans-species efforts to "bring forth a world" across both bio- and culturo-spheres; a world where human language is conceived of as part of a wider natural-cultural semiotic system (Gifford, in Wheeler and Dunkerley 2008). In this Lyotardian understanding, language is heterogeneous, multidimensional, and belongs to humans as well as to animals. Thus, not only each species, but each individual, has its own way of "speaking" to us (Kuperus, in Schaefer 2008), and even if we are unable to "speak" with them, we do have possibilities to, as Bingham (2006) puts it, become articulate with them in various ways. This entails "learn[ing] to be affected," that is, developing a sensitivity and attentiveness to the lifeworld of others (489).

In a call for papers by Asociación Filosófica de México (2009) for a congress on philosophical dialogue, the verb "to dialogue" is defined as "to relate expressively" and posited as a radical praxis. This call for papers envisions dialogues in contingency "sustained precariously in day-to-day existence among agents so different that one can eventually no longer call them all persons in the same way," including different species. These conceptualizations of dialogue thereby move beyond the Habermasian fantasy of deliberation in communicative and democratic processes that is relying on forms of communicative rationality and has been embraced by education scholars in, for instance, curriculum theory (e.g., Englund 2006; Gustafsson and Warner 2008).

A similar view can be applied to the notion of "culture." Nash and Broglio (2006) suggest that animal agency is an approach to reading culture, insofar as what "we" call culture is always already imbued with, affected, resisted, and even changed by animal presences and action. Also here, however, I want to add that human culture in its orthodox anthropocentric manifestations may subordinate, harm, and oppress animals in an endless variety of ways. Education can embrace and develop a multispecies-oriented *ethical* literacy by critically addressing the particularities of engagement of these anthropocentric manifestations, and thereby open up teaching and learning spaces for posing alternative questions.

"THE GLOBALIZED SOCIETY": ADAPTABILITY, PRODUCTIVITY, AND COMPETITIVENESS

The relationship of education to processes of globalization includes dimensions such as migration patterns, the impact of new technologies, and the changing role of the nation state (European Science Foundation 2008). While transnational alliances and networks between educational actors are created, education as such is increasingly seen as a global concern and its products as possible to import and export in a "global knowledge economy." The World Bank (1999) sees globalization as one key trend in the major drivers of change for education:

> Global capital, moveable overnight from one part of the globe to another, is constantly seeking more favorable opportunities, including well-trained, productive, and attractively priced labor forces in market-friendly and politically stable business environments. Employers, seeing local markets more exposed to global competition, are requiring production processes that are much faster, ensure higher quality outputs more reliably, accommodate greater variety and continuous innovation, and cut costs relentlessly, as wafer-thin profit margins drive win-or-die outcomes. These pressures, in turn, are transforming the sorts of workers needed. Tomorrow's workers will need to be able to engage in lifelong education, learn new things quickly, perform non-routine tasks and more complex problem solving, take more decisions, understand more about what they are working on, require less supervision, assume more responsibility, and—as vital tools to those ends—have better reading, quantitative, reasoning, and expository skills. (1)

The World Bank goes on to say that education is a key actor in this process and a failure to recognize the importance of investing in human capital and equipping workers for the challenges ahead will "handicap them severely" (1999, 1–2). Furthermore, it states that in this hypercompetitive global market economy, "knowledge is rapidly replacing raw materials and labor as the input most critical for survival and success" (2). Sloterdijk's "human zoo" with its biopolitical breeding programs does not seem very far away. Economic growth and competitiveness is clearly a major issue at stake for education in a globalized society. Thus, education and the way it is organized contributes to the formation of "the globalized society," but the policy documents fail to recognize the material basis on which this society relies. A significant part of this basis is constituted by the "animal economy," where animals, their bodies, labor, and reproductive capacities are incorporated into globalized commodity chains and in our politico-economic stories of progress and development (Emel and Wolch 1998). Emel and Wolch (1998) have identified the "animal economy" as comprising globalized animal agribusiness; ecological cleansing in the intensification of land use; hunting and fishing; the capturing, trading, and breeding of wild animals for circuses, laboratories, pets, trophies, sport, and other purposes; and biotechnology. Many of these practices are the focus of heavy investments from private and public actors:

> Over the past two decades, the animal economy has become simultaneously both more intensive and more extensive. More profits are squeezed out of each animal life, more quickly, while the reach of animal-based industries has grown to include most of the developing world. (2)

The various ways in which education systems take part in the global web of the animal economy are reflected (and actively reproduced) in everyday school activities, which sometimes get intertwined with corporate branding and identity strategies of big-name companies (Pedersen 2010a). What would it mean for education to examine its own position in the animal (and human) economy? What would be the pedagogical implications of engaging with notions of human/animal corporeality and physicality, structured and interlinked by globalized commodification processes?

"THE GLOBALIZED SOCIETY": CRITICAL INQUIRY INTO FORMS OF BIOCAPITALIZATION

The ways in which animals and their life conditions are intertwined with processes of globalization are numerous, complex, and pervasive. Capital, knowledge, genetic information, disease, and all kinds of material substances are circulated through global networks connecting animal labor and products with human activities and technologies. The global animal economy is implicated in phenomena as diverse as cell phones, zoonoses, and trade patterns, to name but a few, eliciting and accumulating surplus value from every fragment of the bodies needed to keep the machinery prosperous. Shukin (2009) develops an analysis of these processes in such detail and of such a scale that the notions of "animal" and "capital" converge as literally synonymous (see also Watts 2000; Boyd 2001).

One way in which education can respond to these conditions would be to track down, and map, the circulation patterns and flows of capital, materials, and knowledge through animal (and human) bodies and labor at a specific site of production, and locate any educational activities taking place in this chain. If the material foundations of society to a great extent are literally built upon animal bodies and the appropriation of their productive and reproductive properties, an understanding of how this apparatus operates in all its educational dimensions appears urgent. By identifying, and critically analyzing, its own position in capitalist modes of animal production, education can create tools of inquiry into its embeddedness in the nature/technology/society complex in a globalized world: How do animal bodies function as sites of knowledge accumulation and circulation, and how is the biocapital of knowledge predicated on the accessibility and mass production of animal bodies? How are the relations between body, capital, and knowledge played out, and what are the effects? Taking the animal as a unit of analysis and as a point of departure for learning about globalization is a form of "posthuman pedagogy" that starts from the center and periphery of globalization at the same time: The circulation of bodies, labor, knowledge, and capital is a nodal phenomenon in contemporary society; yet the individual animal on whom the entire process is relying is often marginalized, fragmented, and rendered invisible in education discourses and elsewhere.

"THE SUSTAINABLE SOCIETY": (INVESTMENT) CLIMATE CONCERNS AND "OUR" GRANDCHILDREN'S FUTURE

Although the United Nations have announced the period 2005–2014 as the Decade of Education for Sustainable Development, in most policy documents I have reviewed the concept of environmental sustainability is used as little else than a prop. In a special publication the OECD has defined "global environmental challenges" as one trend shaping education in 2008 (OECD 2008b), but it does not address the issue on the Web. Although the World Bank refers to environmental sustainability as part of the 2015 Millennium Development Goals, and despite its view of education as "a dialogue between the present and the future" (2009, 8), the World Bank's concerns about the climate seems largely to be limited to "improving the *investment* climate" (2009, 11, emphasis added). The European Commission (2008a) does acknowledge climate change as one challenge that will require radical adaptation, and mentions support for sustainable development as part of the attitudes related to social and civic competences that education is expected to convey (2007), but the commission's engagement with environmental sustainability does not seem to extend much further.

Education Policy Making for Social Change 69

UNESCO, on the other hand, has produced a number of documents related to the Decade of Education for Sustainable Development, where the issue of the (environmentally) sustainable society is being addressed more specifically. To UNESCO, Education for Sustainable Development means ambitiously "education that enables people to foresee, face up to and solve the problems that threaten life on our planet" (2005b, 5). For what purpose? According to the preface to the same document, in order to have something to pass on, to "promise a sustainable planet and a safer world to our children, our grandchildren and their descendants" (3). In another information document (UNESCO 2005d), sustainable development is defined as fostering peace, fighting against global warming, reducing North–South inequalities, fighting against poverty, and fighting against the marginalization of women and girls. UNESCO (2005a), however, also recognizes the paradox that the most educated nations actually are those that leave the deepest ecological footprints; hence, sustainable societies are not likely to be achieved simply by producing more education, but its content needs to be reoriented.

Although sustainable development to a large extent has focused on the life conditions of present and future generations of humans, some Education for Sustainable Development research has also argued for a stronger recognition of animals beyond their instrumental ecological function as species representatives (e.g., Selby 1995, 2000; Kahn 2003; Andrzejewski, Pedersen, and Wicklund 2009). Kahn (2003) and others have raised critique against sustainability education in many of its present forms for being anthropocentric, technocratic, too tied to governmental and corporate agendas, and failing to adequately address issues of social justice. Given its potential to look beyond the idea of "humanity" and "animality" as fixed and stable categories, how can posthumanism further problematize the role of education in creating a "sustainable society"? And, to paraphrase Haraway (2009): What does it mean to educate in a time of extinction, extermination, and mass-industrial death?

"THE SUSTAINABLE SOCIETY": REPRODUCTIVE FUTURISM?

My suggestion for a posthumanist response to the trope of "sustainability," especially as it is constituted in education policy discourse, includes a profound interrogation of the presumed linearity embedded in the concept. This linearity has several articulations, one appearing in Edelman's (2004) theory on "reproductive futurism." Edelman notes that heterosexuality produces a future embracing "more of the same," an ideology of reproductive necessity of which the hegemonic figure is the Child (not to be confused with the lived experiences of real children) as a symbol of reproduction of the social order in political discourse. According to Edelman, the position and presence of the image of the Child is nonnegotiable, fetishized, universalized, and as compulsory as the future itself. The institution of education, with the Child as its main target *and* basis of subsistence, plays a pivotal role in this process of ideological reiteration. In Edelman's view, the Child produces nothing but predetermination of meaning. His analysis stands in stark opposition to most major philosophers of education, such as Hannah Arendt, to whom "every single [human] birth [is] the hope for something entirely other to come and break the chain of eternal recurrence" (Habermas 2003, 58). I would like to add that the fantasy of the "perpetual new beginning" of natality (Greenaway 1992, 33), and its inherent linearity, is complicated not only by Edelman, but by the limits to its own life-sustaining conditions. Theories of resilience teach us that once being exposed to excessive pressure, social-ecological systems do not necessarily behave in the linear fashion that is the most convenient to conceptualize and handle (Walker and Salt 2006). Reformulated in posthumanist terms, human dominance may be viewed as "not an inherent or essential attribute, but a negotiated position within a system, a position that can be overturned" (Bartlett and Byers 2003, 29). What does this mean for the possibilities of the educational subject to come about? How does the linear time axis built into the logics of education (and the education system) relate to the possibility of planetary destruction and the mass extinction of species (the human species included)? Education, as an elaborate example of an invention of human intervention, may have to address the radical negativity posed against reproductive futurism and come to terms with the idea of the self-regenerative human subject, always already manifested in the reassuring image of the Child, as a hope and a reason to save the world and the future.

CONCLUSIONS

I want to briefly return to the introduction of this chapter, where I refer to four zones of intersection that I have elsewhere suggested connect education theory and animal studies within a posthumanist framework: ontological/epistemological imperfection, "radical" intersubjectivities, open-ended ways of "coming into the world," and decentering of the human subject (Pedersen 2010b). Here, I have used these intersections to perform a critical intervention into the anthropocentric and exclusionary foundations of international educational policy making. In each of the presumably unifying present and future "societies"—that is, the overarching ideas about the relationship between education and social change that I have explored in this chapter—these posthumanist intersections take on particular implications and point to different problems, but also converge in their critique.

I argue that the structural-anthropocentric ideology on which dominant educational policy relies has severe consequences not only for what forms of knowing are enabled to "bring forth a world" (Gifford, in Wheeler and

Dunkerley 2008; Wolfe 2010), but also for *who* is invited to participate in world-forming processes. From this perspective, education policy is involved in a particular form of species performativity by which not only subject positions, but subject *repertoires* are produced and, at the same time, severely restricted. I identify subject repertoires as the range and scope of possibilities available for subjects to emerge, indeed, to *become* subjects in the first place. Subject repertoires in the policy documents reviewed in this chapter typically shape conditions for education so as to produce not only "the human" as its teleological outcome (cf. Boggs 2009), but a certain "species" of *Homo sapiens sapiens* bred, to speak with Sloterdijk (2009), to fulfill the imperatives of global capitalism. In order to fully disclose the disabling force of the knowledge hegemonies from which education policy presently operates, these subject repertoires need critical rethinking from a posthumanist position. From this position, the presence of nonhuman animals makes visible the coercive and exclusionary implications of the policy documents for animals *and* humans alike. It requires education to seriously scrutinize its own embeddedness in reproductive practices and thought patterns and take effective measures toward its transformation. As Wolfe (2010) simply remarks, "we" are not who "we" thought we were.

NOTES

1. By "species performativity," I mean discursive practices and processes that produce and reproduce nonhuman Otherness in specific contexts of human–animal interaction. The term is developed from Birke, Bryld, and Lykke's (2004) application of Judith Butler's notion of gender performativity to human–animal relationships. (For a further account of species performativity, see Pedersen 2010a.)

2. *UNESCO's Medium-Term Strategy 2008–2013 (34 C/4)* (UNESCO 2008); *The OECD Centre for Educational Research and Innovation* (OECD 2008a); *Education Sector Strategy* (World Bank 1999); *Opening Doors: Education and the World Bank* (World Bank 2009); *Improving Competences for the 21st Century* (European Commission 2008a); *Key Competences for Lifelong Learning: European Reference Framework* (European Commission 2007); *An Updated Strategic Framework for European Cooperation in Education and Training* (Commission of the European Communities 2008); *Draft 2008 Joint Progress Report of the Council and the Commission on the Implementation of the "Education and Training 2010" Work Programme "Delivering Lifelong Learning for Knowledge, Creativity and Innovation"—Adoption* (Council of the European Union 2008); *Norden—en ledande, dynamisk kunskaps och kompetensregion* (proposal from Nordic Council of Ministers) (Nordic Council 2007). I have also used the Delors report *Learning: The Treasure Within. Report to UNESCO of the International Commission on Education for the Twenty-First Century* (Delors et al. 1996) as reference material. It should be noted that these texts are not in any way exhaustive nor do they cover all documentation on education policy produced by these actors. They are, however, publicly available on the Web and as such assumed to communicate key ideas of the actors' formal positions on strategies for education policy making.

3. I found the notion of "sustainable development" only in documents of UNESCO and the European Commission.
4. The notion of "social cohesion" has a few different connotations in the documents. The World Bank (1999) mentions social cohesion in relation to equity, but develops the term more specifically in the context of values education by explaining that "education transmits values, beliefs, and traditions. It shapes attitudes and aspirations, and the skills it develops include crucial inter- and intra-personal capabilities" (6). Likewise, the European Commission's (2007) *Key Competences for Lifelong Learning: European Reference Framework* foregrounds social cohesion as a way of combating marginalization, but also mentions it in the context of "social diversity" and the importance of "respect for shared values" (10) (social cohesion in relation to the development of shared values is also emphasized by the OECD 2009). In addition, UNESCO (n.d.) frames social cohesion by intercultural understanding and dialogue.
5. UNESCO (2005c) has produced a report on this topic, but it was not present in the policy documents I studied.
6. See Andrzejewski, Pedersen, and Wicklund (2009) for suggested curriculum development guidelines for critical interspecies education. For a more far-reaching take on nonhumans and education, see Heslep (2009).

REFERENCES

Andrzejewski, J., Pedersen, H., and Wicklund, F. (2009). "Interspecies Education for Humans, Animals, and the Earth." In *Social Justice, Peace, and Environmental Education: Transformative Standards*, ed. J. Andrzejewski, M. Baltodano, and L. Symcox, 136–154. New York: Routledge.
Armstrong, P., and Simmons, L., eds. (2007). "Bestiary: An Introduction." In *Knowing Animals*, ed. L. Simmons and P. Armstrong, 1–24. Leiden: Brill.
Arnot, M., Hopmann, S.T., and Molander, B. (2007). *International Evaluation in Educational Sciences: Democratic Values, Gender and Citizenship. Vetenskapsrådets rapportserie 4: 2007*. Stockholm: Vetenskapsrådet.
Asociación Filosófica de México. (2009). "XV International Congress of Philosophy, Symposium 'Dialogue among Differents, Dialogue in Radicality.'" Mexico City, January 25–29.
Bartkowski, F. (2008). *Kissing Cousins: A New Kinship Bestiary*. New York: Columbia University Press.
Bartlett, L., and Byers, T.B. (2003). "Back to the Future: The Humanist *Matrix*." *Cultural Critique* 53:28–46.
Bergman, C. (2005). "Inventing a Beast with No Body: Radio-Telemetry, the Marginalization of Animals, and the Simulation of Ecology." *Worldviews* 9 (2): 255–270.
Biesta, G.J.J. (1998a). "Pedagogy without Humanism: Foucault and the Subject of Education." *Interchange* 29 (1): 1–16.
Biesta, G.J.J. (1998b). "Say You Want a Revolution . . . Suggestions for the Impossible Future of Critical Pedagogy." *Educational Theory* 48 (4): 499–510.
Biesta, G.J.J. (1999). "Radical Intersubjectivity: Reflections on the 'Different' Foundation of Education." *Studies in Philosophy and Education* 18:203–220.
Biesta, G.J.J. (2006). *Beyond Learning: Democratic Education for a Human Future*. Boulder, CO: Paradigm.
Bingham, N. (2006). "Bees, Butterflies, and Bacteria: Biotechnology and the Politics of Nonhuman Friendship." *Environment and Planning A* 38:483–498.

Birke, L., Bryld, M., and Lykke, N. (2004). "Animal Performances. An Exploration of Intersections between Feminist Science and Studies of Human/Animal Relationships." *Feminist Theory* 5 (2): 167–183.
Boggs, C.G. (2009). "Emily Dickinson's Animal Pedagogies." *PMLA* 124 (2): 533–541.
Boyd, W. (2001). "Making Meat: Science, Technology, and American Poultry Production." *Technology and Culture* 42:631–664.
Braun, B. (2004). "Modalities of Posthumanism." *Environment and Planning A* 36:1352–1355.
Clark, D. (1997). "On Being 'The Last Kantian in Nazi Germany.' Dwelling with Animals after Levinas." In *Animal Acts: Configuring the Human in Western History*, ed. J. Ham and M. Senior, 165–198. New York: Routledge.
Commission of the European Communities. (2008). *An Updated Strategic Framework for European Cooperation in Education and Training.* http://ec.europa.eu/education/lifelong-learning-policy/doc/com865_en.pdf. Accessed June 22, 2010.
Cope, B., and Kalantzis, M. (2000). "Introduction. Multiliteracies: The Beginnings of an Idea." In *Multiliteracies: Literacy Learning and the Design of Social Futures*, ed. B. Cope and M. Kalantzis, 3–8. London: Routledge.
Council of the European Union. (2008). *Draft 2008 Joint Progress Report of the Council and the Commission on the Implementation of the "Education and Training 2010" Work Programme "Delivering Lifelong Learning for Knowledge, Creativity and Innovation"—Adoption. 5723/08.* Brussels: Council of the European Union.
Delors, J., Al Mufti, I., Amagi, I., Carneiro, R., Chung, F., Geremek, B., Gorham, W., Kornhauser, A., Manley, M., Quero, M.P., Savané, M.-A., Singh, K., Stavenhagen, R., Suhr, M.W., and Nanzhao, Z. (1996). *Learning: The Treasure Within. Report to UNESCO of the International Commission on Education for the Twenty-First Century.* Paris: UNESCO.
Edelman, L. (2004). *No Future: Queer Theory and the Death Drive.* Durham, NC: Duke University Press.
Emel, J., and Wolch, J. (1998). "Witnessing the Animal Moment." In *Animal Geographies: Place, Politics, and Identity in the Nature-Culture Borderlands*, ed. J. Wolch and J. Emel, 1–24. London: Verso.
Englund, T. (2006). "Deliberative Communication: A Pragmatist Proposal." *Journal of Curriculum Studies* 38 (5): 503–520.
European Commission. (2007). *Key Competences for Lifelong Learning: European Reference Framework.* Luxembourg: European Communities.
European Commission. (2008a). *Improving Competences for the 21st Century.* Luxembourg: European Communities.
European Commission. (2008b). *School Education: Equipping a New Generation.* http://ec.europa.eu/education/lifelong-learning-policy/doc64_en.htm. Accessed June 22, 2010.
European Science Foundation. (2008). *Call for Outline Proposals: Funding Initiative in the Field of Higher Education and Social Change (EUROHESC).* http://www.esf.org/activities/eurocores/running-programmes/eurohesc.html. Accessed June 22, 2010.
Fudge, E. (2009). "A Project for Animal History." Presentation at the British Animal Studies Network Meeting 10, University College London, February 21.
Gough, N. (2004). "RhizomANTically Becoming-Cyborg: Performing Posthuman Pedagogies." *Educational Philosophy and Theory* 36 (3): 253–265.
Greenaway, P. (1992). *Hundred Objects to Represent the World.* Stuttgart: Hatje.
Gustafsson, B., and Warner, M. (2008). "Participatory Learning and Deliberative Discussion within Education for Sustainable Development." In *Values and*

74   *Helena Pedersen*

Democracy in Education for Sustainable Development—Contributions from Swedish Research, ed. J. Öhman, 75–92. Malmö: Liber.

Habermas, J. (2003). *The Future of Human Nature*. Cambridge: Polity.

Haraway, D.J. (2004). "The Promises of Monsters: A Regenerative Politics for Inappropriate/D Others." In *The Haraway Reader*, 63–124. New York: Routledge.

Haraway, D.J. (2009). "When Species Meet: Ethical Attachment Sites for Out-of-Place Companions." Presentation at the British Animal Studies Network Meeting 10, University College London, February 21.

Heslep, R.D. (2009). "Must an Educated Being Be a Human Being?" *Studies in Philosophy and Education* 28:329–349.

Jones, O. (2000). "(Un)ethical Geographies of Human–Non-Human Relations: Encounters, Collectives and Spaces." In *Animal Spaces, Beastly Places: New Geographies of Human–Animal Relations*, ed. C. Philo and C. Wilbert, 268–291. London: Routledge.

Kahn, R. (2003). "Towards Ecopedagogy: Weaving a Broad-Based Pedagogy of Liberation for Animals, Nature, and the Oppressed People of the Earth." *Journal for Critical Animal Studies* 1 (1). http://www.criticalanimalstudies.org/JCAS/Journal_Articles_download/Issue_1/kahn.pdf. Accessed June 22, 2010.

Latour, B. (1993). *We Have Never Been Modern*. Cambridge, MA: Harvard University Press.

List, C. (2004). "Democracy in Animal Groups: A Political Science Perspective." *Trends in Ecology and Evolution* 19 (4): 168–169.

McLaren, P. (1998). *Life in Schools. An Introduction to Critical Pedagogy in the Foundations of Education*. New York: Longman.

Miller, H.B. (1992). "Not the Only Game in Town: Zoöepistemology and Ontological Pluralism." *Synthese* 92:25–37.

Nash, R., and Broglio, R. (2006). "Introduction to Thinking with Animals." *Configurations* 14 (1–2): 1–7.

Nordic Council. (2007). *Norden—en ledande, dynamisk kunskaps och kompetensregion (Proposal from Nordic Council of Ministers)*. http://www.norden.org/en/nordic-council/sagsarkiv/b-249 kultur/at_download/proposalfile. Accessed June 22, 2010.

Noske, B. (1997). *Beyond Boundaries: Humans and Animals*. Montreal: Black Rose Books.

OECD. (2008a). *Centre for Educational Research and Innovation*. http://www.oecd.org/dataoecd/38/18/38446790.pdf. Accessed June 22, 2010.

OECD. (2008b). *Trends Shaping Education. 2008 Edition*. http://www.oecd.org/document/58/0,3343,en_2649_35845581_41208186_1_1_1_37455,00.html. Accessed June 22, 2010.

OECD. (2009). *Education*. http://www.oecd.org/about/0,3347,en_2649_37455_1_1_1_1_37455,00.html. Accessed June 22, 2010.

Pedersen, H. (2010a). *Animals in Schools: Processes and Strategies in Human–Animal Education*. West Lafayette, IN: Purdue University Press.

Pedersen, H. (2010b). "Is 'the Posthuman' Educable? On the Convergence of Educational Philosophy, Animal Studies, and Posthumanist Theory." *Discourse: Studies in the Cultural Politics of Education* 31 (2): 237–250.

Pickering, A. (2005). "Asian Eels and Global Warming: A Posthumanist Perspective on Society and the Environment." *Ethics and the Environment* 10 (2): 29–43.

Rossini, M. (2006). "To the Dogs: Companion Speciesism and the New Feminist Materialism." *Kritikos* 3 (September). http://intertheory.org/rossini. Accessed November 24, 2008.

Sanders, C.R., and Arluke, A. (1993). "If Lions Could Speak: Investigating the Animal–Human Relationship and the Perspectives of Nonhuman Others." *Sociological Quarterly* 34 (3): 377–390.

Schaefer, D.O. (2008). "Review of Society for Phenomenology and Existential Philosophy's 47th Annual Meeting." Pittsburgh, October 16–18. http://www.h-net.org/~animal/markings10_schaefer.html. Accessed June 22, 2010.

Selby, D. (1995). *Earthkind. A Teachers' Handbook on Humane Education.* Stoke-on-Trent: Trentham Books.

Selby, D. (2000). "Humane Education: Widening the Circle of Compassion and Justice." In *Weaving Connections. Educating for Peace, Social and Environmental Justice,* ed. D. Selby and T. Goldstein, 268–296. Toronto: Sumach Press.

Shukin, N. (2009). *Animal Capital: Rendering Life in Biopolitical Times.* Minneapolis: University of Minnesota Press.

Sloterdijk, P. (2009). "Rules for the Human Zoo: A Response to the *Letter on Humanism.*" *Environment and Planning D: Society and Space* 27:12–28.

UNESCO. (2005a). *Contributing to a More Sustainable Future: Quality Education, Life Skills and Education for Sustainable Development.* Paris: UNESCO.

UNESCO. (2005b). *Promotion of a Global Partnership for the UN Decade of Education for Sustainable Development (2005–2014). The International Implementation Scheme for the Decade in Brief.* Paris: UNESCO.

UNESCO. (2005c). *Towards Knowledge Societies.* Paris: UNESCO.

UNESCO. (2005d). *UN Decade of Education for Sustainable Development 2005–2014: the DESD at a glance.* Paris: UNESCO.

UNESCO. (2008). *Medium-Term Strategy for 2008–2013 (34 C/4).* http://unesdoc.unesco.org/images/0014/001499/149999e.pdf. Accessed June 22, 2010.

UNESCO. (n.d.) *UNESCO and Inter-Religious Dialogue.* http://tiny.cc/h1w3v. Accessed June 22, 2010.

Walker, B., and Salt, D. (2006). *Resilience Thinking: Sustaining Ecosystems and People in a Changing World.* Washington, DC: Island Press.

Watts, M.J. (2000). "Afterword: Enclosure." In *Animal Spaces, Beastly Places: New Geographies of Human–Animal Relations,* ed. C. Philo and C. Wilbert, 292–304. London: Routledge.

Wheeler, W., and Dunkerley, H. (2008). "Introduction to Earthographies: Ecocriticism and Culture." *New Formations* 64:7–14.

Wilbert, C. (2000). "Anti-This—Against-That: Resistances along a Human–Non-Human Axis." In *Entanglements of Power: Geographies of Domination/Resistance,* ed. J.P. Sharp, P. Routledge, C. Philo, and R. Paddison, 238–255. London: Routledge.

Wolfe, C. (2003). *Animal Rites: American Culture, the Discourse of Species, and Posthumanist Theory.* Chicago: University of Chicago Press.

Wolfe, C. (2008). *Posthumanities.* http://www.carywolfe.com/post_about.html. Accessed November 24, 2008.

Wolfe, C. (2009). "Human, All Too Human: 'Animal Studies' and the Humanities." *PMLA* 124 (2): 564–575.

Wolfe, C. (2010). *What Is Posthumanism?* Minneapolis: University of Minnesota Press.

World Bank. (1999). *Education Sector Strategy.* Washington, DC: World Bank.

World Bank. (2009). *Opening Doors: Education and the World Bank.* Washington, DC: World Bank.

5 "Approximate-Rigorous Abstractions"

Propositions of Activation for Posthumanist Research in Education

Stephanie Springgay

> Cleave the notion of the body beyond the human. Connect it to all that co-combines with it to create a movement of thought. (Manning 2013b, 31)

> [There is an] urgent need to supplement humanist methods that rely on generating talk and text, with experimental practices that amplify other sensory, bodily and affective registers and extend the company and modality of what constitutes a research subject. (Whatmore 2006, 606–607)

In her paper *Against Method*, Erin Manning (2013a) argues that the issue with most current models of research is the "bifurcation of nature" (3). Drawing on Alfred Whitehead's work, she contends that there remains a tendency to separate matter from perception, which leads to a fragmentation between awareness and the activity that generates awareness. As such "what emerges is an account of experience that separates out the human subject from the ecologies of encounter" (3). This disciplinary model in which the phenomena of research and the knowing subject are separated shapes knowledge as static, fixed and organized according to preformed categories. In other words, positing the conditions or terms of research *before* the exploration or experimentation "results in stultifying its potential and relegating it to that which already fits within pre-existing schemata of knowledge" (4). We must, Manning contends, find ways of activating thought that is experienced rather than known, and where experience accounts for "more-than-human" encounters.

Perhaps, as a starting place, it is the concept of an encounter that needs further exploration. Encounters between things (human and nonhuman), as Braidotti (2013) argues, cannot be simply defined as an "interaction." Describing an encounter as an interaction, she contends, is inherently neutral, and privileges human–human relationships, communication, and interpretation. Rather the question that needs to be asked concerns itself with the "activation" of a posthuman encounter. Take, for instance, the common practice in education to pair students together to talk about a reading or a topic of study. Once the pairs have discussed the work, typically the teacher asks the pairs to report back to the class as a whole. This interaction between pairs (parts) and class (whole) is unidirectional and determined, and dialectically constitutes humans at the center of the exchange.

Now imagine a classroom of "pairs," each pair singular, heterogeneous, and indeterminate. Each "pair" converges over a concept. After a period of time the pairs break apart and recompose into a new pair. In the new pair formation, there is no reportage, rather the pairing serves to catalyze movement, as the new pair takes up the discussion differently, but already infused with the previous conversation and pairing. The activity or encounter of pair disassembling and reassembling continues for a period of time. This stages a movement exercise where interactions mutate and change through continually displaced pairings. Breaking away from the humanist tradition of explaining what happened in a small group to the larger group requires activation; a modality of affective intensity that generates thought in motion. Moreover, the pair itself is not two human's interacting, but a "more than" encounter between bodies, chairs, floor, desks, pencils, and sensations of yellowness, scratchy wool, and musty paper.

Manning (2013b) often gravitates toward the term "technique" to describe thinking in movement. Techniques are ways of engaging and expressing activities, such as research. They are not tools or methods by which research is defined. Techniques are processual; they are emergent and they constantly reinvent themselves. Thus, in the pairs example, techniques are not a method of pair-share exchange, but rather the movement that sets in motion the activation, and also the modulation of the event as it moves through its various phases. In techniques human actors are not separate from nonhuman elements in the room. Bodies, chairs, floor, clock, sweaters, pencils, yellowness—form technicities of activation. As Braidotti (2013) argues, this technicity "results in relocating difference outside the dialectical scheme, as a complex process of differing which is framed by both internal and external forces and is based on the centrality of the relation to multiple others" (56). Technicities activate new relational fields and new modes of experiencing and knowing. However, these new fields are not complete, they are not fully known or enclosed.

If research, much like the pairs activity, is to loosen its ties to humanist orientations, it needs to untether itself from preprogrammed methods and consider technicities that are immanent to its own research design. We must disrupt the idea that the human/self exists prior to the act of research. Herzog (2000) contends that humanist research operates through "immobilization" where methods assert "correspondences, analogies, and associations between elements at the expense of their differences, their dynamisms, their movements and changes" (9). Posthumanist research cannot take the human subject as the starting point. Rather, as Manning (2013a) argues, "to reorient the question of knowledge away from the idea of subject/object is to rethink the place of *matter* within experience. It is to challenge the idea that what is not known as such is not knowable, emphasizing that knowability may take us off the path of the methodological disciplinary account of experience, propelling us into the midst" (6, emphasis added). We cannot assume to "know" before we enter into research. This emphasis on unknowability means that the conventional understandings of methodology and method need to be undone. Elizabeth St. Pierre (2013) wonders if we can even think about conventional methodologies through new materialist and posthumanist theories. Can we retain the concepts from qualitative research such as interviewing, observation, or data collection? What might these "methods" look like from a posthumanist perspective? Is that even possible? Or, as I argue, do we start anew? Do we think materially from the outset?

There has been an increased attention to matter in social sciences and humanities research. Often referred to as "new materialism" or Deleuzian-informed methodologies, such critical engagements posit affective, machinic, molecular, schizo, nomadic, enfleshed, and vital approaches to research that cut across previously segregated methods (e.g., Barrett and Bolt 2013; Coole and Frost 2010; Coleman and Ringrose 2013; Mazzi 2013; Rotas and Springgay 2013; St. Pierre 2013). Entering into this diverse conversation about materialism and methodologies this chapter will drawn on deleuzeguattarianmassumimanning theories in order to put forth *two propositions of activation for* posthumanist research. A proposition versus an instruction triggers conditions of emergence activating self-organizing potential. This is quite different from giving directions or establishing prior methods of instruction that propose pre-determined interactions. Propositions, according to Manning and Massumi, trigger absolute movement, which they contend is dissimilar to participation or interaction. For example, participation signals out human actors and sets in place a context or a frame of interaction. This preestablishes what can happen and privileges human individualism.

Absolute movement, on the other hand, includes nonhuman elements, such as gravity, technological apparatuses, site conditions, and so on, and does not think in terms of causal relationships—action and reaction. While participatory design typically enables tasks to be oriented toward particular humans, absolute movement is always moving, always already in flux, and composed and recomposed of "more-than-human" intra-actions. Propositions then trigger self-organizing movement that invents its own parameters. In order to think about the implications or the potential of posthumanist research, I develop two propositions of activation: *movement-sensation* and *procedural architecture*. The purpose of the chapter puts materialist, vital, posthumanist theories to work in order to bring matter to the forefront of educational research. This turn to materialism, Hultman and Taguchi (2010) contend, creates a more ethical research practice in which our attentiveness shifts from interpersonal interactions to a more mangled orientation between bodies, things, and sensations.

Propositions, I will argue, are not methods. They cannot be "applied" to research "data," so to speak. One cannot perform materialist posthumanist research from the outside. It is not a matter of collecting research data using qualitative methods and then approaching this data set through a posthuman lens. Thus, the propositions remain irreducible to a method or a methodology. I take St. Pierre's questions seriously, and in concluding the chapter, suggest that we must turn away from conventional questions about of how do we *do* research (methods) *to the how of research*. This requires that we invent not only new language to describe posthumanist research, but "new ways of being research" posthumanistly. Materialist, vitalist, posthuman research is immanent to the research problem itself, and thus remains at the level of a proposition or an activation. Humanist methods operate according to certain spatial dispositions, time parameters, rhythms of transition and modalities of interaction. Embedded within these coordinates is a particular understanding of how a work is experienced. Materialist orientations to research disable and disorient distributive operations. Pulsing with potential technicities, posthumanist research is an event in the making.

PROPOSITION 1: MOVEMENT-SENSATION

In the opening pages of his book *Parables for the Virtual*, Brian Massumi (2002) contends that a body moves and feels simultaneously. "It does both at the same time," he argues, "it moves as it feels, and it feels itself moving" (1). This corporeal connection between movement and sensation, he continues, is a matter of change, or more precisely variation and difference. Every movement invokes a change in feeling, which simultaneously invokes a change in movement so that movement and feeling "have a way of folding into each other, resonating together, interfering with each other, mutually intensifying, all in unquantifiable ways apt to unfold again in action, often unpredictably" (1). The moving-sensing body is indeterminate, open to an elsewhere and an otherwise. It is conjunctive and co-composing, and as such is concerned with issues of collectivity or relationality. Thus, the moving-sensing body gives new urgency to questions of matter, of ontogenetic difference, through materialist, affective frameworks.

According to Erin Manning (2007), movement can be thought of as "relative movement" and "absolute movement." Manning notes that relative movement is where: "form preexists matter. The matter—my body—enters into the form—the room" (15). In this instance, body and room are pre-given and ontologically distinct. Relative movement borrows from a humanist framework. The body is described as active or moving, while the room is viewed as inert and in stasis.

In a relative movement perspective, human bodies and objects are understood separately from the space in which they reside and movement is something that happens in-between, designating an interim between two points that maintains and respects the individuality of these points. In other words, movement that passes between such points (or bodies) does not transform the points/bodies themselves. When a student enters the classroom and sits on a chair, the classroom, chair, and student all preexist each other and movement exists independent of each point, consequently, each entity retains its own self-sameness.

In the instance of absolute movement, a body (human and nonhuman) in movement then, does not simply move between points, rather it exists *in* movement. A body *is* movement, differentiating endlessly. In absolute movement bodies do not precede the classroom, but are in a "ceaseless process of interactive metamorphosis: becoming" (Tianinen and Parikka 2013, 209).

Take for example, the pair-share activity described above. Relative movement would describe movement as the words that flow between students, a student picking up a pencil, moving a chair closer to a desk, or the students' bodies moving between different places in the classroom. And while all of these movements might be considered interconnected, each movement would be understood as discrete and individual, and privilege movement as human-organized and human-controlled. This means that objects in the classroom move because of the actions of the students' bodies. Movement is causal. What sets an object in motion is a body acting upon that object.

Absolute movement shifts this humanist orientation to conceive of all matter as moving, vital, and agential. If bodies (human and nonhuman) are *in* movement, differentiating, and intra-acting, then they are always active, self-creating, productive, and intensive (Barad 2003). Matter becomes "indeterminate, constantly forming and reforming in unexpected ways" (Coole and Frost 2010, 10).

How might absolute movement shift our understanding of research? In humanist research we think of methods (interviews, observation, or images) as external to the research phenomena. Methods enact ways of collecting, documenting, and essentially controlling data. Human bodies enact these methods. How methods are used might depend on particular orientations, such as post-structuralism, feminism, anti-oppression, and so on, but these approaches merely suggest methods of application and analyses. In other words, the methods still insist that there are fixed points between which movement happens.

Braidotti (2013) offers an analogy. She argues that animal rights activists while appearing concerned with post-anthropocentric issues—namely, the ethical rights and treatment of animals—do so from a particular empathetic and political orientation, which is still humanist. Animal rights activists, as an example, end up reinforcing the dualism that is characteristic of the Anthropocene and promotes "full-scale humanization of the environment" (85). Snaza (2013), in writing about posthumanist education, concurs, arguing that acquiring "rights" through inclusion into the category of the human only serves to further demarcate the limits or boundaries of politics. He writes: "to be 'inhuman' or 'nonhuman' or 'less than human' is to be left out of politics" (48). Braidotti argues that what is needed is a "post-individualistic notion of the subject, which is marked by a monistic, relational structure" (87). This, I contend, is what absolute movement offers thought, a conceptualization of politics as "more than."

If research is not "relative"—as in external to its context—but rather "absolute" or immanent, then research emerges as techniques in the midst of the research process. When we think of methods as emanating from outside of research, as something to be applied by humans to a given problem, then we also assume that knowledge can be recognized and studied. This safeguards us from the ineffable. Rather than thinking of research as an organizational structure, as a "form," we need to think about "relations of movement and rest, speed and slowness between unformed elements, or at least between elements that are relatively unformed, molecules and particles of all kinds. There are only haecceities, affects, subjectless individuations that constitute collective assemblages" (Deleuze and Guattari 1987, 266). This leads to an understanding of research as event, or what Manning (2013b) calls a "worlding." Snaza (2013) refers to this as a "'bewildering education' that does not know where it is headed" (49). This not knowing does not mean that research is suspended and immobile. Quite the opposite, it means that we cannot know what our research demands of us before we are in the midst of the research event.

Humanist research promotes movement that is habitual, directional, and predetermined. Movement is something research can "capture" using a video camera, later to be analyzed, potentially coded by a myriad of applications. So while post-structuralist feminist methodologies would argue that knowledge is partial, and would approach video data, for example, reflexively, accounting for power relations and the politicized dimensions of research, the relations between researcher and researched, subject and object, are approached through a humanist orientation. A feminist posthumanist methodology challenges even the category of human as privileged and "looks for subversion not in counter-identity formations, but rather in pure dislocations of identities via the perversion of standardized patterns of sexualized, racialized, and naturalized interaction" (Braidotti 2013, 99). In other words, materialist difference is non-unitarian, indeterminate, and self-differentiating. Posthumanism reminds us that all bodies (human and nonhuman) exist as entanglements, but that they are not defined by such mergings. As such "any entity exists multiply in ways that may not be initially apparent, for entities' entangled and dependent existences mean that none is fully defined by its entanglement in any one particular assemblage" (Bell 2012, 113).

This has enormous implications for thinking about "thought" as ontogenetic and material. Shifting from the Cartesian model of a body coming to thought through consciousness, and the mind severed from or in absence of a moving body, absolute movement underscores "thinking as movement" or, as Manning (2013b) writes, "To move is to think-with a bodying in act" (15). Humanist methods stultify movement. They capture it, record it, and analyze it—cutting into process before it has a chance to engage with the fullness of the technicities it calls forth. Reducing process and extracting movement posits a human subject at the center of research. Posthumanism counters this through movement-sensation, which is affective and intensive. This intensity, Massumi (2002) notes, is nonlinear and unassimilable. Affect, in a deleuzeguattarianwhiteheadmassumimanning inclination, is not congruent with emotions. Emotions, Massumi (2002) would argue, are qualified intensities. Once a body has taken in and formed or shaped an "intensity," and named it so to speak, it becomes an "emotion." "It is intensity owned and recognized" (Massumi 2002, 28). Moreover, affect is not individual; it does not belong to a body/object. Take, for example, the yellowness of a school pencil. The intensity of yellow is already and immediately co-composing with previous and subsequent affects of yellowness (luminosity, warmth, or bitterness). There is a complexity to its intra-actions, an ecology, or a field of relation. "There is no 'body itself' here because the body is always more than 'itself,' always reaching toward that which it is not yet" (Manning 2007, 15).

The yellowness reminds us that every event is intensively relational and collective; it is "pastnesses opening directly onto a future, but with no present to speak of" (Massumi 2002, 30). Movement-sensation then concerns the very dynamism of change or "the being of becoming" (Deleuze and Guattari 1994, 41). This is pure difference—a difference that does not emanate from end points but keeps on differentiating from within itself.

In rethinking what we know as research methodologies, we need to challenge the idea of movement being a move from one position to another, to a movement that opens up possibilities and experimentation. In her work on Deleuzian methodologies, Olsson (2009) notes that education needs to disrupt "positioning." She writes: "Any time positioning comes first, one is allowed to see movement only as intermediate stops on the way towards the goal. In other words, the focus on positions does not allow for movement preceding positions. It creates a grid that permits only the stop-over moments to be seen" (49). Absolute movement, pure difference, enables research to become ontogentic—emergent, vital, and mattering.

Increasingly, educational research has become transdisciplinary, allowing researchers to adopt a multitude of approaches. However, Manning (2013a) contends that this transdisciplinarity still sequesters knowing from doing or activation. Rather, she advocates for a mode of methodological experimentation that emerges from within and is not imposed from without. It must emerge from techniques, she argues, that are unknowable and that heed the uneasiness of categorization. This is what Olsson (2009) means when she writes, "thinking proceeds by laying out its ground at the same time as it thinks" (51). When we move beyond viewing methodologies as preceding movement, thinking shifts from an epistemological formation toward a thinking-in-movement fueled by a pedagogy of infinite variations. Technicity becomes a process of opening up methodology to its own excess, to its more-than.

PROPOSITION 2: PROCEDURAL ARCHITECTURE

The broader engagement with materialist, vitalist, posthumanist research has included the Baradian (2003) notion of "cut" and also concepts such as "contrast" (Manning 2013b), "objectiles" (Rotas and Springgay, forthcoming), and "the figural" (Braidotti 2002) in order to de-naturalize the communicative tendencies in research to tether part to whole. Hughes and Lury's (2013) paper on feminist epistemologies, situatedness, and patterning exemplifies this turn to "cutting," noting that the cut does not "delineate a part as distinct from a whole or cut a part out from a whole but rather that the cut makes a connection" (794) and that this connection/cut "maps where the effects of difference appear" (Haraway 1992, 300). This relationality is thus not causal nor connective. It is, rather, composed.

I want to extend these conjectures about research, and turn to writing by Madeleine Gins and Arakawa (2006) on procedural architecture. Procedural architecture is a process-oriented approach to the way the environment and the body mutually form and extend each other (Keane 2013). In enacting procedures, according to Gins and Arakawa, procedures themselves undergo constant reconstruction. My interest in procedural architecture is not to suggest another "cutting apart" or deviation from the above noted materialist frameworks, but to offer Gins and Arakawa's often undercited writing to questions about the possibilities of posthumanist educational research methodologies.

Common usages of the term "procedure" align with instructive methods, which take as a point of departure a subject. If methods, both pedagogically and in research, enable an evaluation process, which can be extracted from the event itself, how might we envision procedures as a "more than," a tending toward the enactive? The question, then, is, *how is it* a materialist, vitalist, posthuman procedure?

Madeleine Gins and Arakawa (2002; 2006) are best known for their work on "procedural architecture" (see http://www.reversibledestiny.org/). Their theoretical investigations into biotopology frame "approximate-rigorous abstractions" as an important element in thinking procedurally. An approximate-rigorous abstraction is a "holding in place," not in the sense of frozen time frame, but as a site of tentativeness, elusivity, and unknowability. It is in holding in place that "new and different link-ups, fresh points of departure" become breathable, possible, but remain as absolute movement (Gins and Arakawa 2006, 48). Tentativeness, in this sense, is not a hesitation, or where the future has not yet happened, rather holding in place is tentative because the present from which it emerges is yet to be realized (Glazebrook and Conrad 2013). Gins and Arakawa describe this as entering architecture that is not waiting for you. The surround does not preexist the body but co-composes through tentativeness. "The body-in-action and the architectural surround should not be defined apart from each other" (Gins and Arakawa 2006, 50). If we enable their understandings of biotopology to inform the *how* of research, we need to think about entering research as a holding in place.

Research, like architecture, has parts and elements. The tendency in research is to suggest an ordering of these parts. An ordering that is tangential to a whole. Rather, Gins and Arakawa insist that architectural surround and bodily procedure are conjunctive "as soon as someone sets foot into an architectural surround that constrains an action, the architectural procedure it stages gets going. The constraining we are speaking of is so light that it is better thought of as constructive guiding" (55). In other words, the surround does not preexist the procedural way that the body moves through it. Furthermore, as conjunctive, the bodily procedures and movement requires a "sited awareness" (51)—an awareness that is tacit, affective, wittingly, and unknowable. Procedures thus do not separate one aspect of complexity from another. Procedural architecture offers an alternative to research that focuses on communication, accessibility, and delivery of information from human to human and rather considers any object, whether a chair, an artwork, a door, a monitor, a database, or a memory, to be considered as part of holding in place (Keane 2013).

Gins and Arakawa (2002) insist that research exists where living happens within and across the organism-person-environment. Research thus needs to be considered from the start as the site from which procedures emerge, as opposed to applied to; research is immanent to research itself. "Procedures are born of procedures," write Gins and Arakawa (2006, 53). In other words, the ongoing construction of research is the research. Research cannot proceed research. Procedures make space for, but do not determine, the experience of research. Procedures are specific to a situation, and structure an experience of occasion, but in structuring they give way to a pool of potential and thus are open and indeterminate. Moreover, as procedures are constantly evolving, they never end; we can never know their limit. Procedures may exhaust themselves, but at this moment a procedure will emerge into the next. Thus, in thinking about research procedurally, we might ask questions not about what do we archive or collect, but what do we take with us into the next procedure or the next event-making? What tentativeness opens for research is a shift from "This is this" or "Here this is" toward "What's going on? What is it for? What do I do with it?" Not in an instrumental way, but in an ecological or coextensive way.

This approach to procedure considers learning and knowing as emergent and event conditioned. There is an emphasis on enactive processes, which recognize that "one cannot observe the world without participating in its construction, and that modes of construction are purposefully enacted" (Keane 2013, 240). Of vital importance to educational research "methodologies" is co-inventiveness, not as neutral interaction or participatory design, but as emergent in the process of differentiation.

A CONCLUDING PROPOSITION: THERE ARE
NO DATA IN POSTHUMANIST RESEARCH

I'm not convinced that materialist, vitalist, posthuman research requires different apparatuses for doing research. By this I mean the myriad of ways we interact with research such as interviews, journals, art making, images, or videos. However, I argue that these tools for thinking "data" need to shift from "collection" to procedural architecture. St. Pierre (2013) has wondered if we need to do away with the concept of data if we are to work materially. I propose that we shift "data," which always seems to imply something fixed and concrete, to "procedural architectures holding in place." Of course, I've always known to be wordy! However, in renaming them I am not simply casting about a more vague academic terminology, but rather demanding that if we are to take St. Pierre (2013) to heart, to really interrogate this turn to materialism in research, then we need to let go of previously held conventions, such as data. Perhaps the whole point then is to do away with naming at all and to think about "the how of research." There can be no such thing as posthuman data. The etymology of data is "datum," or a "thing given." Nothing can be given in research; it cannot exist beforehand. Rather, it proceeds procedurally. If we are to move forward in rethinking posthuman research, we must let go of our past practices and, as Manning (2013a) argues, begin anew. We are obligated, rather, as Massumi (2011) via Whitehead (1967) contends, to let go of cognitivist approaches that ask what we can know of the world in order to begin with an event-activity. "There is no 'the' subject. There is no subject separate from the event. There is only the event as subject to its occurring to itself. The event itself is a subjective self-creation: the how-now of this singular self-enjoyment of change taking place" (Massumi 2011, 8).

Take, for instance, the use of digital video in qualitative research as a documentary tool. In most instances, the camera functions as a tool that merges humans and machines "in order to enhance or improve human capabilities" (Weaver 2010, 11). The video "data" can be recorded and preserved for future use in interpretive, reflective, and coding strategies. If we approach the use of a video camera in research through the practice of procedural architecture, the camera-body configuration approximates the research tentatively. For instance, if the camera-body is in movement with a student performing a writing task, the camera-body moves as if the student-writing-desk is not a student-writing-desk, but asks questions about the particular moment, the event's shape, its weight, how it behaves under gravity, its solidity, its materiality, its proportion and relatedness to the camera-body. Proceeding procedurally, the camera-body-student-writing-desk become unfixed. Their fixedness exists only in our minds because of the functions that are assigned to them. When we let go of these humanist prior assumptions, surfaces, structures, objects, sensations become open; they become a holding in place and as such co-compose together apart. In this instance, the camera-body becomes an intervention that "brings measured and measurer together so they interact in one single event. Both are changed, constituted anew in that event" (Glazebrook and Conrad 2013, 27). Gins and Arakawa (2002) argue that in always inventing/reinventing, procedures are "not a fixed set of called-for actions, (they are) a spatio-temporal collaboration between a moving body and a tactically posed surround" (73). Moreover, in the video data, typically what is "seen" privileges other bodily configurations. When sound is foregrounded more often, it is discourse that is analyzed because of its humanist role in meaning making. Yet, Gins and Arakawa (2002) note that in breath "the material expands and contracts as we do" (28); thus, the breath, as it passes between camera-body-student-writing-desk, enlarges the tentative possibilities of research.

Thus, a materialist, vitalist, posthuman proposition to research would include stillness, breathing, experimentation, impulse, composition, leaning in, holding and leaning away from, balancing and teetering with the camera-body. What becomes of the camera in procedural architecture is that it stops being a tool for recording research data and exists as a conjunction, where bringing one type of organization near another causes changes in both, which are thick with "indirectness or within the operative clutches of scattered and often not findable action" (Gins and Arakawa 2006, 65). The video camera becomes a proposition about the importance of inventiveness, the production of the new, and aesthetic-political possibilities. Approximate-rigorous abstraction holds open a set of dynamics, or technicities of activation, that propel us forward to another dynamic movement.

Posthumanist research does not need new methods. What it needs are procedures that make felt the unknowability within the unknown. At its best, posthumanist research pulsates with the reverberations of tentativeness, absolute movement, and the openings of a holding in place that engages with the force of the encounter, where propositions of activation are immanent.

REFERENCES

Barad, K. (2003). "Posthumanist Performativity: Toward an Understanding of How Matter Comes to Matter." *Signs* 28 (3): 801–831.

Barrett, E., and Bolt, B., eds. (2013). *Carnal Knowledge: Towards a "New Materialism" through the Arts*. New York: I.B. Tauris.
Bell, V. (2012). "Declining Performativity: Butler, Whitehead and Ecologies of Concern." *Theory, Culture and Society* 29:107–123.
Braidotti, R. (2002). *Metamorphoses: Towards a Materialist Theory of Becoming*. Cambridge: Polity.
Braidotti, R. (2013). *The Posthuman*. Cambridge: Polity.
Coleman, R., and Ringrose, J., eds. (2013). *Deleuze and Research Methodologies*. Edinburgh: Edinburgh University Press.
Coole, D., and Frost, S., eds. (2010). *New Materialisms: Ontology, Agency, and Politics*. Durham, NC: Duke University Press.
Deleuze, G., and Guattari, F. (1987). *A Thousand Plateaus: Capitalism and Schizophrenia*. Minneapolis: University of Minnesota Press.
Deleuze, G., and Guattari, F. (1994). *What Is Philosophy?* London: Verso.
Gins, M., and Arakawa. (2002). *Architectural Body*. Tuscaloosa: University of Alabama Press.
Gins, M., and Arakawa. (2006). *Making Dying Illegal*. New York: Roof Books.
Glazebrook, T., and Conrad, S. (Jun2 2013). "Mapping Reversible Destiny." *Inflexions* 6:22–40. Retrieved February 2014 from http://www.inflexions.org/n6_glazebrook_conrad.html.
Haraway, D. (1992). "The Promises of Monsters: A Regenerative Politics for Inappropriate/D Others." In *Cultural Studies*, ed. L. Grossberg, C. Nelson, and P. Treichler, 295–337. New York: Routledge.
Herzog, A. (June 2 2000). "Images of Thought and Acts of Creation: Deleuze, Bergson, and the Question of Cinema." *Invisible Culture* 3:1–19. Retrieved May 2013 from http://www.rochester.edu/in_visible_culture/issue3/herzog.htm.
Hughes, C. and Lury, C. (2013). "Re-Turning Feminist Methodologies: From a Social to an Ecological Epistemology." *Gender and Education* 25 (6): 786–799.
Hultman, K and Taguchi, L. (2010). "Challenging Anthropocentric Analysis of Visual Data: A Relational Materialist Methodological Approach to Educational Research." *International Journal of Qualitative Studies in Education* 23 (5): 525–542.
Keane, J. (June 2 2013). "An Arakawa and Gins Experimental Teaching Space—A Feasibility Study." *Inflexions* 6:237–252. Retrieved February 2014 from http://www.inflexions.org/n6_keane.html.
Manning, E. (2007). *Politics of Touch: Sense, Movement, Sovereignty*. Minneapolis: University of Minnesota Press.
Manning, E. (2013a). *Against Method*. Unpublished paper.
Manning, E. (2013b). *Always More Than One: Individuation's Dance*. Durham, NC:Duke University Press.
Massumi, Brian. (2002). *Parables for the Virtual*. Durham, NC: Duke University Press.
Massumi, B. (2011). *Semblance and Event: Activist Philosophy and the Occurrent Arts*. Cambridge, MA: MIT Press.
Mazzi, L. (2013). "Materialist Mappings of Knowing in Being: Researchers Constituted in the Production of Knowledge." *Gender and Education* 25 (6): 776–785.
Olsson, L. M. (2009). *Movement and Experimentation in Young Children's Learning: Deleuze and Guattari in Early Childhood Education*. New York: Routledge.
Rotas, N., and Springgay, S. (2013). "'You Go To My Head': Art, Pedagogy and a Politics to Come." *Pedagogies* 8 (3): 278–290.

Rotas, N., and Springgay, S. (Forthcoming). "How Do You Make a Classroom Operate Like a Work of Art." *Journal of Qualitative Studies in Education.*

Snaza, N. (2013). "Bewildering Education." *Journal of Curriculum and Pedagogy* 10:38–54.

St. Pierre, E. (2013). "The Appearance of Data." *Cultural Studies ó Critical Methodologies* 13 (4): 223–227.

Tianinen, M., and Parikka, J. (2013). "The Primacy of Movement: Variation, Intermediality and Biopolitics in Tero Sarrinen's Hunt." In *Carnal Knowledge towards a "New Materialism" through the Arts*, ed. E. Barrett and B. Bolt, 205–224. New York: I.B. Tauris.

Weaver, J. (2010). *Educating the Posthuman: Biosciences, Fiction, and Curriculum Studies.* New York: Sense Publishers.

Whatmore, S. (2006). "Materialist Returns: Practicing Cultural Geography in a More Than Human World." *Cultural Geographies* 13 (4): 600–609.

Whitehead, A.N. (1967). *Adventures of Ideas.* New York: Free Press.

Part II

Attuning to the More-Than-Human Complexities of the Classroom

6 Ecologies of Praxis
Teaching and Learning Against the Obvious

Nikki Rotas

INTRODUCTION

Despite the *obvious* signs of environmental degradation and despite the renewed relation of the environment to curriculum, it is *not obvious* whether environmental education research is reconfiguring school landscapes. Climate disruption, habitat loss and fragmentation, receding shorelines, and contaminated waters have become *so obvious*. Yet, the *obviousness* of environmental degradation and the *not-so-obvious* impact of environmental education is baffling as academics, teachers, administrators, and parents continue to foster ecological thought through environmental education, which is grounded in science-based curriculum. This provokes me to pause and ask two questions: Firstly, *what is being taught*? And secondly, *how are we teaching environmental education*? In a Canadian context, the Grade 3 Science Ontario Curriculum encourages understandings about life systems. A popular way to foster such understandings is through the planting of lima beans in paper cups. Students fill a cup with soil, plant and water the bean, watch it grow, and then it dies. Often, lessons do not extend beyond this scenario, and this is problematic. It becomes limiting when lima beans keep popping up in classrooms, year after year, and decade after decade, serving as mere props. It seems that lima beans have become ecological objects within public school classrooms. They have become artifacts proving ecological commitments grounded in curriculum expectations. It is hopeful that the effort is being made to think and to teach ecologically, but somewhere along the way we smothered ecology with acronyms such as *EE* and terms such as "environmental sustainability," "nature," "the human ecological footprint," and the "web-of-life." We have been smothered by slogans such as "reduce, reuse, and recycle."

Generalizable terms, static definitions, and catchy slogans are also problematic as they affect the ways that ecology is approached within schools. For instance, when ecology is transformed into a school subject, it creates the assumption that ecology is a natural system, that it is universal, and that it is outside, or separate, from human communities (Martusewicz, Edmundson, and Lupinacci 2011). Static definitions further stress scientific approaches to understanding the environment by relying on Darwinian theories of survival and by using metaphors, such as the *web-of-life*, to explain the interdependency of systems in producing life (Martusewicz, Edmundson, and Lupinacci 2011). The natural sciences approach to ecology sustains circular systems theories that favor concepts and practices based in scientific solutions—solutions that disregard the social, political, and economic causes of environmental degradation (Fien 1995). Moreover, definitions of ecology focus on the individual by popularizing concepts, such as the *human ecological footprint* (Martusewicz, Edmundson, and Lupinacci 2011). This concept metaphorically and anthropocentrically refers to one's habits, modes of production and consumption, and the impact of one's living on the environment. While it fosters a sense of responsibility in young school-aged children, the concept positions the individual as capable of "saving" the Earth through the alteration of habits and the reduction of consumption levels. Furthermore, concepts such as the *ecological footprint* irresponsibly claim to be able to measure something that is immeasurable (i.e., environmental degradation) on an individual basis. Such concepts and ways of teaching "about" the environment are well intentioned; however, these concepts do not address environmental issues and the complexity of ecologies on a global, or even local, scale. The theories, theoretical underpinnings, and practices associated with theorizing "about" the environment continue to think and write about the environment as if it is "One" being that needs to be understood and/or repaired.

Research on school gardens is another example of environmental-education-based programming that often develops practices that support theories "about" the environment. The theories and practices that emerge from these research studies focus on the educational value of a school garden, whether it fosters positive attitudes toward food and health or a greater understanding of plant cycles and environmental sustainability. The problem is that these approaches assume a scientific-rationalist, neoliberal, and colonial perspective that suggests communities—labeled "socioeconomically disadvantaged"—need to learn about food, nutrition, health, and environmental sustainability in order to gain economic security. These communities are also perceived as in need of beautification in order to restore them to their "natural" state. Eco-art—the bridging of ecology and art—is yet another example of a practice that often focuses on the production of decorative pieces that "beautify" the school environment. Aesthetic practices in schools are regularly transformed into representational practices, producing objects that satisfy interpretive models. I suggest that environmental and ecological education needs to move away from modernist aesthetic theories and interpretive, solution-based models. McKenzie (2009) suggests that the scope and depth of environmental education should be broadened, and collaborations within and beyond the environmental education field should be fostered. McKenzie also suggests that researchers could reconsider the temporality of their location as the time and place to take a risk

in producing something different. Taking a risk requires breaking from traditional notions of place that tether bodies to concepts of "nature" and
practices of disciplinarity. According to Britzman (1998), it is possible to
"*un*learn" traditions, which I argue should extend to the un/learning of
environmental education as a discipline and/or school subject. Engaging
with deleuze|guattarian philosophy, I propose an un/learning of environ-
mental education through new materialist ontologies (Barad 2007; Bennett
2010). Such a proposal calls for a "vital"-ization and materialization of
environmental education as a bodied act as well as "a not-quite-human
force" that produces "events" of difference (Bennett 2010, 2). Conceiving of ecology in this way entertains a performative understanding that
challenges representational models and the existence of preexisting things.
Resisting definitions of what ecology "is," ecology as *performed* becomes
a relational praxis, a disruptive action, a "contestation of the unexamined
habits of mind that grant language and other forms of representation more
power in determining our ontologies than they deserve" (Barad 2003, 802).
Attending to ecology as performed fosters a becoming praxis of knowledge
creation that is not bounded by the school and does not materialize as the
memorization of knowledge. This shift in thinking and doing disrupts the
repetition of reason and rather asks philosophical, ontological, and empirical questions, as well as attends to the ethical, political, social, and cultural
questions, and questions of agency that produce different ecologies. Questioning thus shifts from solution-based scenarios to questions that foster a
transdisciplinary praxis that is effected by the past but not determined by it
(Ingold and Hallam 2007). Such an emergent praxis sustains curiosity "in
an ongoing generative movement" that is always incomplete (Ingold and
Hallam 2007, 11).

In developing the concept of ecology as *a performed* and as an "event"
of difference, I draw on deleuze|guattarian philosophy, new materialist
ontologies, theories of movement and affect (Manning 2013; Massumi
2011), and the feminist post-structuralist work of Grosz (2011) and Lather
(1998, 1991). Difference, from a Deleuze and Guattari perspective, is a
shift in thinking about difference as discursive *and* material and that which
is constituted *between* the discursive and material (Mazzei 2010). Thus,
newly created concepts do not belong to only discursive systems; they are
reborn in intersubjective experiences as "events" of difference (Semetsky
2009). Attempting to describe the "event," Deleuze (1993) explains that
it is inseparably a process of objectification and subjectification. He further writes that the "event" is a public and private becoming process that
is *in* and *of* potential and actual experience, thus sustaining the capacity to produce another "event." Similar to Deleuze's paradoxical manner,
Lather (1991) describes the event as a praxis of "willful contradiction." She
explains that the event becomes a "self-creative activity through which we
make the world" (11–12). Therefore, events become a way of philosophizing that does not fold back into itself as philosophy, but rather unfolds

as "philosophy becoming practical" (11–12). Lather, however, sharply departs from the Deleuze and Guattari concept of the "event." She argues that theories are nurtured by actions and that theorizing is performative; it grows in and out of practical grounding. To put this in another way, the praxis of willful contradiction is similar to an intervention that Lather further describes as open to "the struggle over truth and reality, and the transcendence [of] non-foundational, post-metaphysical philosophy" (11–12). Taking the above arguments into consideration, Lather departs from deleuze|guattarian philosophy on two accounts. Firstly, deleuze|guattarian philosophies reject notions of becoming practical and/or grounding practice. Secondly, Deleuze and Guattari would argue that "events" of difference have nothing to do with transcendence. I must note that I re/write Lather's words into this fold, not as a means to critique, but to extend her concept of willful contradiction. Attempting to stretch the post-structuralist curricular landscape through new materialist and deleuze|guattarian thought, I begin the chapter by presenting my research context, which is composed of my experience as an occasional teacher within public schools in Canada.[1] I then re/visit the classroom context, not as a means to situate or locate myself "in" and "out" of post-structuralist discourse. Rather, I re/visit the context in a way that re/thinks the classroom as a relational ecology that performs difference (i.e., produces an event). Through theories of movement and affect, and particularly working through notions of intensity brought forth by Massumi (2011) and Grosz (2011), I explore intersubjectivity as an intensive quality of experience that desires crisis, and that potentially evokes a new politics that is nonfoundational and resists representation. Grumet's (1989) work and Kumashiro's (2009) theories of anti-oppressive education contend that classrooms must become chaotic and disruptive spaces. Kumashiro particularly argues that crisis is necessary if students are to become affected and to affect/effect local and global ecologies. In presenting an affective and intensive way of thinking about classroom practice and interaction, I critically examine the political implications of learning as an embodied and intersubjective experience. In the latter section of the chapter, I move toward vitalist theories that consider nonhumans as "agents" of change. Examining notions of agency through a vitalist lens extends an invitation to un/learn what we already know "about" the environment; it provokes us to consider matter as a co-composing agent of knowledge production and change. As Bennett (2010) notes, un/learning is a challenge for many reasons, which include the difficulty to theorize agency outside the acting, human body. In the concluding section of the chapter, I question how we might cultivate a transdisciplinary praxis within schools, classrooms, and scholarship. Touching on Barad's (2007) theory of "intra-action," I lastly contend that posthumanist and/or new materialist methodologies invite new ways of doing ecology in schools that provoke researchers and educators to methodologically re/consider qualitative research and curricular practice as emergent praxis.

RE/VISITING *UGLY* EVENTS

Madeleine Grumet (1989) notes in her paper "The Beauty Full Curriculum" that she taught a *beautiful* class. I found this comment intriguing as I had recently taught a class that I thought was the complete opposite of beautiful or any kind of beauty Grumet was going to outline for me. I had taught an *ugly* class.

> With twenty-two students—ages eleven and twelve in attendance—we began the school day with feelings of outrage over a missing chair, a chair that was supposed to be tucked underneath the student's desk. Feelings of outrage turned into blame and all the bodies within the room were implicated in this blame-game. The day continued and we faced another obstacle impeding access to this beautiful curriculum I had envisioned for this class. An activity involving the use of scissors turned into a bleeding finger and a visit to the hospital emergency room for stitches. Not quite making it to the afternoon bell for lunch, one of my students then decided to run. He ran out the door and would not come back. This required a call to the principal's office, as I could not abandon the rest of the students. What I really wanted to do was run with my student out that door! Why are we having an ugly day? We need an intervention! I thought this class desired one.

INT-E(R)VENT-ION(S)

To intervene (on a basic level) could mean engaging in the act of mediation in order to "mend" what has become damaged and/or gone "wrong." Often, mending practices in schools include sending a student out in the hall and/or to the principal's office. Other mending practices include verbal apologies or lengthy apologies concretized on paper. I have even engaged in the mending of paper, which involved the taping of artwork that had suffered a tear. These "mending" practices are rather Band-Aid solutions that temporarily fix things and/or restabilize environments. Through re/visiting that *ugly* day, I realize that I was not only taping up what had torn, but I was concealing the rupturing and engaging in the suturing of a relational ecology that had reached its limit—the threshold.

Re/writing and reflecting on what had happened within the classroom has prompted me to re/consider my initial desire to intervene. The classroom did not need an intervention after all; it always already had the capacity to un/learn through its own int-e(r)vent-ion. Alive and breathing, the classroom as ecology un/learned through feelings of outrage, the spillage of blood, and the mad dash toward the door. Such behavior would usually be considered "bad" behavior, an *ugly* performance of sorts by most school standards. It is very likely that such events would also be considered the result of "bad" classroom management. Of course, there is nothing rational about my students' behavior; neither is it irrational. *Spilt blood is cause for alarm, is it not? The body's leakiness, its crimson discharge— does it not require attention, perhaps a Band-Aid, a napkin, a suturing practice?* Maybe so, but lingering in reflections and the materiality of what the wound needs, what students need, and what I want does not get us any-where—it will merely suture the wound and return to the Self.

Reflection is a complex practice and perhaps it is a tricky one, as what is reflected could always soothe our bodily habits. Reflection is also a prac-tice that smothers the intensity of immediate experience. It smothers the flicker, the spark, the *something* that begs bodies to attune to the co-com-posing, temporal moments of relation that are always already perform-ing, not as prior to existence but existing as potential—potential "that is lived and felt in the pulsating rhythms of life itself" (Ingold and Hal-lam 2007, 10). Engaging in a reflective practice, as I have done here, does not serve the purpose of reliving the experience as it was lived; nor am I interested in determining best practices for future teaching. I view the act of reflecting and writing as extending what had happened. Phillips and Larson (2012) similarly argue that reflective writing and the act of re/ writing extends data, or "invites" new data. Ingold and Vergunst (2012), too, refer to a similar praxis as the "gestural present"—a generative move-ment that recalls the past, not as it was, but as it presses forward into the present, producing future entanglements. The future always becomes an unpredictable place and our environments will always already be different before we can pin anything down. In that case, the point could also be made that teachers should put a stop to lesson-planning, for unpredict-ability will trump best practices for teaching anyway! It is perhaps this latter point in regard to lesson-planning that is of issue here. Ingold and Hallam suggest that "a system that was strictly bound to the execution of a pre-composed script [i.e., lesson plan and/or curriculum document] would be unable to respond and would be thrown off course by the slight-est deviation" (2007, 12). Responding to their argument, I am questioning whether classroom practices are sticking to the script that directs the same story lines year after year. Within the Canadian public school system there is a considerable amount of freedom in "how" curriculum is delivered, so the shredding of lesson plans and/or curriculum documents is not the radical solution. My point is that there are social scripts that have yet to be shredded and there are curricular expectations to be managed, but learn-ing can also be unscripted (Ingold and Hallam 2007). In re/thinking the classroom as a relational ecology that is always already performing, teach-ers open their classrooms to unscripted moments that potentially alter how we think and act *with* and *in* environments. Therefore, "how" we learn is not determined by best practices, but rather "how" we learn becomes an emergent praxis that desires collectivities, new knowledges, and differ-ences that perform change.

PERFORMING ECOLOGY:
MOVEMENT, DESIRE, AND INTENSITY

In their collaborative work, Deleuze and Guattari (1977) attempt to describe a transdisciplinary praxis that attends to the temporality of place, yet moves beyond territorializations (i.e., static relations). Such a praxis enables deterritorialized movements that lead to infinite relations elsewhere. Deleuze and Guattari refer to "deterritorialized flows of desire" as temporal potentialities that dismantle the colonizing practices of capitalism, including the "interior colony" of the individual that teaches the subject to desire their own repression and the oppression of other beings, places, and things. From an ecological perspective, I further argue that the colonizing practices of capitalist production and consumption teach individuals to ignore the *obviousness* of environmental degradation and/or to assume their *powerlessness* in dealing with environmental issues on a global and local scale. Working with and against the capitalist machine, Deleuze and Guattari propose a "machinic" performance that is similar to the proposed notion of ecology as performed, in that performance calls for a collective action "here and now" (xxiii). This is, however, not a call for "a" collective movement. Rather, it is *in* and *of* movement that agency is performed. This understanding can be clarified through deleuze|guattarian and Massumian notions of "agency" (although they do not use this term). For Deleuze and Guattari, agency is not solely human; it is potential that is expressed as movement, intensity, and as difference. Attempting to describe the intensity of movement, Massumi (2011) explains that it bleeds outward like an ink spot on paper, intensifying its capacity to combine with its surroundings. The practice of gardening can work in this way. Consider, for example, the shoveling of soil, the smell of grass, and the texture of tomato plants—taking this into consideration affectively, gardening becomes a co-composing movement, a praxis that does not fall back into itself as gardening with a desired effect. The act of gardening can move beyond the material process of plant growth and vegetative production and consumption. This is not a transcendent move; it is a move toward thinking about gardening (and ecology) as a praxis that attends to agency as materializing and "mattering" (Barad 2011). Such movement attends to the smell and texture of grass, soil, and plants, and to the materializing effects that territorialize movement and evoke fixed identities, such as human or nonhuman. Attending to mattering is not a radical move to include nonhumans, but rather is a way, as Barad states, "to think about the nature of causality, origin, relationality, and change without taking these distinctions to be foundational or holding them in place" (124). It is a way of experiencing ecology as an intensive quality of experience that fosters an emergent praxis that bears material implications, yet has the capacity to undo itself.

Grosz's (2011) writing on Darwinian sexual selection, and an ontology associated with Bergson and Deleuze and Guattari, is influenced by new materialist frameworks. Grosz's work is not quite new materialist, as Bennett (2010) would say, but her work entangles feminist materialist theories in ways that offer readers a politicized feminist theory. Grosz's politics philosophize life and support a becoming practice that undoes ecologies. She describes the process of "becoming undone" as a self-differentiating movement that is created within and/or in-between humans, nonhumans, and/or systems. This process actualizes in duration: a space of potential that creates futurity through "the fracturing and opening up of the past and the present to what is virtual in them, to what in them differs from the actual, to what in them can bring forth the new" (43). Matter thus carries duration and it is the experience of space-time that potentializes difference. It is also this idea of movement and change that enables us to think differently, rather than to seek things and a fixed state of being (Grosz 2011). Borrowing from Bergsonian thought, Grosz evokes the image of the female swollen body, the mother-to-be, as a way to think about life and matter as different tendencies that create difference within space-time. She describes contraction and dilation as two tendencies that intensively—through a continuous and discontinuous movement—produce something else. The human is indeed actualized as a result of contraction and dilation; however, it is not the infant that becomes. Becoming produces matter—matter that cannot be contained in the human infant or female body. Becoming is rather the convergence of tendencies, a flickering and dynamic experience that moves beyond the subject. Grosz writes:

> It is not things, either subjects or objects, which become, but rather the virtualities latent in them, whose (future) actualizations cannot be contained in the present. Thus it is not an object or subject that becomes—indeed there is no subject of becoming or a thing that is the result of becoming—but only something in objects and subjects that transforms them and makes them other than what they used to be. (2011, 51)

Grosz's understanding of becoming complicates perceptions of what is real. It further works to complexify relations by attending to intersubjective experiences as well as to the capacity of nonhumans and things in producing future moments. Bennett further complicates matters by asking the very question: "Can worms be considered members of a public . . . even if a convincing case is made for worms as active members of, say, the ecosystem of a rainforest?" (94).

THE POLITICS OF FLESH

The difference between ecosystems and publics, political systems and political participation is something to be considered, according to Bennett. Returning to her question above, it is perhaps *obvious* that worms do not have the capacity to speak and so questioning their participation in politics is notably a bit of a stretch. Of course worms are not producers of human culture, but, as Bennett points out, they do "make history." Darwin (1881) studied worms for many years. He observed where they went, what they did, and he particularly paid attention to their spontaneous movements (Bennett 2010). Darwin was fascinated by worms and insisted on their importance in history. The return to Darwinian theories, here, is, however, not to prove that worms are important because they remain in the histories of thought; nor is it my intention to sustain such theories. Rather, the contribution of worms to history and to culture is the "unplanned result" of worms co-composing with other biological and bacterial agents (Bennett 2010). Deleuze and Guattari refer to such a process as an assemblage, and Bennett similarly explains that worm behavior affects/effects the composition of ecologies. What is perhaps a fascinating point about worms is that they unpredictably respond to the temporality of place, not reducing their interactions to mechanical instinct (Bennett 2010). For example, worms do not gather leaves and drag them to their burrows in the same manner each time; they adjust their behavior in accordance with the situation and the possibilities that could potentialize (Bennett 2010). This is not to say that worms do not have habits and engage in repetitive movements. What I do think this brief note about worm behavior does is provoke researchers and classroom teachers to take note of the relational movement of things. It further provokes us to rethink "agency" in terms that realize that nature and culture never stop relating and/or mattering (Barad 2011).

Theorizations of agency are often relayed through interventionist methods that are strictly embodied and thus ignore the capacity of nonhuman assemblages (Bennett 2010). Bennett explains that this is in part attributable to the difficulty humans have in understanding that "the human" is not special or superior to material nature. Notions of agency are, of course, debatable, and there are ontological and social questions to be raised that do not deny the machinations of rational agents and/or individuals (Coole 2005). However, I must note that conventional understandings of agency in environmental education discourse propose that reflective practices will generate concern about global warming. This interventionist approach assumes that awareness will in turn provoke individuals to act—this is *obviously* not working. The *not-so-obvious* behavior of worms and their unpredictable acts keep me curious. I think that there is something to be learned from worms that can also lead to lengthy debates about freedom of choice and power, but can also lead to discussions that refrain from anthropomorphism and anthropocentrism. The entanglement of worms, classroom praxis, and politics may perhaps potentialize an int-e(r)vent-ion of sorts and/or spark a "vibrant political theory" (Bennett 2010). Referring to Rancière's (1999) disruptive politics, Bennett argues that the political act does not lie in the interjection of the affective body in a preexisting public. The political is not a revelation of bodies, nor does it involve a public insurgence. What can be learned from the entanglement of politics and worms is not that worms have been there all along, or because we now know they are there we will even care. Formed notions of politics, practices, people, places, and things keep us thinking that there is something or someone out there to become *aware* of like Darwin's worms. Such thinking forms a "wait-and-see" approach that waits for someone to find out that environmental degradation is *really* happening. Furthermore, such passivity lends to thoughts of the "Other" as someone to learn about and to fully know. If environmental education research is going to matter in a different way, then a re/consideration of *what* matters and what *could* matter is significant in ecological thought. It is such thought that provokes a praxis that unravels what it "is" we consider to be human, politics, classroom practice, and environmental education.

THE CRISIS OF FLESH

To seriously consider that worms are more than just worms risks what we know. Risking what we know could mean encountering my student's act of outrage (over a missing chair) as an intimate int-e(r)vent-ion that "make[s] felt the coming-into-eventness of the field of relations" (Manning 2013, 101). From this perspective, the student becomes an "intensive participant" *with* an *in* the classroom as ecology, rather than a perpetrator of bad behavior (Manning 2013). As an intensive participant, a relational capacity is always already stretching the limit and working to exceed predictability, practices, and form (Manning 2013). And yet, participation is not mandatory. Ecologies do not require participation, and, for that matter, notions of participation must also be re/thought. In sticking to the social scripts that assume a human world, environmental education research will continue to be *not-so-obvious*. Bennett gives us something to think about by stating: "To assume a world of active subjects and passive objects begins to appear as thin descriptions at a time when the interactions between human, viral, animal, and technological bodies are becoming more and more intense" (2010, 108). To re/think environmental education does not involve the addition of knowledge, nor does it assume that a lack of knowledge exists. Environmental education as ecological desires creativity and works horizontally across disciplines in order to disrupt the disciplinary practices that end with a culminating task that evaluates an art-object, or a written report "about" the environment. Disruptive knowledge, Kumashiro (2009) contends, involves resisting the desire to know through the un/learning of others and ourselves. Kumashiro argues that "the goal is not final knowledge (and satisfaction), but disruption, dissatisfaction, and the desire for more change" (34). Through the work of Felman (1995), Kumashiro describes un/learning as entering into crisis, which moves students to different spaces—intellectual, emotional, and political. Crisis does not only enable cognitive differences; crisis is also a performative action, in that it has the capacity to create new associations through its expression (Kumashiro 2009).

It is understandably challenging to cultivate a praxis that views teaching and learning as an emergent event that constitutes "reality as it names it" (Kumashiro 2009, 46). In a paradoxical manner, not unlike Lather's notion of "willful contradiction," such a praxis acknowledges that whatever materializes is never controllable, neutral, and unproblematic (Kumashiro 2009). It was this wildness and unpredictability that I thought was *ugly* and that shattered *beautiful* illusions of my class. The classroom as ecology is a paradoxical place that desires an "unknowable" space in-between beautiful *and* ugly (Lather 1998). It is this performative space that works against the oppressive realities that desire repetition, sameness, and the same harmful histories, lesson plans, and practices that are already in place (Kumashiro 2009).

A NOTE ON POSTHUMANIST METHODOLOGIES

Ecology is not a radical move to erase the disciplines, or the theoretical and methodological frameworks, that have served to guide and produce significant research in the curriculum and environmental education field. Curriculum research has greatly focused on subjectivity in relation to power, and tremendous work has been done to radicalize notions of subjectivity (Coole and Frost 2010). Inquiring into new landscapes does not, however, mean that oppressive pasts, presents, and futures can be erased or prevented. Neither does ecology dismiss phenomenological, epistemological, and post-frameworks of the past, for it is this work throughout the years that has challenged and developed new approaches to research (Coole and Frost 2010). In order to rethink what already "is," posthumanist and/or new materialist methodologies keep on asking new questions. This means asking:

> fundamental questions about the nature of matter and the place of embodied humans within a material world; it means taking heed of developments in the natural sciences as well as tending to transformations in the ways we currently produce, reproduce, and consume our material environment. It entails sensitivity to contemporary shifts in the bio- and eco-spheres, as well as to changes in global economies in structures and technologies. (Coole and Frost 2010, 3)

The above questions and suggestions should not evoke checklists and mobilize efforts to take heed of these things in humanist ways. This is what I hope will not happen. The developing field of posthumanist and/or new materialist research calls for an affirmative approach that undoes binary logic by *thinking* and *doing* simultaneously (i.e., performing ecology) (St.

Pierre 2013). If we begin to see ourselves and the work that we do in schools and in scholarship as "always already" entangled with matter, "our responsibility to being becomes urgent and constant" (St. Pierre 2013, 655). There is an intra-active element at play here, rather than a participatory one. Barad's (2007) theory of "intra-action" similarly argues that "knowing entails differential responsiveness and accountability as part of a network of performances. Knowing is not a bounded or closed practice but an ongoing performance of the world" (149). With Barad and through an ecological lens, I have argued that ecology is "a comprehensive process, a process of comprehension, a material reality" that critically examines corporeality, yet does not dismiss the intangible (Kirby 2008, 234). Posthumanist and/or new materialist methodologies are thus aligned with ecological understandings that are not embedded in reflective practices, but rather invented *with* and *in* environments that affect/effect bodies. This suggests that human beings are not the only "participants" within a research study. Simply put, posthumanist and/or new materialist methodologies urge researchers and teachers to look at data and classrooms differently. As Kumashiro points out, the goal is not "to move to a better place; rather, we are just trying to move" (2009, 46). Such praxis becomes *obvious* in ways that affect/effect student engagement and perception of place.

NOTES

1. The term "occasional teacher" is used interchangeably with "substitute" and/or "supply teacher." The role of the occasional teacher is to fulfill temporary teaching assignments throughout the school year.

REFERENCES

Barad, K. (2003). "Posthumanist Performativity: Toward an Understanding of How Matter Comes to Matter." *Signs: Journal of Women in Culture and Society* 28 (3): 801–831.
Barad, K. (2007). *Meeting the Universe Halfway: Quantum Physics and the Entanglement of Matter and Meaning.* Durham, NC: Duke University Press.
Barad, K. (2011). "Nature's Queer Performativity." *Qui Parle: Critical Humanities and Social Sciences* 19 (2): 121–158.
Bennett, J. (2010). *Vibrant Matter.* Durham, NC: Duke University Press.
Britzman, D.P. (1998). *Lost Subjects, Contested Objects: Toward a Psychoanalytic Inquiry of Learning.* Albany: State University of New York Press.
Coole, D. (2005). "Rethinking Agency: A Phenomenological Approach to Embodiment and Agentic Capacities." *Political Studies* 53:124–142.
Coole, D., and Frost, S., eds. (2010). *New Materialisms: Ontology, Agency, and Politics.* Durham, NC: Duke University Press.
Darwin, C. (1881). *The Formation of Vegetable Mould, through the Action of Worms, with Observations on Their Habits.* London: John Murray.
Deleuze, G. (1993). *The Fold: Leibniz and the Baroque.* Minneapolis: University of Minnesota Press.

Deleuze, G., and Guattari, F. (1977). *Anti-Oedipus: Capitalism and Schizophrenia*. New York: Penguin.

Felman, S. (1995). "Education and Crisis, or the Vicissitudes of Teaching." In *Trauma: Explorations in Memory*, ed. C. Careuth, 13–60. Baltimore, MD: Johns Hopkins University Press.

Fien, J. (1995). "Teaching for a Sustainable World: The Environmental and Development Education Project for Teacher Education." *Environmental Education Research* 1 (1): 21–33.

Grosz, E. (2011). *Becoming Undone: Darwinian Reflections on Life, Politics, and Art*. Durham, NC: Duke University Press.

Grumet, M. (1989). "The Beauty Full Curriculum." *Educational Theory* 39 (3): 225–230.

Ingold, T., and Hallam, E. (2007). "Creativity and Cultural Improvisation: An Introduction." In *Creativity and Cultural Improvisation*, ed. T. Ingold and E. Hallam, 1–24. New York: Berg Publishers.

Ingold, T., and Vergunst, J.L., eds. (2012). *Ways of Walking: Ethnography and Practice on Foot*. Hampshire, UK: Ashgate.

Kirby, V. (2008). "Natural Convers(at)ions: Or, What If Culture Was Really Nature All Along?" In *Material Feminism*, ed. S. Alaimo and S.J. Hekman, 214–236. Bloomington: Indiana University Press.

Kumashiro, K. (2009). "Toward a Theory of Anti-Oppressive Education." *Review of Educational Research* 70 (1): 25–53.

Lather, P. (1991). *Getting Smart: Feminist Research and Pedagogy with/in the Postmodern*. New York: Routledge.

Lather, P. (1998). "Critical Pedagogy and Its Complicities: A Praxis of Stuck Places." *Educational Theory* 48 (4): 487–497.

Manning, E. (2013). *Always More Than One: Individuation's Dance*. Durham, NC: Duke University Press.

Martusewicz, R., Edmundson, J., and Lupinacci, J. (2011). *Ecojustice Education: Toward Diverse, Democratic, and Sustainable Communities*. New York: Routledge.

Massumi, B. (2011). *Semblance and Event: Activist Philosophy and the Occurrent Arts*. Cambridge, MA: MIT Press.

Mazzei, L. (2010). "Thinking Data with Deleuze." *International Journal of Qualitative Studies in Education* 23 (5): 511–523.

McKenzie, M. (2009). "Scholarship as Intervention: Critique, Collaboration and the Research Imagination." *Environmental Education Research* 15 (2): 217–226.

Phillips, D., and Larson, M. (2012). "The Teacher–Student Writing Conference Entangled: Thinking Data with Material Feminisms." *Cultural Studies⊠Critical Methodologies* 12 (3): 225–234.

Rancière, J. (1999). *Disagreement: Politics and Philosophy*. Minneapolis: University of Minnesota Press.

Semetsky, I. (2009). "Deleuze as a Philosopher of Education: Affective Knowledge/Effective Learning." *European Legacy* 14 (4): 443–456.

St. Pierre, E.A. (2013). "The Posts Continue: Becoming." *International Journal of Qualitative Studies in Education* 26 (6): 646–657.

7 Losing Animals
Ethics And Care in a Pedagogy of Recovery

Alyce Miller

In an increasingly urbanized, industrialized West, most people have little contact with living animals beyond interactions with "pets," a trip to the zoo or the occasional encounter with urban wildlife, often viewed as pests. Farmed animals, once commonly seen grazing in open fields, are now bred and raised in cramped conditions behind the walls of factory farms. In 1862, 90 percent of the American population were family farmers, living in close proximity to their free-range cows, sheep, goats, and chickens. That figure declined over the next few decades and into the early twentieth century, so that by 1920, with growing urbanization and migration to cities, only 30 percent of Americans were farmers. Corporate farming gradually replaced small family outdoor farms with enclosed confined animal feeding operations. Today, only 2 percent of the current population are farmers. Likewise, numbers of those engaged in hunting and fishing show a slow decline, attributed in part to suburban sprawl that leads to reduced habitat, as well as a younger generation less interested in spending time outdoors.

Though social media saturate us with videoed and photographed representations of animals, bodies of nonhuman animals are more and more removed from ours, relegated to the realm of cyberspace and our imaginations. Even as images of animals proliferate, human-caused mass suffering of animals is pushed into invisibility: the thousands of caged puppy mill breeding dogs whose lives of misery remain hidden from the pet shop buyer who sees only a cute puppy on the other end; the ten billion land animals slaughtered for food each year in the United States alone.[1]

In an essay originally published in 1990 in her book on the sexual politics of the meat industry, "The Rape of Animals, the Butchering of Women" (1990/2010), Carol Adams turned her attention to this invisibility of the flesh-and-blood animal body—lost in the rhetoric of "cuisine," packaged and disguised as "meat," thereby masking the precipitating violence—what she calls the "absent referent." Additionally, Adams's insightful comparisons between the violences inflicted on women's bodies and animals' bodies have certainly contributed to the significant body of work known as "feminist care" theory. These theories also amplify other interconnected oppressions, as evident in sociopolitical overlaps such as the ones social historian Charles Patterson (2002) illuminates in his book *Eternal Tre-blinka*, which demonstrates the deep connections among bigoted Ameri-can industrialist Henry Ford, the processing and killing of animals in the Chicago stockyards, and the mass executions of Jews during the Holo-caust,[2] or the historic brutalities committed against black and brown bod-ies during the slave trade and other conquests, often conflating people with "animals," thereby obliterating their humanity. But such analogies require careful grounding. One goal has been to provide critical lenses allowing them to recognize the problems of a well-intentioned film exposé of dolphin slaughter like *The Cove* that inadvertently demonizes Japanese fisherman while overlooking a similar slaughter in Scandinavia. As a result, I have begun including more work by feminists who engage with multiple phe-nomenological lenses of "Otherness," even as their work has been largely eclipsed by the likes of scholars Cary Wolfe and Matthew Calarco and the Derrideans. There are two major underlying pedagogical challenges, which I will address throughout: keeping the animal body in our sight, and recog-nizing interrelationships with other "Othered" bodies.

First, a little background on the course. In 2006, after organizing and chairing Kindred Spirits, an international, interdisciplinary conference on animals, I was asked by then dean of our Honors College to develop a course on animals and ethics at Indiana University, where I teach in the English department and graduate creative writing program. A philoso-pher herself, she didn't explain further, and I didn't ask for specifics. What seemed obvious, though, is that various human interactions with animals could form the basis for an intriguing study of ethics. Yet I knew I couldn't do justice to the subject if we were to use an applied ethics framework focused on rights arguments. Just as I'd done with the conference, I wanted to put into dialogue active thinkers from a number of disciplines, placing primarily Western philosophers in conversation with scientists, anthropol-ogists, literary writers, legal scholars, religious thinkers, and ethologists.

What was less obvious was the journey on which I myself was about to embark, including the fact that I became a vegan during the second time I taught the course, prompted by an essay by philosopher Bernard Rol-lin. Two major imperatives began to emerge: not to lose animal bodies to abstractions and theories, and to actively keep in sight the historical and rhetorical connections in structures of oppression, affecting both human and nonhuman animals. As a woman professor, I have also had to work around what I call "the sympathy trap," a dismissive accusation that has plagued the wide spectrum of animal rights advocates since their earliest days, the majority of whom were women activists. The historic undercut-ting of compassion for animal suffering as feminizing and too sentimentally inclined continues today.[3]

Teaching an animals and ethics class in the twenty-first century poses a number of other challenges, as well, not the least of which is the common response that until all human beings are equal, we should not be so focused on nonhuman animals ("you care more about the suffering of animals than you do the suffering people"). But this ignores the interrelated nature of oppressions.[4] Human and nonhuman animals share in the stakes.

Evidence that contemporary views of animals are more enlightened can be found in protection laws for pets, the legislative work of animal advocacy groups, and a lower tolerance for farmed animal suffering, that is, legislation to ban corporate farming cruelties such as gestation crates for pigs and battery cages for chickens. Under public pressure, some zoos have modified the more egregious practices (the inbreeding that produces white tigers, the selling off of aging and "surplus animals" to canned hunting businesses) and added enrichment programs and improved enclosures for animals. The nastier practices of corporate farms that also affect human health have led to small-scale alternatives, often known colloquially as "compassionate meat," which, while admittedly giving farmed animals "better lives" and supplying meat eaters safer food, still results in the animal's death. The Animal Welfare Act, despite its name, covers around only 5 percent of the animals used by human beings, and excludes most animals used in research experiments, such as rats, mice, and birds, from necessarily being given basic care, such as food, water, and shelter. Farmed animals known as "livestock" are not covered under the act, nor are cold-blooded animals such as turtles, snakes, and fish. Even the federal Humane Slaughter Act offers little or no legal protection to farmed animals and excludes poultry who suffer unthinkable cruelties. The act also does not cover the conditions animals are kept in or how they are transported or treated in the slaughterhouse.[5] As long as animals remain profitable commodities, the interests of those benefiting will clash with those who wish to protect.

The very pervasiveness of corporate farming practices, the destruction of habitat and wilderness, overfishing, and so on, adds to the urgency. Our treatment of animals is not isolated from our treatment of the environment and of other people. In very basic ways, our lives and survivals remain intertwined, in much the way many Native American religions have for so long traditionally recognized. Whether it's an appeal to enlightened self-interest or inherent concern for the well-being of other living beings, our treatment of nonhuman animals matters.

Animals and Ethics is a fifteen-week-long interdisciplinary course meeting twice a week for thirty sessions. Because of its popularity, it now has its own course number.

Readings for Animals and Ethics jump-start discussions around a series of basic questions, beginning with a definition (legal definitions of "animal" vary, particularly those found in case law and state statutes, but all exclude humans). Philosophical and religious views of animals have shaped both our behavior toward animals and the laws governing their treatment.

The various disciplinary approaches provide multiple contexts and 360-degree perspectives for more nuanced discussions than possible in, say, the Literary and Legal Animal, a course I taught a few years earlier.

An ethologist observing primates in the wild, for example, will think and write differently about the value of animal lives than a social scientist using those same primates in laboratory experiments. Both their purposes, and their outlook and relationships with the animals are different.

Course texts typically include philosopher David DeGrazia's *Animal Rights: A Very Short Introduction*; various selections from *The Animal Ethics Reader*, edited by Susan J. Armstrong and Richard Botzler; *The Lives of Animals* by novelist J.M. Coetzee; and the memoir *A Pack of Two: The Intricate Bond between People and Dogs* by Carolyn Knapp. More than a hundred readings from a range of genres include poems, essays, stories, scientific articles, case law, and journalistic inquiries. We also screen and discuss three documentary films, *Grizzly Man*, *The Wild Parrots of Telegraph Hill*, and *The Tiger Next Door*, all of which feature men who, to varying complicated degrees, interact with or live among wild animals. An intense week is devoted to animals as food, with arguments for and against vegetarianism, as well as differing views on meat eating and factory farms versus small farms by such writers as Jim and Mary Ann Mason, Breeze Harper, Jonathan Safer Foer, and Michael Pollan. It is one of the most challenging weeks, given the strong emotions that meat eating arouses on both sides of the plate.[6]

The course foundation is laid with contemporary philosophers and their antagonists (and their intellectual lineages), such as moral philosopher Peter Singer's utilitarianism and animal rights theorist Tom Regan's debt to and expansion on Kant. Then comes the backward leap to Aristotle for whom animals lacked the rational souls of humans, before fast-forwarding to Kant, who thought that while it might be good for our moral character to be nice to animals, animals are machines and have no reason or feeling. Empiricists Hobbes and Locke conceded that animals have feelings and some rationality, and Hume found sympathy toward animals to be appropriate since sympathy forms the basis of ethics. While it is well known that Descartes did not believe animals actually felt pain and their cries were simply autonomic reflexes, Bentham explicitly observed that they can suffer. We then fast-forward to read contemporary philosophers, such as David DeGrazia and Bernard Rollin, comparing and contrasting them with Singer and Regan. Singer, of course, authored what is considered the seminal work on animal rights, *Animal Liberation*. We work through the rational questions about moral patients and moral agents, about theories of moral obligation and duty on the part of humans and the kinds of moral status that might be appropriately conferred on animals. Various animal rights theories emerge to create a foundation, replete with a kaleidoscope of terms, concepts, and a "who's who" of philosophical reasoning.

This strategy erects the scaffolding for what follows. As philosopher Kelly Oliver points out, while the predominantly male Western tradition of philosophy historically draws a clear dividing line between human and nonhuman animals, much of what makes us human is directly and even mutually constituted by our relations with animals. This creates something of a two-sided coin: If we assign ourselves to an elevated category of human, we separate ourselves not just from animals, but from our own animality; alternatively, if we acknowledge through mutual relationships with animals that we are also "animal" and therefore interconnected, we are likely to bring a very different set of views to our treatment of animals. According to Oliver, "What we need is to move from an ethics of sameness, through an ethics of difference, toward an ethics of *relationality* and *responsivity*." [7] And this gets to the heart of the theory behind this class.

Students who enroll in Animals and Ethics typically represent a variety of majors, from humanities and the sciences to journalism and business. Some have read and thought a great deal about animals, some have worked with volunteer groups, such as wildlife rescue and spay and neuter clinics, and others sign up out of passing curiosity. Some self-describe as ethical vegetarians; some come from hunting backgrounds or farming families. The latter are often the ones to quickly (and helpfully) point out to the well-intentioned urbanized vegetarians in the class that they don't know what it's like to live closely with animals you raise and care for, even if they are eventually to be sold and eaten.

Roughly half of the students plan to go on to professional schools: medicine, law, and veterinary. Others are headed to graduate programs in the humanities and sciences. Not unlike the readings assigned, the students themselves represent a range of interests and expertise. Discussion is enlivened by biology students who can talk firsthand about the use of nonanimal models in research, or philosophy students who can further expound on Kant and Descartes.

Because my own academic expertise lies within and law and literature, I rely on roughly six to eight guest speakers to join us for formal presentations, followed by Q&As. First on the list is a philosophy professor who performs her "greatest philosophical animal hits" presentation in the third week, after students have a basic foundation in the various theories from Aristotle to Singer and Regan. Other guest speakers have included the Indiana state director of the Humane Association of the United States to discuss current animal legislation and pressing issues within the state (most recently, these involved dog fighting, puppy mills, coyote penning, and canned hunting); a licensed wildlife rescue rehabilitator; a published and experienced cetacean activist who offers a slide show and startling look into the practices of organizations such as Sea World; and so on. Additionally, at least half of the human guest speakers have real-life experience outside the Academy.

Last year, I sponsored a mini-symposium featuring a moral philosopher from another institution who presented on both the immorality as well as the sheer scientific folly inherent in relying on nonhuman animals to test drugs for human use.[8] The debate took on a particularly interesting cast when a sharp biology student (not a member of the class) challenged him repeatedly, all occasions to which he rose eloquently and knowledgeably. The impromptu conversation that unfolded exemplifies the sort of valuable exchange this kind of course can foster.

Any study of ethics can feel deeply personal and, at times, disruptive. Worldviews and senses of morality are often tightly held, connecting to culture, community, and family. But these disruptions have led to some of the most intensely intimate moments of any class I've taught outside of creative writing. Each year I join my students, not simply as their "teacher," but as a fellow learner. Success in the course rests not on students' viewpoints, but on their abilities to engage with a vast array of material in meaningful ways and produce three papers, two of which are responses to "ethical problems" I have designed and the third on any subject of their choice; all rely heavily on secondary sources. One of the most recently assigned ethical problems, for example, focuses on the fictional Rudiger, who asks whether it is more ethical to shoot wild deer to feed his pet dog for the next year or buy commercial pet food. The student writer advises Rudiger while working through the various ethical frameworks and applying them (e.g., "Callicott might say ___, or Adams would argue ____"). The point is not to settle on "the right decision," of course, but to think through the ethically bumpy terrains of daily choices. Final paper topics run from indictments of corporate farming and support of small family farms to the importance of preserving traditional hunting practices to the human–horse connection. But all must be grounded in theory, and all arguments must be supported by credible secondary sources. The final essay exam, composed of more holistic questions, puts students in close conversations with a number of the writers and thinkers discussed in class.

Of course, almost no real animals appear in any of these initial readings, just ideas about animals, debates on whether they experience pain or emotion or consciousness, and how we should weigh their moral value as determined by human standards. We sit in a university classroom discussing animals in the abstract, weighing theories of equal consideration and moral agency. But as animals cannot themselves enter these debates, how do we make room for their presence in the classroom?

Emerging was an inherent irony that in Animals and Ethics we were risking "losing animals." In the last couple of decades, "the animal" has grown into a hot academic topic. In my own experience, so often when a "subject " grabs the attention of academics, the "subject" seems to disappear and become instead an object to be written and thought about. There are parallels in other disciplines. Departments like Women's Studies and Black Studies in their earliest inceptions arose out of political urgency and social necessity to challenge uneven power relations and oppression, providing counternarratives to misrepresented and underrepresented histories. But in the last decade and a half, Women's Studies has been replaced by Gender Studies and even Masculinist Studies. And not dissimilarly, Black Studies morphed into variations on African Diaspora Studies, sometimes even upstaged by Whiteness Studies. Thinkers like Tania Modleski and bell hooks were already observing these shifts with concern in the 1990s. Modleski's *Feminism without Women* smartly challenges the false notion that "our work is done," and we are now comfortably "postfeminist." And perhaps anticipating the current claims that our American society is now "postracial," hooks argues presciently in "Postmodern Blackness" that the rhetoric of postmodernism feels exclusionary to those for whom ongoing marginalization continues, perhaps less visibly.

In a similar way, much of academic writing about animals removes us from the particular vulnerable bodies of those we study and think about.

According to scholar Cary Wolfe, an important voice in animal studies, one needn't even particularly like or care about nonhuman animals to write about them. In her 2012 essay, "Pussy Panic," feminist scholar Susan Fraiman critiques Wolfe's claim that liking animals has nothing to do with the imperative to challenge speciesism as "disingenuous" and "puzzling" (14).

Fraiman points to a common distancing strategy by a number of male animal scholars such as Peter Singer, who eschews emotionality and feeling. She attributes this refusal to what she and a number of other feminists suspect is considered feminizing and implicitly anti-intellectual.

She writes:

> As we have seen, however superfluous in logical terms, not-needing-to-like-animals has obvious advantages in strategic terms, as long as one assumes the bundling of nonemotionality and nonfemininity with intellectual credibility. That this assumption continues to hold sway is suggested by several other strategies fending off not only affection for animals but also association with two intellectual formations marked as feminine: ecofeminism and contemporary gender studies. (102)

This resistance to "caring" plagues a long intellectual tradition of reason and rationality that presumes their primacy. As both response and enhancement, the radicalizing sorts of compassion and empathy espoused by the feminist care ethicists draw on a fully embodied world of emotions and feeling that joins intellectual discernment and precision. The two are not mutually exclusive. We need to not just "think with and about animals," as current theoretical lingo directs us to do, in a kind of ongoing intellectual meditation, but to acknowledge our direct engagements with animal bodies and lives, in specific ways that resists what Carol Adams terms "massification."[9]

So where to begin? How to particularize the problem?

I start with what is familiar. Though we focus attention on a wide variety of animals (from cetaceans to reptiles to farmed animals to wildlife to pets), the fifth week of class is devoted exclusively to dogs. I rely on the affinity most of the class readily feel with dogs (making them, in my students' lingo, "relatable"), as well as the imbricated histories of human–dog coevolution that includes the extremes of exploitation and companionship. Carolyn Knapp's 1992 memoir, *Pack of Two: The Intricate Bond between People and Dogs*, falls into a long tradition of writers extolling the virtues of dog–human interactions, but distinguishes itself by offering up a smart critique of anthropomorphism and human need. Knapp focuses her attention on her own intimate, loving, and often complex relationship with her dog Lucille as a way of exploring the expectations and needs humans place on their animal companions, which often puts animals at risk when reality intervenes. Written in intimate prose, the book also celebrates the embodied connection between human and dog, while examining cross-species communications.

We discuss Knapp's willingness to risk sentimentality, as she examines her own human need to be loved unconditionally. "This is love, pure but not simple, not all," she writes in *A Pack of Two* (41). After describing a chaotic personal life, Knapp calls s Lucille "an agent of structure" (189). Knapp's vision provides an important counterweight to the rationalism of thinkers such as Singer and Regan and Wise, as she brings to life on the page the physicality of her love and emotional devotion to Lucille. Knapp is hardly alone.[10] Anthropologist Barbara Smuts, known for recording her interactions with primates in the field, like primatologists Jane Goodall and Dian Fossey, also writes about living with her dog Safi. In "Reflections" (2001), Smuts asserts that she and Safi "are equals," while clarifying this does not mean they are the same. Safi, Smut says is a "person," "albeit of another species." She writes:

In the language I am developing here, relating to other beings as person has nothing to do with whether or not we attribute human characteristics to them. It has to do, instead, with recognizing that they are social subjects, like us, whose idiosyncratic, subjective experience of us plays the same role in their relations with us that our subjective experience of them plays in our relations with them. If we relate to them as individuals, it is possible for us to have a *personal* relationship . . . personhood connotes a way of being *in relation to others*, and thus no one other than the subject can give it or take it away. (118)

For strategic reasons, I pair writings by male ethologists, such as Jonathan Balcombe and Marc Bekoff, who both speak of experience and feeling and compassion and loving animals. This helps bridge the move to the feminist care ethicist tradition that Carol Adams and Josephine Donovan assert "recognizes the importance of each individual animal while developing a more comprehensive analysis of her situation. Unlike 'welfare' approaches, therefore, the feminist care tradition in animal ethics includes a political analysis of the reasons why animals are abused in the first place" (3). This extends to important intersections among gender, race, and class, permitting the larger picture view of losing animals and animality within social and economic systems.

J.M. Coetzee's provocative 2001 novel of ideas, *The Lives of Animals*, features as his protagonist the unforgettable aging novelist Elizabeth Costello, who has been invited by a small Midwestern college to speak, where she chooses to talk about the suffering of animals. She urges her stunned audience to "open your heart and listen to what your heart says" (37). Condemning as cowards those philosophers who waste time philosophizing about whether nonhuman animals can reason, or if they share sufficient qualities with human animals to justify ending their suffering, Elizabeth takes no prisoners. "Even Immanuel Kant, of whom I would have expected better has a failure of nerve . . . Even Kant does not pursue, with regard to animals, the implication of his intuition that reason may be not the being of the universe, but . . . merely the being of the human brain" (23). She is opinionated, and irascible, and not particularly likable. But if frankness and facts don't work, how do you make people listen and pay attention? Do you turn people off by confronting them directly? In a world of so much human suffering, how do you make an argument that animal suffering matters, too? Is it either/or? Can it be both? I ask my students, do you agree with Elizabeth that if you can't get people to empathize with animals, they have lost sight of their souls? Why does there seem to be such urgency in what she is saying? How does she understand that un-cruel people can contribute to such cruelties? What other examples might we find?

In truth, there are moments that Elizabeth comes very close to a feminist care position and, in fact, one might argue that is the basis for her philosophy, but Coetzee then puts on the brakes.[11] While the fictional Elizabeth is given some of the best lines for one arguing for the rights of animals, she is also subject to her emotions and often teary, and by the end of the short novel, collapses in her son's arms in a kind of defeated grief over the seemingly unstoppable cruelties and suffering visited upon animals.

I am haunted by Coetzee's choice to leave us with a pathetic image of Elizabeth collapsing under the weight of her grief and helplessness, rather than finding strength and resolve in emotions. If compassion begins with feeling, and feeling is communicated with language, then what does Elizabeth's silence mean at the end? In a novel so powerfully built on words, is it possible that there is simply nothing left to say?

Indeed, there is plenty.

Coetzee's book is deeply valuable for laying out various arguments illustrated by Costello's reactive audience. For example, despite Costello's plea to stop harming animals, one member rightly points out that while she refuses to consume the flesh of other beings she still wears leather shoes and carryiesa leather purse. To this accusation, Costello famously responds that we're all complicit in "degrees of obscenity," a theme that eventually begins to run through our course. It's a powerful moment in a powerful book. And yet the absence of actual animals and their bodies is palpable.

Even Coetzee's alter ego, Elizabeth Costello, lecturing away on the rights of animals, relies on mostly literary animals to make her points. She never once describes interacting directly with animal bodies, something critic Barbara Smuts points out in her essay in a final section of the book devoted to critical responses.

This is why throughout the semester we host an array of animal visitors, including snakes, possums, raptors, pit bulls, ferrets, and rats, many of whom are marginalized and associated with the "abject." And while logistics make larger or less social animals next to impossible to include in a classroom setting, my plan is to add other animal visitors, such as farmed chickens and rabbits whom we consider "edible."

Obviously simply bringing animals into the classroom without a carefully erected intellectual framework would be a very different experience—worthwhile, perhaps, but not nearly as thought-provoking. A good illustration of this is the week we spend reading essays about and discussing the practice of dog fighting, a nasty "sport" initially brought to the New World by the British colonists. In particular, a reading on dog fighting and masculinity targets both the symbolic and the financial gains. Though illegal, dog fighting thrives. Once primarily a predominantly white male rural activity, it has entered the urban realm, with pit bulls the most commonly fought dog. Pit bulls, of course, are not a breed, but a type of dog. And while the high-profile case of Michael Vick brought dog fighting to mainstream attention, the fact is Michael Vick was hardly an anomaly. (That Vick is black engendered angry websites posts raging against black men and calling Vick "an animal," demanding that he be "castrated" and so on.[12])

Class discussions preceding the arrival of ex–fighting dog Fred prompted everyone to think about Fred in particular and his damaged body in a much more complicated way. Unsurprisingly, Fred was not well socialized. When he wasn't being fought, he spent his life on a chain. Initially, his presence inspired some fear and reticence. The visibly scarred Fred paced and circled the large room as if he didn't know what to make of so much new space. As students may always opt out for animal visits, and are never required to interact with any animal guest, I was pleasantly surprised that no one chose to leave when Fred appeared (as of this writing, no student has ever asked to be excused during animal visits). Still, Fred's agitated movements, his obsessive sniffing of furniture and walls, and his utter lack of "manners" like knocking over a large garbage container understandably inspired caution on the part of the students.

Eventually, as Fred's "handler" and rescuer, experienced in rehabilitating fighting dogs, offered important personal accounts of dog fighting and its consequences, the room visibly relaxed. And how that he had time to investigate the room thoroughly and rule out obvious dangers, Fred took notice of the students, some of whom began tentatively to hold out their hands. And like many fighting dogs, bred and selected not only for easily exploited willingness to aggress, but for submission to humans, Fred was a risk only to other dogs. Students expressed pity until the rescuer explained that Fred didn't need pity; what he needed most was a chance to "be a dog." As dis-ease shifted to curiosity, Fred slowed down and paused before each of the proffered hands, sometimes offering a lick, sometimes a sniff. Many students moved closer to him, encouraging interaction. The rescuer assured them they were helping Fred to learn that human hands were not always hurtful. Several students expressed interest in adopting Fred, whereupon the practical and unsentimental rescuer explained the responsibilities in adopting a rehabilitated fighting dog. The readings and the talk helped contextualize the sympathy students felt, while Fred provided the missing component—the animal body on whom suffering was so directly written, and about whom so much was being historicized, theorized, and pondered.

Additionally, Fred's story and physical presence stood in sharp contrast to the relationship between Carolyn Knapp and her precious Lucille. In an essay on Buddhism in her 2003 book, *Pedagogy of Buddhism: Touching Feeling*, Eve Sedgwick demonstrates that animals can be our teachers. Using as an example the cat who brings her human companion "small, wounded animals into the house," Sedgwick writes that "most people interpret these deposits as offerings or gifts . . . meant to please or propitiate us" (153–154). Quite the contrary. An anthropologist she cites reads the gesture very differently—as a pedagogical or teaching moment for the human. Sedgwick acknowledges the wound to the human ego, the idea that we are teachable when we are least aware, that a cat may actually have more to teach us than we her. This distinction between learning *from* animals and not simply *about* is crucial, which is another function of the animal guests.

After we read about the exotic pet trade,[13] some of it illegal, another animal guest arrives for further contemplationThe sight of the humane educator removing Lucille, the elegantly marked yellow ball python, from the pillowcase she travels in always creates a sensation. This is because Lucille is about as "Other" as one can get, and unlikely to be as readily anthropomorphized. Audible gasps, even some groans of disgust are common as her four-foot-plus body fully emerges. Ball pythons are indigenous to Africa, but bred and sold as pets in various parts of the world, in part, because of their relatively docile natures.[14] While the humane educator talks, I sit with Lucille draped over my shoulders and arms. Of all the animal guests who have visited, Lucille causes the most stir. Little by little, driven by curiosity, students begin to inch forward to inspect, then touch Lucille, not unlike the way Fred approached them. They are deferential and careful, surprised by her skin texture. "Not slimy at all," some remark. They explore Lucille's vestigial feet on her underside, and the beautiful patterns marking her skin. Lucille's presence offers more than a simple natural history lesson on snakes. Confronted by her body, students begin to imagine what it means to confine her and provide a "comparable life." By the end of class, at least several students take turns holding her. What makes these moments remarkable is the careful attention students are engaged in. Even the feel of Lucille's physical body engenders observations about difference and capability.

For me, posthumanism remains embodied and entails a committed engagement with the very materiality of the lives of nonhuman animals and our own animality, as well as the "gendered" and "raced" aspects of the way we live with and treat and think about animals.[15] "Posthumanism" does not mean simply transcending humanism, or standing in opposition to lingering Enlightenment fantasies about human superiority and the privilege accorded to our evolution. Nor does it eliminate problems of rights arguments. The most commonly summoned voices in animal rights and welfare still belong to white men, and most of the national animal advocacy organizations are headed by men, while historically much larger numbers of women have served in the capacity of "foot soldiers."[16]

Given the artificial limits of a semester, less time than I like is devoted to animals used in experimentation, though it's mostly because I have yet to find an animal experimenter willing to speak to the class. The final two weeks are devoted to law and activism. Students read scholarship, legislation, and samples from case law.

A good focal point is animals' legal status as property and arguments on the pros and cons Wild animals of course belong to no one, and some like philosopher Grace Clement have argued that they are more appropriately served by an ethic of justice than an ethic of care. Other thinkers like Steven Wise, propose extending personhood to certain animals like the great apes. Legal scholar David Favre suggests a concept he calls "equitable self-interest," which would legally elevate the interest the animal has in herself, while being protected by human guardianship. Other writers argue that "human law" (codified worldview) is simply not appropriate for "animal law." While some animals may benefit from shifts in legal status, such as the great apes or companion animals whom some courts are recognizing as "sentient property," such distinctions may only further the divide between those animals on whom we confer moral status and those we don't: the chicken we love as a pet and the chicken we slaughter for the dinner plate.

Postscript: There is nothing like a discussion of animal bodies to underscore my own animal body as a biological woman teaching a university class on animals. Following the aforementioned mini-symposium, a woman faculty member in philosophy and I went to dinner with our guest, who is male, and white, and smart and engaging. He readily announces to his classes that he's vegan, and tells them throughout the course why it is morally wrong to harm animals. Based on my own students' enthusiastic reactions, he must be an extremely popular teacher. The other woman and I pressed him for details about his strategies. Yes, of course he shows slides of slaughterhouses; he seemed surprised that neither of us would. He confronts his students much more directly and has no problems including the "other f-word," feminist theories. Same approach. Recognizing our dilemma, he conceded easily, he probably gets away with a lot more than we can.

My own journey teaching the class continues. In its most recent incarnation, I told the students I am vegan, but found myself quickly apologizing that I didn't expect any of them to become vegan. And then I stopped myself. Why this caution and hesitation? It's the same caution and hesitation I feel about losing the animal. What maybe also deserves recovery is the fierceness and fearlessness of the feminist care ethicists who remind us that this enterprise demands both head and heart, that the two are mutually dependent and essential.

NOTES

1. The number worldwide is around sixty-five billion.
2. Patterson offers the following succinct quotes from writer Isaac Bashevis Singer: "There is only one little step from killing animals to creating gas chambers a la Hitler" and philosopher Theodor Adorno: "Auschwitz begins whenever someone looks at a slaughterhouse and thinks: they're only animals."
3. Carol Adams's essay "The War on Compassion," in *The Feminist Care Tradition in Animal Ethics*, addresses such misconceptions as the problem is too overwhelming, or if we feel sympathy we won't be able to bear it, or our treatment of humans needs to be addressed and solved first.
4. Consider the meat industry: consumer health, animal suffering, the plight of slaughterhouse workers, and so on.
5. According to advocacy groups, such as the Animal Legal Defense Fund, the act is also rarely enforced.
6. An entire semester could easily be devoted to the troubled food industry, the perceived elitism of veganism, as well as the role of GMOs, corporate control of seeds, and food access challenges in this country for rural and urban poor, in particular.
7. Oliver, K. (2010). "Animal Ethics: Toward an Ethics of Responsiveness." *Research in* Phenomenology 40:269
8. It has been well proven that nonhuman animals do not respond to drugs and other products the same way that humans do, and not all nonhuman animals respond the same way. This has led to numerous false positives and false negatives (e.g., ibuprofen can be an effective drug for humans, but deadly to animals). Not only do these tests cause animals tremendous suffering, distress, and even death; they do not reliably predict outcomes for human beings. Many countries are turning to more reliable nonanimal models, such as in vitro research, computer models, and micro-dosing.
9. "Massification," as used by Adams and others, roughly refers to the erasure of the individual experience through the sheer force of volume of numbers. Decades ago, John Hersey's *Hiroshima*, first published in *The New Yorker*, attempted to personalize the bombing experience by focusing on individual lives, not aggregate numbers, to access the horror.
10. In her 2003 *Companion Species Manifesto: Dogs, People, and Significant Otherness*, posthumanist science and feminist scholar Donna Haraway speculates that she and her dog, Ms. Cayenne Pepper, through the saliva exchange of kisses, or "oral intercourse," have managed to find "potent transfections" in each other's DNA.

11. In a not dissimilar gesture, Jacques Derrida, in the famous cat anecdote found in "The Animal That Therefore I Am (More to Follow)," which certainly argues for the importance of compassion, stops short of fully engaging with the cat's gender (even while acknowledging as an aside that she is a "she"), or otherwise reflecting on all the other "Othernesses" confronting him in that moment of "startle." I make this argument in an unpublished essay, "What If Derrida's Cat Had Been a Dog?"

12. Melissa Harris-Perry offers a provocative look at the nasty history of equating black people and animals, that "implied that all subjugated persons and all animals could be used and abused at the will of those who were more powerful. The effects were pernicious for both black people and for animals." Dogs were used to chase down slaves, as well as during Civil Rights demonstrations, and speaks to one general view that white people care more about animals than they do the suffering of their fellow black humans. She ends by suggesting that outrage over Vick was as much about his race as it was about concern for animals.

13. Though relative, "exotic" typically denotes animals who are either geographically nonnative or not typical companion animals. Privately owned wild animals include lion and tiger cubs, tarantulas, monkeys, foxes, and raccoons. In the few states where these animals can be kept legally, licensing schemes, some of them federally mandated, apply.

14. The "herp" pet trade, as it is called, is one of the cruelest (some of it is legal and some illegal). Snakes do not bond with human beings the way more common companion animals do; they are delicate creatures with specific dietary and health needs that can be difficult to manage properly, and many end up neglected and mistreated. Also sold in pet stores, snakes are easy impulse buys.

15. In "Toward a Postcolonial, Posthumanist Feminist Theory: Centralizing Race and Culture in Feminist Work on Nonhuman Animals," Maneesha Deckha observes that posthumanist feminists have focused primarily on the interconnected oppressions of animals and women, while overlooking the equally significant intersections of race and culture.

16. Large national organizations, such as the ASPCA, the Animal Legal Defense Fund, and the Humane Society of the United States, are currently headed by men.

REFERENCES

Adams, C. (2010. The Rape of Animals, the Butchering of Women." *The Sexual Politics of Meat (20th Anniversary Edition)*, 64–91. New York and London: The Continuum International Publishing Group.

Adams, C., and Donovan, J. , eds, (2007). "Introduction." In *The Feminist Care Tradition in Animal Ethics*, 1–20. New York: Columbia University Press.

Armstrong, S., and Botzler, R., (2008)*The Animal Ethics Reader*, 2nd Edition, London and New York: Routledge.Clement, G. (2003). "The Ethic of Care and the Problem of Wild Animals." In *The Feminist Care Tradition in Animal Ethics*, 301–315. New York: Columbia University Press.

Coetzee, J.M. (2001). *The Lives of Animals*. Princeton, NJ: Princeton University Press.

DeGrazia, D. (2012). *Animal Rights: A Very Short Introduction*. Oxford: Oxford University Press.

Deckha, M. (2012). "Toward a Postcolonial, Posthumanist Feminist Theory: Centralizing Race and Culture in Feminist Work on Nonhuman Animals." *Hypatia* 27 (3): 527–545.

Derrida, J. (2002). "The Animal That Therefore I Am (More to Follow)." Trans. D. Wills. *Critical Inquiry* 28:369–418.

Fraiman, S. (2012). "Pussy Panic versus Liking Animals: Tracking Gender in Animal Studies." *Critical Inquiry* 39:89–115.

Haraway, D. (2003). *The Companion Species Manifesto: Dogs, People, and Significant Otherness*. Chicago: Prickly Paradigm Press.

Harris-Perry's, M. (December 30, 2010). "Michael Vick, Racial History, and Animal Rights." In *The Nation*. http://www.thenation.com/blog/157372/michael-vick-racial-history-and-animal-rights

Hersey, J.(2010), *Hiroshima*. New York and Tokyo: Ishi Press.

hooks, bell. (2001). "Postmodern Blackness." In *The Norton Anthology: Theory and Criticism*, ed. V.B. Leitch. New York: W.W. Norton: 2478–84.

Knapp, C. (1999) *Pack of Two:The Intricate Bond Between People and Dogs*. New York: Delta.

Modleski, T. (1991). *Feminism without Women*. New York: Routledge.

Oliver, K. (2010). "Animal Ethics: Toward an Ethics of Responsiveness." *Research in Phenomenology* 40:267–280.

Patterson, C. (2005). "Animals, Slavery, and the Holocaust." *Logos: A Journal of Modern Society and Culture, v. 4 issue2*, http://www.logosjournal.com/issue_4.2/main.htm Sedgwick, E. (2003). *Pedagogy of Buddhism. Touching Feeling*. Durham, NC: Duke University Press.

Smuts, B. (2001). *Reflections. Commentary in the Lives of Animals*. Princeton, NJ: Princeton University Press.

Part III
Ecological Aesthetics

8 Affirmations and Limitations of Rancière's Aesthetics

Questions for Art and its Education in the Anthropocene

jan jagodzinski

The force of Jacques Rancière's thought on art and aesthetics has slowly penetrated into the mainstream philosophy of education, and art education in particular. The U.S.-based flagship research journal, *Studies in Art Education*, has a splattering of articles that reference Rancière's sweeping claims to aesthetics (e.g., Trafi-Prats 2012). Educational philosophy is equally enamored with his theory, spearheaded by Biesta (2010; Biesta and Bingham 2010). Bright rising scholars such as Tyson (2009) have tried to maintain that Rancière's theoretical vision offers a way of grasping Paolo Freire's long-standing claims to "conscientization." Freire's failure to provide an unconscious foundation for its conceptualization is thereby vindicated by Rancière.

In this chapter, I want to address Rancière's stance on the aesthetics of politics, and the politics of aesthetics in relation to art educational research. Rancière seemingly provides educators a way to further the politics of representation bequeathed to them by the legacy of critical theory. Equality and social justice remain on the table, but he avoids the more obvious traps of representational thought where the binary of sameness and difference is still maintained throughout educational research paradigms as developed by arts-based research (jagodzinski and Wallin 2013). Critical theory remains deadlocked with neoliberalism in a lose-lose game. Political subjectivity is aligned with critical oppositional consciousness that simply leads to negativity. Art and politics usually fall into the two bookends that hold up this discourse: Either it is political content of art that is forwarded or it is the politics of form that is found to be ideological. Rancière offers one line of flight out of this dilemma, as did Gilles Deleuze, Fèlix Guattari, and Jean-François Lyotard. The extension of his work, however, that I would like to make is to attempt to radicalize it further by questioning his *humanism*, and to raise the implications of his thesis for a radical deanthropomorphization into the realms of the inhuman and the nonhuman that posthuman theorists have taken. Without this reorientation, education research, especially arts-based educational research, will continue to reiterate the above deadlock. This is the primary thesis that is explored here. In other words, as much as Rancière offers new openings to old questions of emancipation and social justice, they come up short in relation to educational research in the arts given the historical period we find ourselves in—the Anthropocene.

RANCIÈRE'S POSITION

One of Rancière's redeeming features is that, like Deleuze and Guattari (1994), he is interested in the question as to what art can *do*. But this is not a problematic that simply falls into various forms of praxis or pragmatism so that art is made to be useful again; rather the axis is turned toward aesthetics, which is now understood as the human sensorium that can have transformative effects at the structural level. According to Rancière, the Situationist International (SI), in their uncompromising purity of conduct toward spectacular capitalism, made art impotent and the spectator passive (2009a, 2009b). According to SI, many critically creative efforts by artists were denounced as simply being part of the spectacle. Being spectacularly critical was commodified and sold back to the public. FCUK is my favorite example, which plays on the misrecognition of a glance aesthetics. Contemporary art and its research can no longer easily play the role of radical negation. It becomes part of the creative mill of designer capitalism (jagodzinski 2010). The outrageous can be easily accommodated.

Rancière's (2004b) aesthetics is best understood in terms of Immanuel Kant's 1781 grounding achievement, *Critique of Pure Reason* as "the system of a priori forms determining what presents itself to sense experience" (13). It is here where politics and aesthetics come together. The *a priori forms* (which are historically conditioned) determine the organization of human experience, and thereby determine the *common sense* of the world as to who is privileged to partake in it and who is not—as the "part that has no part" as he terms it (2001, 5–6). What is sensible and insensible is politicized by *a priori* categories. Those who are heard and who remain visible set the agenda in the way the sensible is distributed. Yet, it is within Kant's third critique written in 1790, *Critique of Judgment* where an aesthetics is posited that can erupt immanently from within, changing the distribution of the sensible and, hence, offers the possibility of a "minoritarian politics" as developed by Deleuze and Guattari (1987). Although Rancière, through his historical aesthetic regimes, seems to suggest that "politics" only applies when the "part that has no part" becomes heard and visible in a "molar" revolutionary way. His notion of a democratic political change that redistributes the sensible is a *rare event*, closer to Alain Badiou's (2005) notion of an Event proper. Only major critical changes characterize the shift of the sensible.[1] This is not a minoritarian multiple and multiplied incremental politics; rather it is more of a regime change as such. Lyotard, Deleuze, and Guattari, *and not Rancière*, make the move to a minoritarian political position.[2] The two notions of aesthetics in Kant are precisely what Deleuze (1984) queries. Yet, Rancière (2004a) has no use for Deleuze, or rather he is unable to see the Deleuzian move to a radical aesthetic—or rather, an aesthetic that targets the affect at the bodily unconscious level—as being a politically charged position.[3] As many scholars do, and Rancière is no exception, to differentiate his stance from those such as Badiou, Deleuze, and Lyotard, he misinterprets their positions through selective choice.

The heart of Rancière's theory is the way the sensible (that is, subjectivity) is distributed politically. In what is a rather quirky and selective read, Rancière historically outlines three aesthetic "regimes"—that is, structures—as to how the sensible is distributed throughout the populace and maintained as a form of common sense: Briefly, these are the ethical regime of images, the representational regime of art, and the aesthetic regime of art. In a nutshell the ethical scheme belongs to the Platonic age, where art does not yet "exist." Plato blocks its existence by downgrading mimesis since imitation as simulacra (as Deleuze [1990, 253] was to show) can upset the distribution of the sensible. *Poiesis*, as bringing something new into being, was judged subversive to the harmonic distribution of time and space where everyone had their place according to the distinct categorizations of gold (the landowners), silver (the seafaring class), and copper (the artisans and slaves). The representative regime of art emerges with Aristotle. The long historical stretch of this visual regime places the representation of deeds within the framework of tragedy. Character development and description have to fit the expected role. This sets up a hierarchy of genres—high and low divisions in the arts. Art imitates proper action. Finally, the aesthetic regime abolishes the hierarchies, redefining what can be seen and said. It does this primarily by collapsing the division between active reason and passive sense. A "sensorium" emerges, negating any strict relationship between form and content by an insistence upon the equality of all subject matter. All "life" is open for contemplation.

These regimes are not chronological as much as they form a repertoire of existing positions, a way of discursively ordering the arts; so, for example, for Rancière, cinema negotiates both the representative and aesthetic regimes. "Le partage du sensible," as a number of scholars (Chambers 2010, 202) have pointed out, has a double meaning: "as a distribution of the sensible" as well as a "partition of the sensible." *Partage*, stemming from the verb *partager*, means that the activity being distributed is also shared. There is a sharing taking place. So, a distribution of the sensible is a sharing of the sensible. A world that is "common" is being defined.

This highlights the claim that politics is aesthetic and aesthetics political in the way that both activities define forms of inclusion and exclusion at the level of what is perceptible. A given distributive regime delimits, that is, frames, the forms of participation and subjectivity; it does so by defining what is visible or invisible, audible or inaudible, and what is said and unsaid. The parallels to a Foucauldian epistemé are evident. The French sociological and philosophical use of the complex term *dispositif* identifies the various networked linkages that exist and are held together within a regime. Rancière is also close to Deleuze and Guattari's (1987) notion of the "assemblage"; however, as remarked earlier, Rancière's regime is theorized within the contextuality of humanism. There is no recognition of the Other to the human, which is why Rancière draws more from the Kantian *Critique of Pure Reason* while still recognizing the radicality of *The Critique of Judgment*. The strength of this move is that the redistribution of the sensible requires the redistribution of both time and space as transcendental categories. Turning day into night, for instance, would be a radical shift in sensibility, a reconfiguration of the *partition* of experience. However, these transcendental conditions are not to be located in the subject, as my example suggests; rather they are embodied in practices, institutions, and cultural divisions. Time and space become political questions because their distributions define forms of subjectivity and political participation. To quote Rancière (2009a) here:

> Politics consists of reconfiguring the distribution of the sensible that defines the common of a community, by introducing into it subjects and new objects, in rendering visible those who were not, and of making understood as speakers those who were understood as *noisy animals*. (38, emphasis added)

Humans are "noisy animals." Animals as Other, for example, are *not* part of Rancière's political and aesthetic theory. Basically, art is political and politics artistic because both practices contest the historical-transcendental factors that delimit the social, ascribing to individuals a particular mode of subjectivity.

For Rancière, this shared aspect of a distribution of the sensible enables the possibility for art to institute practices of equality. In the *Ignorant Schoolmaster*, Rancière (1991) presents the life and writing of Joseph Jacotot, who demonstrated that all intellects were equal and found a way to teach for intellectual emancipation. Rancière (2009b) makes a strong commitment to this position throughout his writings, maintaining that there are no passive spectators; all spectators can be involved in emancipatory work.

Rancière hinges the politics of aesthetics on the third regime—the aesthetic regime. This sets up art as playing a role in creating a new world of communal life. Art and life are connected by what he calls the "heterogeneous sensible." Rancière is against the effacement of the boundary between art and life. Art fails if art becomes life and life becomes art. In a recent book (jagodzinski 2010), I turned to Rancière explorations of Schiller's *Letters on the Aesthetic Education of Mankind* to claim that a fundamental antagonism emerged between art *and* design—why the ampersand began to appear between (art&design) them as a result of this transformative potential of art, which remains with us today. The crucial paragraph is to be found in an essay that Rancière (2002) published and translated in the *New Left Review*, "The Aesthetic Revolution and Its Outcomes." Rancière writes:

> In a sense, the whole problem lies in a very small preposition. Schiller says that aesthetic experience will bear the edifice of the art of the beautiful *and* the art of the living. The entire question of the "politics of aesthetics"—in other words, of the aesthetic regime of art—turns on this short conjunction [the "and"]. The aesthetic experience is effective inasmuch as it is the experience of that *and*. (134, original emphasis)

The internal tension of this ampersand generates the extremes of art becoming life and life becoming art where the political potential of the sensorium—namely, the transformative nature of art, is done away with. I argue (jagodzinski 2010) that when art becomes life, it is subsumed in the consumerism of designer capitalism, and when life becomes art, it falls into the excesses of aestheticization of the gallery machine. In the latter case, art's autonomy, to follow Rancière, falls into being *mere* art; in the former case, where the differences between aesthetic experience and the practice of life are denied, art falls into *mere* life. The dichotomy is maintained whereby all the outside becomes designed life and all the inside (the cathedrals to art—that is, the galleries and museums) become empty forms, the transcendentalism of unachievable spirituality to save art from the ravages of kitsch. Both options end art's political possibilities of redistributing the sensorium for further equality.

Rancière does not deny that the aesthetic regime has produced an ambiguous political destiny of art since it has to navigate these extremes. In my estimation, Deleuze and Guattari, throughout their writings, are able to keep this ambiguity open because they dwell on the unthought, the "outside" to this aesthetic regime. This has consequences for arts-based research (jagodzinski and Wallin 2013). The outside refers to a *virtual dimension* that recognizes a sense of time that Rancière has no knowledge of. Deleuze (1990) refers this to the time of Aion, a time that is "out of joint" with chronological time. It is a time that arrives either too early or too late but never manifests itself in the present. Rancière's humanism, his heavy stress on human agency and political action, blocks him from exploring this direction of time and space that exists on the virtual level. In this last section I will try to articulate what I mean by this, and the consequences for art, its education, and research in relation to the Anthropocene.

RANCIÈRE'S POSTHUMANIST LIMITATIONS

Rancière (2004b) is right to reinvigorate art and politics on a different axis. Art instructs viewers in alternative temporalities and spacings. *This is its research directive.* It is called upon to question what is taken for granted.

By challenging the apportionment of time and space, it also contests the allotment of subjectivity. Politics, however, as stated earlier, is not about the exercise of power, or the justifications of power. Rather, it is an intervention at the level of what is visible and audible, and *should be extended to what is "feelable."* It is an action by which the very distribution of the sensible is called into question; artistic research then becomes a process by which the exclusions embodied in sensible configurations are made explicit and their allotments of identity challenged. This view, as it stands within Rancière and arts research in general, remains *highly anthropomorphic.*

In our contemporary world, ecological issues have come to fore, raising questions of global survival. The "subjects" that inhabit the world need to be extended to both the *inhuman and nonhuman world,* to radically de-anthropomorphize Rancière's political posthumanism and arts-based research in general. Those that have no voice and cannot be seen require the limits of affective feeling to be changed and include the posthuman sensibility of *their* sensorium. Our species needs to develop new symbiotic relationships with them. Aesthetic acts, as interventions within the distribution of the sensible, have to be opened up further than what Rancière currently theorizes. "A part that has no part" has to be extended to include the inhuman (anorganic life) and nonhuman (artificial intelligence). This is the "outside" that forms the assemblages within technological and biological circuits that affect and modify our species. These are intelligences that we are unable to comprehend as yet. It is for this reason that the agency of aesthetic regime that Rancière champions is too limited. The re-creation of social life must now extend to include inhuman and nonhuman life.

To redistribute the sensible beyond the limitations of Rancière's humanism is a task that confronts arts-based research in an age of the Anthropocene, where our species has come to realize that our productivity, via the so-called democratic exploitations of capitalism, has jeopardized our survival (Steffen et al. 2011). Boldly put, if our species' survival depends on recognizing this historical juncture, then the Event of the Anthropocene has *already happened* as there is agreement among a global community of scientists that the Earth may go into a phase change that does *not* repeat its fluctuations of cooling and melting as in the past. Of the *nine indicators* that this is happening (ocean acidification, the nitrogen cycle, the phosphorous cycle, atmospheric aerosol loading, chemical pollution, stratospheric ozone depletion, global fresh water use, change in land use, and the loss of biodiversity), three thresholds have already been crossed: climate change, the nitrogen cycle, and biodiversity loss (Foster, Clark, and York 2010).

There is no other position for art educational research to take other than an *eco-ontological one* that copes with the impending catastrophes that are about to amplify in the next fifty years if the partition (*partage*) of the sensible is to take place. Climate change, a euphemism for this transformative change, has become globally visible—even to skeptics. Added to this glum scenario is the militaristic state of the geopolitical world today where global paranoia is met with surveillance and the "war on terror" rages on.

AN AVANT-GARDE *WITHOUT AUTHORITY*

The eco-ontology confronted by arts based research can only be raised problematically from the outside. The most radical position possible is one that emerges from a "dark ecology" that faces the abyss of human extinction (e.g., Morton 2007). My argument is that the formation of an "avant-garde *without authority*" (jagodzinski, 2014, forthcoming) is perhaps all that is left to raise the psychic unconscious to a level where it might become viral in recognizing that we, the fish who are swimming in the earth-tank, are slowly suffocating as the water is heating up, and the oxygen that we breath is quickly escaping, replaced by carbon dioxide. It's only a question of projected time before we float belly-up. An *affirmative* ethico-politics, in line with theorists such as Deleuze and Guattari, should theoretically inform an *avant-garde without authority to help change the distribution of the sensible globally via a posthuman arts-based research paradigm that activates a public pedagogically.*

Such a shift is strongly anti-Hegelian. It turns away from Rancière's (2007) overcoding of negativity when he criticizes Lyotard's (1991) views on sublimity, and especially Deleuze's (1989) nonhuman developments on the "machinic eye" of cinema (Rancière 2006). An artistic education and research paradigm that is governed by the eco-ontological issues of the Anthropocene locates political practice that attempts to reinvent what is understood as "life" from its current anthropocentric view that has been bequeathed to us by humanism, and furthered by posthumanist positions such as phenomenology, ethnography, and deconstruction.[4] This requires a neo-vitalist view of subjectivity that engenders modes of becoming along the conflicting lines of the effects of repressive power (*potestas*), as well as power in its potential (*potentia*) for affirmative change. "Without authority" speaks to a position where the emphasis is placed on the latter position—given that the force of power is generally understood and placed oppositionally or dialectically in our posthumanist capitalist democracies. In Heideggerian terms, power as *machen* and power as *lassen* are paradoxically in play with one another, opening up a future that is not yet closed by probabilities and possibilities (see Ziarek 2004). The logics of *both/and*, as well as *and/and* but avoiding *either/or*, are in play, alluding to the same paradox Rancière identifies in Schiller. A radical relationality of subjectivity extends into assemblages of flows of desire that make up the two sides that "frame" what we believe to be "human." On the one side is Nature, as defined by anorganic forms of consciousness, and on the other side by the artifices of technology—Nature "doubled" so to speak through our own ingenuity. Both assemblages *modify* what becomes "human" historically.

As Bruno Latour (1993) rightly put it, "we have never been modern," as we have always been part of Nature.

How might art and its education and research help cultivate an increase in the relations with these multiple Others? Interrelations need to be furthered with inhuman (anorganic) and nonhuman (technological artifice) in ways that promote a well-being that offers a sustainable future that eliminates the competitiveness and negativity inherent in capitalist forces of production. Without new modes of interrelations that *must* emerge, we are truly a doomed species. Ultimately this means a new attitude toward Life as *zoe* rather than *bios*, the latter has already been explored via the biopolitics of Foucault and Agamben. *A Life* that one inhabits is not something to be possessed (Deleuze 2011); such *A Life* (*zoe*) does not bear one's name; rather *A Life* is a force of becoming, of individuation (and not individualism); it is *A Life* of differentiation (and not difference in relation to sameness). *A Life* is a-personal, indifferent, and generative. Such a position is difficult to grasp within a culture of schizophrenic narcissism where humanity is held together by the negativity of a common threat via the xenophobia of migration, the terror of religious zealots and the impending "climate change."

TRAJECTORIES OF CURRENT ARTISTIC FLOWS

How to rethink art, its education, and research where the trans-subjective and transhuman forces come into play? Where the logics of both/and and and/and assert themselves for the purposes of an affirmative ethico-political economy, which addresses at least the problematic of a dying species such as ours who is on a trajectory to extinction. Mainstream artic exhibitions that address the Anthropocene are rather weak in their response for providing such exemplars that would provide a nervous shock of fear to a visiting public pedagogically.[5] As is well known, "pedagogy" and "art research" have become a curatorial imperative in contemporary times to "educate" the public, as spearheaded first by Documenta XIII (Frimer 2011). Museum and gallery educators take pride in "participatory" installations that are to (somehow) "teach" visitors about the dangers of the Anthropocene.[6]

On the level of freeing up *A Life* as *zoe*—that is, the blockages to libidinal arrest and rigidification when it comes to *anthropocentric forms of activism*, which in many ways support Rancière's call for the politicization of the "part that has no part"—the artistic exemplars of research and pedagogy that are most notable are the one's which draw on Deleuze and Guattari's text on "The Apparatus of Capture" in *A Thousand Plateaus* (1987). Such artistic research explorations addresses the geophilosophy of power that pits the state against the subversions of the "nomadic war machine."[7] At the heart of this is the concept of overcoding that speaks directly to power as *potestas* in Spinozian terms, or *machen* in Heideggarian terms. The many writings of Brian Holmes (e.g., 2009) offers many exemplars in the way activist art in the service of pedagogy and research has attempted to decode and uncode the structures that are in place. However, this is not enough in relation to recognizing that it is human extinction that is at issue, and that, as Guattari and Deleuze maintained, the way capitalism relies on crisis states, disasters, and wars in order to feed its own creative drives for profit. How can a "new Earth" be abetted by an eco-ontological sensibility through other forms of art, its education, and research?

AFFIRMATIVE TRAJECTORIES?

The first trajectory requires an avant-garde without authority involved in art, education, and research to make the public aware of the way global capitalist activity is leading our species down the road of extinction. I choose an exemplary example that shows a commitment to *A Life* by showing *death* in the living present. In the installation *Black Shoals Stock Market Planetarium* (2001–2004), the London-based artists Lise Autogena and Joshua Portway projected an array of otherworldly constellations onto a planetarium-style dome, making the night sky disturbingly different than the one a public is used to looking at. Each astral body corresponds not to a "star" in the night sky, but to a publicly traded company, as a computer program translates the real-time financial activity of the world's stock exchanges into what appear to be glimmering stars. In 2001, the artwork was connected to a Reuters news feed. In 2004, when the artwork was displayed at the Nikolaj Copenhagen Contemporary Art Center, it was wired to the local stock exchange. The "stars" flashed more brightly whenever stock was traded. They gathered into clusters or dispersed according to market momentum.

Added to the complexity of this celestial panorama, the artists introduced digital creatures into this luminous ecosystem. The "celestial ecosystem" that was created was solely artificial, devoid of any natural life. Cefn Hoile, an artificial-life researcher and programmer, designed evolutionary algorithms so that these creatures fed on the energy of the fluctuating stars; they grew into complex beings and reproduced in order to better survive in this media ecology. With a market downturn they experienced "famine" and died out, overcome by darkness.

The project puns on the so-called Black-Scholes option-pricing formula, published in 1973 by University of Chicago professors Fischer Black and Myron Scholes, which set the course for the trading of financial derivatives on an unprecedented scale. *Black Shoals Stock Market Planetarium* reduces such complex calculations to the level of a video game's seductive visual logic, whereby the ravenous AI animals simulate the speculative passions that have led to real-life suffering and disasters.

The *Black Shoals*'s creatures are nothing but a purified expression of self-entrepreneurship—approximating the biopolitics of Homo economicus, the subject of neoliberalism. Picturing a lifeworld merged with capital, Autogena and Portway's starry sky presents the activity of the stock market via a technology of visualization, showing just how artificial the financial system is—and revealing the vulnerability of life exposed to a purely economic rationality. The market is seen as a second Nature, as if global capitalism and trade is the "natural" economic activity of our species. The piece is not just a means of visualizing abstract data, but an existential model for predatory life under advanced capitalism, within a zone where nothing else—not bodies, social life, religion, or aesthetics—matters. The fact that the "creatures" have repeatedly rendered themselves extinct during the running of the piece proposes that, at its most extreme, the project be taken as a dark allegory—and a stark warning—for our precarious existence as a species whose actions are putting our very viability at risk via neoliberalist capitalist economics that is governed by a necro-politics.

An attempt to get out of the gallery and into the streets for the purposes of pedagogy, an avant-garde without authority, is exemplified by *Army of Melting Men* by Brazilian artist Néle Azevedo. *Army of Melting Men* is a repeated installation performed in Brazil, France, Japan, Italy, and Germany. It addresses global warming, and presents the precariousness of existence under climate change. One thousand to thirteen hundred cast mold ice figurines, generically male and female, approximately eighteen inches high, are placed on-site, usually on the steps of some well-known state building of legislative authority (but not necessarily) by a participating public. Like the melting of the Arctic ice in Greenland and Antarctica (sea levels will rise more than a meter by 2100), these statuettes begin to "disappear" as they melt—as quickly as twenty minutes. During this duration, the melting "sculpturines" undergo subtle differences of form before "becoming extinct." Their inactivity as they melt away speaks directly to the inactivity of humankind toward climate change. The sculptural minimalism and autonomy addresses "every[man]" who cannot escape, regardless of class, wealth, and power, the impeding apocalypse.

Such artic installations illustrate the *haecceity*, the "thisness," of art's ephemeral existence once its force as a potentiality has been exhausted or dispelled. *This is an affirmative sense of zoe in death.* Such art harbors within itself the seeds of its own destruction via catastrophe as a meltdown, and it is this "breakdown," as breakthrough, or "chaosmosis," in Deleuze and Guattari's terms, that is underplayed in school art and its education. What these examples shows is the need for an art that experiments with different lines of "becoming death," a dark ecology that is affirmative in its notion of *zoe*, precisely because it rethinks death.

Given this gloomy scenario, I have come to my own conclusion that the contemporary affective force in art places a fixation on Thanatos, a negative notion of *zoe* as forwarded by Giorgio's Agamben's (1998) conceptualization of "bare life." This is not the way to proceed forward. To change the partitioning of the sensible that includes both inhuman and nonhuman assemblages, an avant-garde *without authority* needs to persist with a trajectory that paradoxically plays with death—the end of our species—but does so in an affirmative way as my examples show, so that the affects of pedagogy can penetrate at the unconscious level where the nerves are most vulnerable, for humanity has much to be anxious about.

NOTES

1. The terms "minoritarian politics" and "molar" are developed by Deleuze and Guattari (1987, 106, 291) and not by Rancière. However, "molar" equates closest to Rancière's notion of "police order" as the actions of bureaucracies, parliaments, and courts, while "minoritarian" equates with Rancière's "part that has no part."
2. For a counterargument to this general consensus of Rancière's *la politique*, see Chambers (2011). If Chambers's claims are accepted, then Rancière is merely poaching Deleuze and Guattarian ideas on minoritarian politics without acknowledgment. There is a slippage between *politics* (molar) and the *political* (minoritarian) in his writing.
3. Deleuze and Guattari's (1987) notion of "becoming-imperceptible," identifies a realm of sensibility that is 'beyond' the accepted common sense of the community, *must* (not ought or should) be politicized much like Rancière's part that has no part. This brings these two desperate positions together politically, but within a minoritarian politics (see, Wolfe 2006).
4. To qualify this statement: Derrida (2008) comes very late in his career to recognizing the inhuman of animality, but he is unable to carry this thought any further to the anorganic level before his death.
5. Contrasting examples would be "EXPO 1: New York," held at MoMA PS1, in Queens, Long Island, in the summer of 2013, and the more successful *Yes Naturally: How Art Saves the World*, curated by Ine Gevers in 2013 at Gemeentemuseum Den Hague (Gevers 2013).
6. One example of many was *The Anthropocene Project*, held at the Haus der Kultern de Welt, (HWK), January 13, 2013–December 31, 2014.
7. The nomadic was machine is developed by Deleuze and Guattari (1987) to explore the many ways a minoritarian position of power is able to subvert and resist what they call molar forces of the state.

REFERENCES

Agamben, G. (1998). *Homo sacrer: Sovereign Power and Bare Life*. Trans. D. Heller-Roazen. Stanford, CA: Stanford University Press.
Badiou, A. (2005). *Being and Event*. Trans. O. Feltham. London and New York: Continuum.
Biesta, G. (2010). "A New Logic of Emancipation: The Methodology of Jacques Rancière." *Educational Theory* 60 (1): 39–59.
Biesta, G., and Bingham, C.W. (2010). *Jacques Rancière: Education, Truth, Emancipation*. London: Continuum.
Chambers, S.A. (2010). "Jacques Rancière (1940–)." In *From Agamben to Žižek: Contemporary Critical Theorists*, ed. J. Simons, 194–209. Edinburgh: Edinburgh University Press.

Chambers, S.A. (2011). "Jacques Rancière and the Problem of Politics." *European Journal of Theory* 10 (3): 303–326.

Deleuze, G. (1984). *Kant's Critical Philosophy: The Doctrine of the Faculties.* Trans. H. Tomlinson and B. Habberjam. London: Athlone Press.

Deleuze, G. (1989). *Cinema 2: The Time Image.* Trans. H. Tomlinson and R. Galeta. Minneapolis: University of Minnesota Press.

Deleuze, G. (1990). *The Logic of Sense.* Trans. M. Lester. New York: Columbia University Press.

Deleuze, G. (2011). *Pure Immanence: Essays on a Life.* Trans. A. Boyman. New York: Zone Books.

Deleuze, G., and Guattari, F. (1987). *A Thousand Plateaus.* Trans. B. Massumi. Minneapolis: University of Minnesota Press.

Deleuze, G., and Guattari, F. (1994). *What Is Philosophy?* Trans. H. Tomlinson and G. Burchell. New York: Columbia University Press.

Derrida, J. (2008). *The Animal That Therefore I Am.* Ed. Marie-Louis Mallet. Trans. D. Willis. New York: Fordham University Press.

Foster, J.B., Clark, B., and York, R. (2010). *The Ecological Rift: Capitalism's War on Earth.* New York: Monthly Review of Books.

Frimer, D. (2011). "Pedagogical Paradigms: Document's Reinvention." *Art and Education.* Retrieved February 19, 2014, from http://www.artandeducation. net/paper/pedagogical-paradigms-documenta%E2%80%99s-reinvention/.

Gevers, I. (2013). *Yes Naturally: How Art Saves the World.* Rotterdam: Nai010 publishers.

Holmes, B. (2009). *Escape the Overcode: Activist Art in Control Society.* Eindhoven: Van Abbe Museum and Zagreb: WHW (What How and for Whom?).

jagodzinski, j. (2010). *Art and Education in an Era of Designer Capitalism: Deconstructing the Oral Eye.* New York: Palgrave McMillan.

jagodzinski, j. (2014). "An Avant-Garde 'Without Authority': Towards a Future Oekoumene—If There Is a Future?" In *States of Crisis and Post-Capitalist Scenarios*, ed. H. Felder and F. Vighi, 219–239. Wey Court East: Ashgate.

jagodzinski, j. (Forthcoming). "1780 and 1945: An Avant-Garde without Authority: Addressing the Anthropocene." In *Deleuze and Schizoanalysis of Visual Art*, ed. I. Buchanan and L. Collins, 149–171. London: Bloomsbury.

jagodzinski, j., and Wallin, J. (2013). *Arts Based Research: A Critique and a Proposal.* Rotterdam: Sense Publishers.

Latour, B. (1993). *We Have Never Been Modern.* Trans. C. Porter. Cambridge, MA: Harvard University Press.

Lyotard, J-F. (1991). *The Inhuman: Reflections on Time.* Trans. G. Bennington and R. Bowlby. Cambridge: Polity.

Morton, T. (2007). *Ecology without Nature: Rethinking Environmental Aesthetics.* Cambridge, MA: Harvard University Press.

Rancière, J. (1991). *The Ignorant Schoolmaster: Five Lessons in Intellectual Emancipation.* Trans. and intro. K. Ross. Stanford, CA: Stanford University Press.

Rancière, J. (2001). "Ten Theses on Politics." *Theory and Event* 5 (3). Retrieved February 2, 2014, from http://muse.jhu.edu/journals/tae/toc/index.html.

Rancière, J. (2002). "The Aesthetic Revolution and Its Outcomes." *New Left Review* 14 (March–April): 133–151.

Rancière, J. (2004a). "Is There a Deleuzian Aesthetics?" Trans. R. Djordjevic. *Qui Parle* 14 (2): 1–14.

Rancière, J. (2004b). *The Politics of Aesthetics: The Distribution of the Sensible.* Trans. and intro. G. Rockhill. New York: Continuum Press.

Rancière, J. (2006). *Film Fables.* Trans. E. Battist. Oxford: Berg.

Rancière, J. (2007). "Are Some Things Unrepresentable?" In *Jacques Rancière, The Future of the Image*, trans. G. Elliot, 109–138. New York: Verso.

Rancière, J. (2009a). *Aesthetics and Its Discontents*. Trans. S. Corcoran. Cambridge: Polity.

Rancière, J. (2009b). *The Emancipated Spectator*. Trans. G. Elliot. New York: Verso.

Steffen, W., Grinevald, J., Crutzen, P., and McNeill, J. (2011). "The Anthropocene: Conceptual and Historical Perspectives." *Philosophical Transactions of the Royal Society* 369:842–867.

Trafi-Prats, L. (2012). "Urban Children and Intellectual Emancipation: Video Narratives of Self and Place in the City of Milwaukee." *Studies in Art Education* 53 (2): 125–138.

Tyson, E.L. (2009). "Education in the Realm of the Senses: Understanding Paolo Freire's Aesthetic Unconscious through Jacques Rancière." *Journal of Philosophy of Education* 43 (2): 285–299.

Wolfe, K. (2006). "From Aesthetics to Politics: Rancière, Kant and Deleuze." *Contemporary Aesthetics* 4. Retrieved February 15, 2014, from http://www.contempaesthetics.org/newvolume/pages/article.php?articleID=382.

Ziarek, K. (2004). *The Force of Art*. Stanford, CA: Stanford University Press.

9 Dark Posthumanism, Unthinking Education, and Ecology at the End of the Anthropocene

Jason J. Wallin

What is an end? It is this very question that drives the speculative horror of zombie fiction, for ostensibly disabused of romantic idealism and the conceit of anthropocentric dominion, the figure of the zombie advances a denuded speculation on the end of planetary life *as it is for humans.* Immanent throughout its allegorical transformations to "the unsettled ecology in which it dwells," the zombie has *become* a contemporary harbinger of eco-catastrophe and the accelerated collapse of the Anthropocene (Cohen 2012).[1] Decomposing the homeostatic, equilibrated, and "bounded" image of the human, the zombie emerges counterpart to a hostile ecology in which the human organism faces its immanent obsolescence (Colebrook 2011). In perverse nuptials to viral contagion (*Plague of the Zombies, 28 Days Later, Ponypool*), radioactive contamination (*Night of the Living Dead*), toxic poisons (*Dawn of the Dead, Return of the Living Dead*), and bio-engineered disease (*28 Weeks Later*), zombie-life speculates on life by other means, or, rather, on an unthought alter-ecology out of step with the anthropocentric conceit that the *world* is *as it is for us* (Thacker 2011). McKibben (2011) points to this virulent dark ecology in his assertion that we are *already* living on a "strange new Earth." Non-resemblant with the certain and stable image of the planet's *Earthrise*, photographed by William Anders of *Apollo 8*, the "strange new Earth" articulated by McKibben describes an inhospitable and alien environment dominated by violent storms, mega-fires, acidic oceans, and accelerated glacial erosion (McKibben 2011; Adam 2008; Harris 2009).[2] *It is too late to go back.* The world *as it is for us* is at an end.

THE WORLD-FOR-US

While *Earthrise* constitutes a paradigmatic point of reference for human life on the planet,[3] it is nevertheless one that is imbricated within an anthropocentric philosophical legacy intimate to contemporary educational thought. Quentin Meillassoux (2010) articulates this legacy in *Beyond Finitude: An Essay on the Necessity of Contingency*, in which he outlines the problem of *correlationism*, or, rather, the idea that access to the world is only ever access to the *correlation* between thought and its object. Correlationism marks an invisible philosophical presumption that objects can only be thought as they are given and further, as they are given *for a subject*. As Meillassoux writes, the thesis of correlationism asserts "the essential inseperability of the act of thinking from its content [such that] [a]ll we ever engage with is what is given-to-thought, never an entity subsisting by itself" (36). The problem of correlationism hence pertains to a presupposed philosophy of access that assumes things cannot exist without their *a priori* givenness to thought, or rather, the presumption that the world exists only to the extent that we think it. Here, correlationism founds an anthropocentric conceit that the world is as it is *for us* (Thacker 2011). Despite its shock to perception, for example, *Earthrise* becomes neither an image of the world independent of human existence or an object that recedes from its givenness to thought. Framed against the desolate alien terrain of outer space, *Earthrise* signals an image of the Earth in its givenness for human life. That is, the *Apollo 8* mission's nostalgic characterization of the "good Earth" as a bounded oasis inscribed within the theological mytheme of Genesis correlates the world to its meaning for a given human subject, obfuscating an occulted and unthinkable planet prior to and beyond human perception.[4]

CORRELATIONISM AND EDUCATION

Exhibiting what Meillassoux (2010, 36) refers to as "strong" correlationism, orthodox educational processes assume as their fundamental task the coordination of the world according to *a priori* categories and forms. From the youngest age, we learn that there is no X without the givenness of X, or, rather, no entities without their having already been given to thought. In this system of "strong" correlationism, learning might be defined as the discovery and coordination of things to given transcendent indexes, systems of identification, and taxonomies of thought. Accelerated in an era of standardization, such correlationism presumes the *a priori* reflection of learning according to prescribed epistemological forms. This closed correlationist loop might otherwise be known through the significance attributed to representation in schooling, where representation *always-already* presumes the "fact" of *a priori* categories through which *datum* (the singularity of data) are deduced (Laruelle 2013). To represent is to postulate a world in conformity with thought's *a priori* forms, where the world (datum) and its givenness to thought are unified through their submission to transcendent meaning. That the process of education is continually implicated in producing a representational image of the world *as it is for us* points to the circle of correlationism in which thought itself becomes habituated. It is not just that we are taught that things have proper categorical meanings or epistemic states, but, more fundamentally, that human consciousness constitutes privileged access to the world.

THE HUMANIST FACE OF EDUCATION

The anthropocentric philosophy of access intimate to correlationism inheres Rousseau's (1979) treatise on education *Emile*, which articulates the "natural" teloi of education correlative to universal humanism. That for Rousseau life is naturally oriented to its realization in the ideals of civic and individual perfectability presumes an *a priori* image in which "natural education" is itself conditioned. For what is "natural" about education, Rousseau avers, is its power to transcend contingency, or rather, to "denature" the human from its nonhuman impulses (Lewis and Kahn 2012). What is human about humanity in Rousseau's treatise is its correspondence with universal attributes of rational progress and perfectibility *above* and *beyond* the mutative aspects of material life. Herein, Rousseau's philosophy of education palpates a dual teloi. For what distinguishes the human from nonhuman life is its ability to both deterritorialize from and be realized in a position of dominion over the mutable (Steel 2012). In givenness to this dual teleology, the world is presumed not only to be human-centered, but governed by the values and morals of transcendent humanism as a measure of all things. In this way, *Emile* not only reifies a human-centered image of "natural order," but founds difference as pejoration. As Rousseau articulates, "natural education" must become recalcitrant to the horrors of "mixing," "disfigurement," and "deformity" as perversions of the spirit in which education is thought *ought to* labor (Lewis and Kahn 2012, 10). Herein, education presumes an ideal "face" of the world according to which life itself becomes correlated.

The anthropocentric desire to eclipse the materiality of the Earth evident in *Emile* has its corollary in the Neoplatonic *Great Chain of Being* and its hierarchical division and subdivision of living and nonliving entities. While the *Great Chain of Being* conveys the knotted relation of the human organism to the Earth, it concomitantly establishes human life as an ontological strata divided from the animal, vegetable, and mineral entities it is imagined to dominate and for whom such entities are presumed to exist. The representational stratification of life conveyed through the *Great Chain of Being* might be thought alongside the coding machine Deleuze and Guattari (1987) dub faciality, where faciality makes sense of bodies by overcoding and regulating their expressive potentials in the image of a "limit face" defined according to the "model enforcing grid of [W]hite [Man]" (Watson 2008, 209). Beginning with the image of Jesus Christ or that of "the typical European" spread by Renaissance and colonial missionaries, facialization functions to absorb traces of singularization through the exertion of a majoritarian model of signification (178). Under the semiotic regime of faciality, difference becomes reduced to degrees of deviancy from the face of White Man as a transcendent index (Opondo 2013). Here, Deleuze and Guattari (1987) link the imperial semiotics of faciality to colonial racism, for it is in faciality that the species is both recognized and distributed in proximity to White Man as the image of what others *ought to become* and according to which deviancies are absorbed by "waves of sameness" (Saldanha 2013).[5]

While the biopolitical backdrop of *faciality* is implicate with the molarizing powers of racism and coloniality,[6] the deviances against which faciality functions equally pertain to a biopolitics of anthropocentrism (Saldanha 2013, 19). That is, faciality not only functions to molarize human life according to the Christ-White-Man face, but as Deleuze and Guattari (1987) suggest, the correlationist imperialism of faciality extends to the landscape itself. Herein, the historical invention of the face during the Renaissance becomes contracted with the Earth "populated by a loved or dreamed of face" (171). Projected upon the schizo-materiality of the landscape, the image of human dominion and order figured in the *Great Chain of Being* overcodes the Earth from the perspective of White Man, in whose image the landscape is both absorbed and idealized. Renaissance landscape painting exemplifies such overcoding in its pastoral and utilitarian image of the world *as it is for humans*. Here, the "loved face" of Renaissance landscape painting is linked to the domestication and control of animal, vegetable, and mineral life, as if the landscape were always-already destined to an image of life given anthropocentrically (171). Such glorification of human centrality is registered throughout Renaissance landscape painting via the facialized image of heroic idealism, "natural" order, and the submission of life to the superiority of human activity. As with da Vinci's *Vitruvian Man* (c. 1490) and the image of progress and perfectibility it symbolizes for human culture, the facialization of the planet is informed by a Renaissance "civilizational ideal" ensconced in the moral, spiritual, and discursive values of humanism (Braidotti 2013, 15). Modelized in the Neoplatonic Chain of Being, the Renaissance Earth is conceptualized as a *world-for-us*—facialized as different, but by degree from the imperial regime of humanism as its ultimate arbiter of significance (Thacker 2011). Put differently, the world is made thinkable from the perspective of an idealized species relative to which it is both recuperated and reduced in potential.

EAARTHRISE

As a corollary to the unsettled ecology in which it dwells, zombie-life might be linked to the "dark ecology" of a decoding planet and the threat to anthropocentrism such dark ecology portends in its corruption of transcendent optimism and the romantic idealization of human dominion over the planet (Morton 2010; Thacker 2011). As McKibben (2011) articulates, the Earth is no longer recognizable as that stable oasis pictured in Anders's *Earthrise*, nor does the planet reflect in the utopian face of imperial progress intimate to humanist ideals. Falling out of sync with the image of the "Earth" *as it is for humans*, the unsettled and mutative transformation of the planet marks the emergence of a planetary-becoming not yet given to human thought.[7] Here, McKibben palpates the image of an Earth that is no longer *for-us* by speculating on an alter-planetary "Eaarthrise" that both breaks from anthropocentric faciality and the presupposition that reality is given to a human subject (2011, 1). Opposed to its transcendent correspondence with an image of the Earth given *a priori*, "Eaarthrise" palpates the planet's immanent schizo-materiality, o, rather, the intensive rise and assemblage of inhuman life non-correspondent to the image of the human or the ideal of human dominion. Herein, "Eaarthrise" becomes a speculation on what Thacker (2011) dubs the *planet-without-us*, or, rather, a planet that breaks from the face of anthropocentrism by palpating both the collapse of the Anthropocene and the realization that the world is replete with strange life non-conformant with its supposed "enlivenment" by humans (Morton 2010).

DARK EAARTH

From its modern reconceptualization, the zombie has often figured in special relationship with a decaying Earth. Across a litany of films, including Romero's seminal *Night of the Living Dead* (1968), *Zombi 2* (1979), and *Resident Evil: Apocalypse* (2004), zombies burrow from their hidden subterranean internment into the terrestrial world, producing an anexact relation to the inhuman life of invertebrates, microbial life, and the unfathomable inhuman movements of Chthon. The emergence of the zombie's contaminated and putrefied body might hence be delinked from the allegory of Christian resurrection and rethought as an indexical figure of the "shifting visage of the planet" beyond human history and biology (MacKay 2012, 18). This is to say that the Earth to which the zombie has become an index is not the stable and homeostatic oasis of *Earthrise* apprehended from a human vantage 384,400 kilometers *above and beyond* this planet. Rather, the unsettled ecology of the zombie portends to an unthought and inhuman world that soils the transcendent gaze of *anthropos* by drawing it back into material nuptials with the dark ecology of the planet (Cohen 2012; Steel 2012). It is this *immanent* ecological fold that is diagrammed in *Return of the Living Dead* (1985), *Mud Zombies* (2008), and *The Bay* (2012), each of which articulates a rapidly decoding planet accelerated through molecular forces of contamination and decay. Herein, the image of the Earth *as it is for us* is confronted by a subterranean dark world closer to the "strange new Earth" of leachate-contaminated soil, toxic swamps, airborne poisons, and vitriolic viral life described by McKibben (2011). As an indexical figure of this planetary geotrauma, the zombie fulminates a diagram of inhuman affective life subtending the anthropocentric conceit that *the face of man* constitutes a horizon of planetary life. Against correlationism, zombie-life recedes from human comprehension in articulation of an alter-life born of the horrific plastic forces of planetary decoding and its triggering of a strange ecosophical unconsciousness unthinkable under anthropocentrism (MacKay 2012, 22).

PLANETARY SCHIZOANALYSIS

Zombie-life deterritorializes the anthropocentric facialization of the planet by diagramming an unthought dark ecology, or, rather, a malevolent assemblage of the dispersed *life-and-death* forms subtending the image of human life, its orders of arrangement and identitarian *telos* (Colebrook 2011, 12). Put differently, the subterranean ecology fabulated in zombie fiction questions not only how a life might go, but also what thinks and of what things might think *where we are not*. The dark ecology of the zombie speculates on a posthuman "horde ontology" in which humans are divested of their presumed status as dominant planetary actants transcendent to material life (Bennett 2012). Reterritorialized in intimate relation to dark ecology, the zombie is "triggered" through the conjoined actions of viroid transmission (*Dawn of the Dead*), molecular parasitism, accumulative chemical pollution (*Mud Zombies*), disavowed industrial effluent (*The Bay*), capitalist expansionism (*Land of the Dead*), and so on. This is to say that the zombie speculates on the obsolescence of the Anthropocene and the rise of an alter-Eaarth that no longer repeats in the narrative of anthropocentric dominion. Rather, the zombie produces speculative resources for thinking an ecosophy at the end of the humanity, figuring as a noir realist harbinger to what Thacker (2011) dubs the "anonymous, impersonal 'in itself' of the world" indifferent to the hopes and desires of human life (17).

Breaking from the correlationist conceit of anthropocentrism, the dark ecology of which the zombie is an indexical figure commences a schizoanalytic program that brings both inhuman materialism and a dilated account of geological spatio-temporality into the purview of analysis (MacKay 2012). This is to follow Professor Challenger's provocation that analysis must necessarily supplant history and biology in its detection of an unconscious that fails to repeat in the overcoded terrain of the *human-all-too-human* (Land 2011). Such a schizoanalytic account is nascently articulated in Morton's (2010) *The Ecological Thought*, in which the bounded image of human life is superseded by massively distributed and nonlocalizable "hyperobjects" (global warming, radioactive plutonium, UV rays) with which life itself is *always-already* enfolded.[8] This schizoanalytic dilation of ecology produces an inherent challenge to contemporary education insofar as it delinks the world from its givenness to human thought. As Morton (2013) articulates, such hyperobjects as UV rays are not a function of knowledge, but act despite our thinking them. This notion is redoubled in contemporary epigenetic research that suggests that human life is always-already being "thought" by the composite inhuman life of waste, chemical composites, radiation, and environmental mutation (Morton 2013; Thacker 2012).

Breaking from both human history and biology by palpating the finitude of anthropocentric thought, the zombie's *horde-life* is assembled upon an onto-ecological diagram divorced from the speciesist ordering of things, inverting the anthropocentric ideals of human perfectibility and progress in which schooling is "ought" to labor (Bennett 2012). That is, the speculative world of the zombie breaks the humanist conceit of progress and perfection by actualizing the occulted unconscious background of horror and decay with which human life is imbricated. This is to suggest that where schooling remains wedded to the correlationist idea that our understanding of the world is equal to the world, it negates an ethical account of material life without humans, hence reifying the implicate forms of violence and exploitation coextensive of thinking the world as always-already given to a human subject. Populated by the powers of nonhuman and differently abled "bodies," the speculative world of the zombie proposes both an inhuman sensorium impossible to apprehend via human means and the expansion of spatiotemporal experience outside human thought (Bennett 2012). Such noir speculation marks an engagement with the inherent speciesism of contemporary education in its articulation of superabundant material realities unthinkable by humans. Here, the anti-correlationist dark ecology of the zombie functions to break from the epistemological question of *what knowledge is of most worth* insofar as it suggests both forms of life and realities to which humans have *no access*. To presume the correlationist unification of thought and being coextensive of education's epistemological reverence for *best knowledge*, or, rather, the *best* correspondence of thought and reality, is to continue to found a denial of life that exceeds our ability to think it.

WHAT IS AN END?

That the task of education continues to be oriented to the discovery of constants, rules, and axioms suggests its habituation in correlationism. Yet, the forces of standardization and discovery whereby we *learn what everyone already knows* is not correlationism's limit. Battles over epistemological and interpretive terrain in education are likewise informed by an albeit weak correlationism, whereby the world's givenness to thought is nevertheless assumed. Such weak correlationism might otherwise be known via the automatic interpretation machines rife in the field of educational thought, whereby *events* are given automatic form and meaning for us. As with the central premise of correlationism, education teaches over and again that thought and its object are inseparable. While such inseparability is a hallmark of education's post-structural turn, the very conceptualization risks reterritorializing anthropocentrically. That meaning continues to be wed to the task of representing reality as it is *for us* marks an analytic commitment that establishes as its expressive limit point the face of human life—and perhaps necessarily so, for is our inability to think beyond the human not an unavoidable aspect of our being human? This posed, if science is correct in its demonstration that human and inhuman life are enfolded at varying scales of existence, then why might this imbrication not be extended to human thought? That is, why should it be that thought is *necessarily* human (Thacker 2012)? It is perhaps already too late for education to confront the hideous gnosis that is the end of the Anthropocene (Shakespeare 2010). It seems today that the presumption of human dominion over the Earth remains a thoroughly entrenched ontological perspective of orthodox education. Humanist mantras of hope and optimism remain moral mainstays, and at the end of the day it often still suffices to acquiesce that "we are all human." Even the most forward-thinking critical approaches in educational research have yet to fully apprehend our inherently speciesist orientation to reality and the exploitative impacts of such speciesism as it both consciously and unconsciously informs upon the gendered, racial, and social divisions implicate in our own species (Monson 2005).

For education to become adequate to posthuman thought necessitates its investment in the destruction of the face, for "if the face is politics," Deleuze and Guattari (1987) write, "dismantling the face is also a politics involving real becomings, an entire becoming-clandestine" (188). The question of how a face might be dismantled has become intimate to the broadly defined "movement" of speculative realism, for it is within speculative realism that the correlationist impulse of philosophical thought to account for reality is vigorously defrayed via the fabulation of ecologies, analytic approaches, and realisms for which no system of thought preexists as an apparatus of capture or overcoding. This is not simply to court the tired educational cliché that "there is more to learn" or to redouble the postmodern valorization of uncertainty, but to take seriously that the privileged image of human access to reality intimate to education must be *unthought* (MacCormack 2013). An outside to anthropos persists in the strange hyper-assemblage of "horde life," in the unfathomable life of nonhuman entities, in the dilated unconsciousness of planetary schizo-decay, and the horror of dark ecology. Preserving the autonomy of reality from its overdetermination in interpretation or underdetermination as superfluous excess to human reason, speculative realism produces a dilated account of ontology divested of its reliance upon human enlivenment.

PESSIMISM

Where education functions to territorialize the world in an image *for-us*, speculative realism assumes instead a pessimistic approach to the privileged place of the human knower. Such pessimism pertains not only to the finitude of human epistemology and its anthropocentric obliteration of strange life, but to the stratification of biological orders and physical structures that presume in advance a human face upon the world. To produce a mode of analysis capable of giving expression to alter-ecologies necessitates first the liquidation of the face as a dominant ground of meaning and foundation for thought. The dark ecology of "Eaarthrise" portends this very liquidation by suggesting the obsolescence of the Anthropocene and emergence of inhuman planetary assemblages that "think" where we are not. Herein, pessimism is not simply equivalent to inaction, but to the creation of conditions for the surrender of the anthropocentric imaginary and an ethical "letting-be" of life-forms non-resemblant with human life (MacCormack 2012). This is to suggest that education be rethought not only in terms of its material ecological consequences, but with utter pessimism for the philosophy of access reified via its implicate commitment to anthropocentric correlationism. This is to mobilize pessimism as an ethical force for warding against the false optimism of transcendence and the obfuscation of ecological forces of "negativity, introversion . . . ambiguity, darkness . . . fragmentation, and sickness" (Morton 2010, 16). Put differently, posthumanist education's break from the face of man necessitates thinking without privileging the holistic and healthy image of "nature" produced by humanism and redoubled in the "green" movement's fetishization of nature in the 1960s. That the "ugliness . . . and horror of ecology" be confronted requires that posthumanist education delink from the anthropocentric representation of "nature" *for us* (17). We are but one species among many (*things*).

DARK ECOSOPHY

If education is to become posthumanist, it must become capable of forging an encounter with eco-catastrophe that does not reterritorialize upon an *all-too-human* image of life. This is to recommence the educational project in a manner capable of apprehending that the image of life hitherto reified in educational thought has fallen gravely out of sync with a rapidly decoding planetary ecology. Herein, posthumanist education must be rethought by dint of a planetary schizoanalysis, or, rather, alongside forces of planetary decay, mutation, and violent upheaval obfuscated by education's subjugation of the unconscious in an image of romantic humanism. Herein, a posthumanist education must become capable of *unthinking* anthropocentrism by taking seriously both the collapse of human and nonhuman "things" as well as that which is already inhuman within the human.[9] As contemporary science reveals, what we call the human body is in fact composed of 90 percent inhuman organisms (Thacker 2012). This is to produce a thoroughly strange analytic reorientation to history, biology, and geology relinked to the schizo-material triggers of planetary change with which we are imbricated but remain cleaved insofar as the human remains a privileged ground from which thinking is made to emanate. This is to suggest a dark ecosophical turn for educational thought linked not only to the failure of correlationism and its production of speciesist violence, but to the realization that the face of man as a "measure of all things" lingers as but a "petrified fiction" amid the dark ecology of planetary decay (Land 1992, 131).

The pedagogy of such dark ecosophy would of necessity become anti-prophetic in its attenuation to both the illusion of self-importance and the transcendence of human life and meaning over the world (Cioran 2012). Where the correlationist impulse of epistemology to unify the world *for-us* perseveres, a pedagogical dark ecosophy might aim to render such presumptions into both objects of inquiry and as a fulcrum for the introjection of speculative and untimely thinking on alien difference. Schooling's civilizational ideal and image of civic subjects might be rethought against the background of a dark ecosophical *chaosmopolis*, or, rather, decoding lines of the "civilized world" always-already linked to planetary "triggers" and "tipping points" (Cioran 2012). This is all to suggest that where posthumanist education might eclipse the abuses of romantic humanism, it might dare imagine a moment when human life and vitality "will no longer be the fashion," but rather, apprehended as a prejudice against all that is inhuman, "unthinking," and dead (90). It is only at the point of being able to think an end that is the *end of the all-too-human* that a posthumanist education might be commenced with sincerity for the occulted planet subtending anthropocentrism.

A contemporary posthumanist turn in education must be one capable of thinking with death, and, more specifically, the death of the anthropocentric conceit that the world is *as it is for us*. This posits an immense challenge insofar as educational thought remains habitually contracted to anthropocentric philosophies of access and their presumed reflection of human vitalism. In ways that support the continuation of speciesism, the exploitation of animal and inhuman life, and the illusion of human centrality, education continues to apprehend the Earth from 384,400 kilometers *above and beyond* the planet. This is to say that where educational processes continue to produce a world given to a human subject, it remains implicate with only that which is revealed, collected as data, produced as models, and measured by value (Thacker 2012). Herein, education continues to think life from the perspective of a single species. It is this very problematic that posthumanist education must become capable of overcoming in an account of ontological forms that resist "the ambit of human wants and desires" (4). As we today witness the emergence of a horrific occulted Earth, we must contend with *its* prescient thought of humanity's end. No sincere answer will come in the form of a new transcendence, or in the continuation of *all-too-human* morals and values complicit in the stratification of life and modelization of the Earth in the image of man as the "measure of all things."

TO DIE WELL

Posthumanist education must palpate a different quality of response, and, by way of conclusion, I would like to rejoin in this consideration the zombie as an indexical figure of a decaying planet. That is, where the humans of zombie fiction clamor to reterritorialize in *all-too-human* social and familial formations, it is the zombie that commits to the unthought horrors of planetary contamination, toxification, purification, and decay. It is in this way that the zombie might be thought as a melancholic figure for its ethical commitment to the dark ecology of the planet, refusing as it does to leave this dying "Eaarth." Wandering, digging, and occupying the sub-astral recesses of the planet, the zombie oozes melancholic black bile from its corporeal,[10] sundered body. This is significant, for as Morton (2011) describes, melancholy is linked to the Earth, or rather, a particular Earth—*cold and dry, sour, and black* (16). Herein, melancholy is inherently ecological or rather, intimate to the dark ecology of the planet, for the melancholic is resolved to stay with this planet without optimism for a *way out*. It is in this regard that the zombie marks a posthumanist ethical commitment to stay with the occulted life of *this* planet and, hence, to break from the aspirations of transcendence in which the face of humanism continues to be forged.

NOTES

1. The dark ecology palpated by zombie-life has been counterposed by an inventory of (popular) pedagogical responses. In such video games as *Alive 4-Ever*, *Call of Duty: Black Ops: Zombies*, *Dead Rising*, and *Red Dead Redemption: Undead Nightmare*, zombies have become fodder in a simulated war for human dominance and preservation. AMC's immensely popular *The Walking Dead* reifies this desire in its restaging of familial melodrama and xenophobic anxiety for difference. In popular film, Jonathan Levine's *Warm Bodies* (2013) recolonizes such inhuman difference by dramatizing the zombie's salvation through heteronormative romantic love. Across these varied mediums, there insists a prejudice against the zombie, or, rather, against the schizo-affects of zombie-life and their accelerative dilation of an onto-ecological dark ecology.
2. Symptoms of this mutating Holocene suprabound. Increases in oceanic temperature over the past half decade have been linked to a fourfold intensification in the frequency of disasters related to violent weather and the concomitant emergence of so-called mega-storms of unanticipated virulence and intensity (McKibben 2011). The ocean today is more corrosive than at any point in the past eight hundred thousand years, with pH fluctuations accelerating ten times faster than forecast. Familial ice core marker layers containing fallout from atomic testing in the 1960s have begun to disappear from ancient Himalayan glaciers, marking the accelerated erosion of glacial sheets.
3. *Earthrise* was described by wilderness photographer Galen Rowell as "the most influential environmental photograph ever taken." U.S. photo specialist Richard Underwood argued that of the multibillion-dollar cost of the *Apollo 8* mission, it would be the nineteen cents of film featuring the eponymously

named *Earthrise* that would constitute its most significant artifact (Spier, 2002). Historian Fred Spier attributes Anders's *Earthrise* to a mutation in the human imaginary, catalyzing a new conceptualization of the Earth as a certain and stable "oasis" (McKibben 2011).

4. On its ninth pass from behind the moon's dark side, the crew of *Apollo 8* live broadcasted a reading of the book of Genesis.

5. We might think here of the popular fairy-tale cliché in which the *inhuman* face of the animal is "positively" transformed into the image of *prince charming*, or otherwise, where the unformed head (in Pinocchio, for example) is seen as a transitory phase on its way to becoming realized in an orthodox image of humanity (Genosko 2002).

6. As Watson (2008) notes, it is through the production of majoritarian models that a white European, secularized Christian majority has protected its dominance (209).

7. As jagodzinski (2014) articulates, research emerging from the work of such leading climatologists as James Hansen of the Stockholm Resilience Center have identified that no less than three of nine planetary tipping points have now been eclipsed. These include global warming, transformations of the nitrogen cycle, biodiversity loss, and the radical transgression of the planetary "carrying capacity" by upward of 30 percent.

8. Emerging inquiry in the field of epigenetics suggests that human genes are being "triggered" by planetary transformations and environmental factors such as global warming (http://rspb.royalsocietypublishing.org/content/early/2010/11/19/rspb.2010.1890).

9. As jagodzinski (2014) articulates, human and natural history are now undifferentiable.

10. The corporeality of the zombie is significant for its virulent embodiment and must in this regard be distinguished from other modern monsters.

REFERENCES

Adam, D. (2008). Too late: Why scientists say we should expect the worst. Retrieved from http://www.theguardian.com/environment/2008/dec/09/poznan-copenhagen-global-warming-targets-climate-change on January 3, 2014.

Abraham, M. (producer), Newman, E. (producer), Rubinstein, R.P. (producer), and Snyder, Z. (director). (2004). *Dawn of the Dead* (motion picture). Brazil: Fábulas Negras.

Aragão, R. (director). (2008). *Mud Zombies* (motion picture). Canada: Lionsgate Entertainment.

Bennett, J. (2012). "Powers of the Hoard: Further Notes on Material Agency." In *Animal Vegetable, Mineral*, ed. J.J. Cohen, 237–272. Washington, DC: Oliphant Books.

Braidotti, R. (2013). *The Posthuman*. Cambridge: Polity.

Cioran, E.M. (2012). *A Short History of Decay*. Trans. R. Howard. New York: Arcade Publishing.

Cohen, J.J. (2012). *Grey: A Zombie Ecology*. Retrieved September 13, 2012, from http://www.inthemedievalmiddle.com/2012/06/grey-zombie-ecology.html.

Colebrook, C. (2011). "Time and Autopoeisis: The Organism Has No Future." In *Deleuze and the Body*, ed. L. Giallaume and J. Hughes, 9–28. Edinburgh: Edinburgh University Press.

Deleuze, G., and Guattari, F. (1987). *A Thousand Plateaus*. Trans. R. Hurley, M. Seem, and H.R. Lane. Minneapolis: University of Minnesota Press.

Fresnadillo, J.C. (director). (2007). *28 Weeks Later* (motion picture). United Kingdom, Spain: 20th Century Fox.
Fulci, L. (director). (1979). *Zombi 2* (motion picture). United States: Studio Mafera.
Genosko, G. (2002). *Felix Guattari: An aberrant introduction*. New York: Continuum.
Harris, R. (2009). Global Warming is irreversible, study says. *All things considered*, January 26, 2009.
jagodzinski, j. (2014). An Avant-garde 'without Authority': Towards a Future Oekoumene—if there is a Future?" In Heiko Felder, Fabio Vighi and Slavoj Žižek (Eds.). *States of Crisis and Post-Capitalist Scenarios* (pp. 219–239). Wey Court East: Ashgate Press.
Land, N. (1992). *The Thirst for Annihilation: George Bataille and Virulent Nihilism*. New York: Routledge.
Land, N. (2011). *Fanged noumena: Collected Writings 1987–2007*. New York: Sequence Press.
Laruelle, F. (2013). *Principles of Non-Philosophy*. Trans. A.P. Smith and N. Rubczak. New York: Bloomsbury.
Levine, J. [Director]. (2013). *Warm bodies* (Motion Picture). USA: Summit Entertainment.
Levinson, B. (director). (2012). *The Bay* (motion picture). United States: Automatik Entertainment.
Lewis, T., and Khan, R. (2012). *Education Out of Bounds: Reimagining Cultural Studies for a Posthuman Age*. New York: Palgrave Macmillan.
MacCormack, P. (2012). *Posthuman Ethics*. Burlington, VT: Ashgate.
MacCormack, P. (2013). "Gracious Pedagogy." *Journal of Curriculum and Pedagogy* 9 (2): 13–17.
MacKay, R. (2012). "A Brief History of Geotrauma." In *Leper Creativity: Cyclonopedia Symposium*, ed. E. Keller, N. Masciandaro, and E. Thacker, 1–38. Brooklyn, NY: Punctum Press.
McKibben, B. (2011). *Eaarth: Making a Life on a Tough New Planet*. New York: St. Martin's Griffin.
Meillassoux, Q. (2010). *After Finitude: An Essay on the Necessity of Contingency*. New York: Bloomsbury.
Monson, S. (director). (2005). *Earthlings* (documentary film). United States: Nation Earth.
Morton, T. (2010). *The Ecological Thought*. Cambridge, MA: Harvard University Press.
Morton, T. (2013). *Hyperobjects: Philosophy and Ecology after the End of the World*. Minneapolis: Minnesota University Press.
O'Bannon, D [Director]. (1985). The return of the living dead (motion picture). United States: Fox Films Ltd.
Opondo, S.O. (2013). "Cinema-Body-Thought: Race-Habits and the Ethics of Encounter." In *Deleuze and Race*, ed. A. Saldanha and J.M. Adams, 247–268. Edinburgh: Edinburgh University Press.
Romero, G.A. (director). (1968). *Night of the Living Dead* (motion picture). United States: Walter Reade Organization.
Romero, G.A. (director). (1978). *Dawn of the Dead* (motion picture). United States, Italy: Laurel Group.
Romero, G.A. (director). (2005). *Land of the Dead* (motion picture). United States: Universal Pictures.
Rouseau, J.J (1979). Emile or on education. In Bloom, A. (Trans.). New York: Basic Books.

Saldanha, A. (2013). "Introduction: Bastard and Mixed-Blood and the True Names of Race." In *Deleuze and Race*, ed. A. Saldanha and J.M. Adams, 6–34. Edinburgh: Edinburgh University Press.

Shakespeare, S. (2010). "The Light That Illuminates Itself, the Dark Soil That Soils Itself: Blackened Notes from Schelling's Underground." In *Hideous Gnosis*, ed. N. Masciandaro, 5–22. United States: Createspace.

Steel, K. (2012). "With the World, or Bound to Face the Sky: The Postures of the Wolf-Child Hesse." In *Animal Vegetable, Mineral*, ed. J.J. Cohen, 9–34. Washington, DC: Oliphant Books.

Spier, F. (2002). The apollo 8 earthrise photo. Retrieved from http://www.sfu.ca/physics/ugrad/courses/2007–3old/p190/Apollo%208%20Earthrise%20Photo%20-%20Fred%20Spier.pdf on February 12, 2014.

Thacker, E. (2011). *In the Dust of This Planet: Horror of Philosophy Vol. 1*. Washington, DC: Zero Books.

Thacker, E. (2012). "Black Infinity; Or, Oil Discovers Humans." In *Leper Creativity: Cyclonopedia Symposium*, ed. E. Keller, N. Masciandaro, and E. Thacker, 173–180. Brooklyn, NY: Punctum Press.

Watson, J. (2008). "Theorizing European Ethnic Politics with Deleuze and Guattari." In *Deleuze and Politics*, ed. I. Buchanan and N. Thorburn, 196–217. Edinburgh: Edinburgh University Press.

Witt, A. (director). (2004). *Resident Evil: Apocalypse* (motion picture). United States: Constantin Film.

Part IV

What Posthumanist
Education Will Have Been

10 Undoing Anthropocentrism in Educational Inquiry
A Phildickian Space Odyssey?

Noel Gough

> phildickian: Having the qualities of a story by Philip K. Dick, a 20th century writer who regularly asked readers to consider the nature of reality and humanity. Films directly based on his work include "A Scanner Darkly," [and] "Blade Runner," but many other films and novels at the turn of the century have adopted a phildickian tone.[1]

> In posthuman terms, Noel Gough is our forefather, he is the Robocop (first cyborg in film) and the Philip K. Dick (innovative, visionary SF writer) of curriculum studies. (Weaver 2010, 32)

When I first read John Weaver's (2010) generous appraisal of my position as a "forefather" to the posthumanist curriculum scholarship he so capably represents, I was grateful, humbled, and curious.[2] Reading further in his text satisfied my curiosity to some extent. I appreciate Weaver's perceptive interpretations and critiques of my work, but I am also aware that the publications on which he bases his judgments represent somewhat static positions rather than the messy flux of their becomings. This chapter therefore offers an autobiographical account of how my posthumanist standpoints on educational inquiry emerged. Despite the risks of solipsism that can attend autobiographical accounts, I privilege autobiographical approaches to curriculum inquiry for two related reasons. Firstly, I began teaching graduate studies in curriculum during the year following the publication of William Pinar's (1975b) influential *Curriculum Theorizing: The Reconceptualists*, and his autobiographical method of curriculum inquiry—also known as *currere* (see Pinar 1975a)—became a significant component of my teaching and research repertoires from the late 1970s onward.

I also privilege autobiography in this chapter because I believe that it might be more informative for readers than a less personal account. As William Reid (1981) writes:

> When people are asked why they support certain positions and reject others, they usually point to some kind of logical justification. Often, however, this fails to produce an advance in understanding. Logical systems tend towards closure. If you are in them, everything hangs

together quite nicely. If you are outside them, the logic is opaque. It is rather like having someone show you how he [*sic*] won a game of chess when you don't know the moves. An awkward paradox comes into play: only the expert can really have a "feel" for the system within which he operates, but his very familiarity puts a barrier between him and the outsider looking for enlightenment. A deeper question is why people "buy into" particular systems in the first place, and that is, literally, a deeper question, in that the reasons (if indeed it makes sense to speak of "reasons") are hidden even to the individuals concerned. Partly they inhere in character, partly in the accidents of experience, and even that kind of distinction may not hold up very well. (168)

I will account as best I can for the "reasons," personal characteristics, and "accidents of experience" that have led me to "buy into" posthumanist curriculum inquiry and to write curriculum inquiry in a phildickian voice that questions understandings and representations of reality and humanity.

An additional reason for offering these autobiographical reflections is that I interpret being named as a "forefather" to posthumanist curriculum scholarship by the coeditor of this volume as an invitation to take up a subject position consistent with that of a tribal elder.

AN ACCIDENTAL ASTRONAUT

In 1989 I received an invitation to contribute a chapter to an edited collection, *Reflections from the Heart of Educational Inquiry: Understanding Curriculum and Teaching through the Arts* (Willis and Schubert 1991), which provided the impetus for me to *perform* autobiographical curriculum inquiry (as distinct from merely using it in my teaching of curriculum studies). The book has two parts. Part I focuses on the influence of the arts on school curricula and curriculum inquiry and includes substantial chapters by prominent arts educators, including Elliot Eisner and Madeleine Grumet. Part II consists of short autobiographical accounts by twenty-seven curriculum scholars who recount how a work (or limited number of works) of art contributed to their understandings of curriculum and teaching. My chapter, "An Accidental Astronaut: Learning with Science Fiction" (Gough 1991), reflects upon a succession of fortunate accidents through which particular SF stories influenced my personal and academic development, and how SF eventually became significant in my work as a teacher educator and curriculum scholar.[3] Beginning with my "childhood dreams," inspired by the comic strip "Dan Dare: Pilot of the Future," I recalled how the influence of my elder brother's fondness for SF predisposed me to notice the incongruous location of Arthur C. Clarke's (1953) SF novel *Childhood's End* in an education library and how the experience of reading it quite literally changed my life. Clarke led me to an academic interest in futures study and to other SF authors, notably Ursula Le Guin, whose work exemplified the capacity of SF to generate questions for curriculum inquiry (see Gough 1987). I concluded my chapter by reflecting on what I learned from authors like Clarke and Le Guin, noting especially my self-realization as "a child in time" and the ways in which SF stories helped me to appreciate the "imaginative perspectives of space and time future" that shaped the stories I was then telling to my children, colleagues, and colearners.

The experience of writing "An Accidental Astronaut" powerfully demonstrated to me that Grumet's (1981) claims for *currere* were not farfetched—that it indeed has the capacity to reveal how our collective and individual histories and hopes permeate our stories of educational experiences and to ask how our interpretations of them influence curriculum thought and action. Grumet (1981) also draws attention to the ways in which an individual's attitudes, choices, and values might be rendered invisible by our personal involvement in our stories:

> The problem of studying the curriculum is that we are the curriculum. It is we who have raised our hands before speaking, who have learned to hear only one voice at a time, and to look past the backs of the heads of our peers to the eyes of the adult in authority. It is we who have learned to offer answers rather than questions, not to make people feel uncomfortable, to tailor enquiry to bells, buzzers and nods. (122)

Although autobiography provided me (and many of my students) with an accessible and flexible frame for ordering and critically analyzing educational experiences, I sometimes found reason to doubt the method's capacity to address Grumet's "we are the curriculum" problem. Both Pinar and Grumet clearly sought to rescue autobiography from the self-absorption that fuels many positivist researchers' mistrust of subjectivity. But I suspected that some students were using autobiography to reinforce a unitary sense of an essential humanist self rather than seek a critical perspective on educational experiences that they might otherwise have taken for granted. It was not until I worked through the implications of post-structuralist understandings of subjectivity for *currere* that I saw how I might ameliorate this difficulty. My conceptual breakthrough was recognizing the contradiction inherent in the title of William Pinar and William Reynolds's (1992) edited collection, *Understanding Curriculum as Phenomenological and Deconstructed Text*, namely, that post-structuralist understandings of subjectivity as multiple and continually contested irreversibly destabilize the phenomenological quest for essential meanings (see Gough 1994).

LABORATORIES IN FICTION AND MANIFESTING CYBORGS IN CURRICULUM INQUIRY

In the early 1990s, two further accidents of experience provided the motive and opportunity for me to explore further ways of learning with SF and of enacting autobiographical curriculum inquiry. In 1991 I was invited to write a research monograph, *Laboratories in Fiction: Science Education and Popular Media* (Gough 1993), as part of the study materials for a new subject, Educational Issues in Science and Technology, to be offered in Deakin University's Open Campus Program. This monograph set out my vision for what I then called a postmodern science education. I argued that the science textbooks of late twentieth-century schooling retained a Newtonian worldview and a nineteenth-century image of science as the study of material structures of simple systems. I provided evidence that SF in comics, books, movies, and even popular music offered more plausible representations of twentieth-century science as the study of informational structures of complex systems and more realistic representations of the ways in which contemporary scientists work. Scientists in SF are not the objective, value-neutral, and apolitical creatures of textbooks who work in disciplinary silos but, rather, are more lifelike people who struggle with moral and political issues and improvise their interactions with colleagues in their own and other disciplines, other organisms, materials, and machines. I did not argue that SF is simply a more palatable way of introducing or illustrating textbook science. Rather, I argued that SF gives imaginative form to the limits of our own constructed knowledge (and particularly to what might lie beyond them) and is thereby a conceptual territory in which to explore ideas and issues that may be more significant to learners than those to be found in conventional science textbooks.

At around the same time as I was researching *Laboratories in Fiction*, my partner, Annette Gough, was undertaking a PhD—a feminist post-structuralist analysis of the discourses of environmental education's "founding fathers"—and I was intrigued by the relevance of some of the sources on which she drew for my burgeoning explorations of potentially generative links between SF, *currere*, and other methodologies for curriculum inquiry. I was especially inspired by Donna Haraway's cyborg manifesto (1985, 1991) and her deployment of SF in *Primate Visions* (1989). Haraway's (1985) assertion that "the boundary between science fiction and social reality is an optical illusion" (66) was pivotal to developing the strategy I describe as an alternative to *currere* in "Manifesting Cyborgs in Curriculum Inquiry" (1995), namely, to *diffract* stories of personal experience by reading them within and against examples of postmodernist SF, and then to rewrite these stories (and/or write new stories) in ways that self-consciously display their intertextuality.[4]

I did not consciously acknowledge the posthumanist dimensions of my work until Weaver (1999) drew attention to them in an essay review, "Synthetically Growing a Post-Human Curriculum: Noel Gough's Curriculum as a Popular Cultural Text":

Gough's work is no idle exercise in the techno-worship of cyberspace. Instead, he (re)makes the future of curriculum theory and information technology as he critically enters into a dialogue with the post-human condition and the manifestation of this condition in popular culture texts. In this dialogue Gough not only theorizes the impact of information technology on our identity, environment, and curriculum but also establishes a post-structural, postmodern practice in order to understand the impact on students, teachers, and the world of genetic cloning, cosmetic surgery, prostheses, synthesized drugs, memory altering devices, bio-hazardous conditions, and post-Fordist economics. (162)

I regret that I did not immediately take up Weaver's implicit invitation to explore the posthuman dimensions of my work more thoroughly, but at the time I was involved in a capacity-building project with environmental education colleagues in southern Africa and I focused much of my academic attention on issues of postcolonialism and globalization (Gough 2000, 2002). However, in 2001 my partner was diagnosed with a rare form of breast cancer and underwent a mastectomy and breast reconstruction. Somewhat predictably, given our mutual interest in Haraway's work, we began to interpret her experience and changing subjectivity in posthuman terms—her breast implant rapidly became known as "cyberboob" (see Gough 2003). Notice of a then forthcoming conference titled "Body Modification: Changing Bodies, Changing Selves," to be held in April 2003, provided further impetus to our respective academic interests in the posthuman as we each prepared proposals for papers. My abstract for the conference paper, "Becoming-Cyborg: Performing Posthuman Pedagogies," was the first time I consciously used the term "posthuman" in an academic context.

NARRATIVE EXPERIMENTS, RHIZOSEMIOTIC PLAY, AND DELEUZE AND GUATTARI'S GEOPHILOSOPHY

At the time I began to research and write "Becoming-Cyborg," my approach to writing educational inquiry was increasingly being shaped by a methodological disposition to produce texts of the kind that Laurel Richardson (2001) calls "writing-stories" and that I came to call "narrative experiments" (Gough 2008). Richardson (2001) argues:

Writing is a method of discovery, a way of finding out about yourself and your world. When we view writing as a *method*, we experience "language-in-use," how we "word the world" into existence . . . And then we "reword" the world, erase the computer screen, check the thesaurus, move a paragraph, again and again. This "worded world" never accurately, precisely, completely captures the studied world, yet we persist in trying. Writing as a method of inquiry honors and encourages the trying, recognizing it as emblematic of the significance of language. (35, original emphases)

Like Richardson (2001), I found myself writing *essays* "to find something out . . . to learn something that I did not know before I wrote it" (35), and I found it increasingly generative to bring objects of inquiry into intertextual play with Deleuze and Guattari's geophilosophy and "fictions" in the broadest sense of the term. I use the term "essay" here both as a verb—to attempt, to try, to test—and as a noun. In theoretical inquiry, an essay serves similar purposes to an experiment in empirical research—a methodical way of investigating a question or problem—although I find more appropriate analogies for my work in the experimental arts than in the experimental sciences.[5] Both "essay" and the related term "assay" come to English through the French *essayer* from the Latin *exigere*, to weigh. I now write essays to test ideas, to "weigh" them up, to give me (and I hope others) a sense of their worth.

The narrative experiment that emerged as my "Becoming-Cyborg" conference paper was inspired by Deleuze and Guattari's (1987) figuration of the rhizome—a process that I now characterize as *rhizosemiotic play* (Gough 2007). My "report" of this experiment is available elsewhere (Gough 2004), and here I will simply demonstrate some textual strategies that I used in writing it, with particular reference to the generativity of intertextual readings of selected fictions.

Deleuze and Guattari (1994) map the "geography of reason" from pre-Socratic times to the present, a geophilosophy describing relations between particular spatial configurations and locations and the philosophical formations that arise in them (the spatiality of Deleuze and Guattari's geophilosophy is one reason for titling this chapter "A Phildickian *Space Odyssey*"). "Philosophy," they write, "is the discipline that involves creating concepts" (5) through which knowledge can be generated. This differs from the approaches taken by many analytic and linguistic philosophers who are more concerned with the *clarification* of concepts.

Deleuze and Guattari (1987) created a new critical language for analyzing thinking as flows or movements across space. Concepts such as *assemblage, deterritorialization, lines of flight, nomadology,* and *rhizomatics* refer to ways of conceiving ourselves and other objects moving in space. For example, Deleuze and Guattari (1987) distinguish the "sedentary point of view" (23) of much Western philosophy, history, and science from a nomadic subjectivity that allows thought to move across conventional categories and move against "settled" concepts and theories. They distinguish "rhizomatic" thinking from "arborescent" conceptions of knowledge as hierarchically articulated branches of a central stem or trunk rooted in firm foundations. As Umberto Eco (1984) explains, "the rhizome is so constructed that every path can be connected with every other one. It has no center, no periphery, no exit, because it is potentially infinite. The space of conjecture is a rhizome space" (57). In a world of increasingly complex information/communication/knowledge technologies, the space of educational inquiry is also becoming a "rhizome space" more hospitable to nomadic than to sedentary thought.

RHIZOMANTICS

My "Becoming-Cyborg" conference paper eventually became a journal article, "RhizomANTically Becoming-Cyborg: Performing Posthuman Pedagogies" (2004), which began as follows:

> Make a rhizome. But you don't know what you can make a rhizome with, you don't know which subterranean stem is going to make a rhizome, or enter a becoming, people your desert. So experiment (Deleuze and Guattari, 1987: 246).
>
> So I shall. This paper is a narrative experiment inspired by Deleuze and Guattari's (1987) figuration of the rhizome. It is a textual assemblage of popular and academic representations of cyborgs that I hope might question, provoke and challenge some of the dominant discourses and assumptions of curriculum, teaching and learning.[6]
>
> Emboldened by Deleuze's penchant for inventing new terms for his figurations,[7] I have coined the term "rhizomANTic" (sometimes "rhizomantic") to name a methodological disposition that connects Deleuze's rhizomatics, ANT (actor-network theory), and Donna Haraway's (1997, p. 16) "invented category of semANTics, *diffractions*" (my caps.).[8] Diffraction is "an optical metaphor for the effort to make a difference in the world," which Haraway (1994) also represents by the activity of making a "cat's cradle"—a metaphor that imagines the performance of sociotechnical relations as a less orderly and less functionalist activity than the word "network" often conveys. As my reference to Haraway's work suggests, my engagement with ANT leans towards those aspects of the theory that John Law (1999) characterizes as "after-ANT." In an annotated bibliography on Law's ANT Resource Home Page, he refers to Haraway's (1997) *Modest_Witness@Second_Millennium.FemaleMan©_Meets_OncoMouse™* as "the best-known example of the different and partially related radical feminist technoscience alternative to actor-network theory. The 'after-ANT' studies in this resource in many cases owe as much or more to Haraway as to ANT itself."[9]
>
> I also use the term rhizomantic because much of this essay is about ants. (253)

Why ants? Ants came to my rescue when I was struggling to expand my hastily written abstract into a presentable conference paper. My abstract did little more than point to the proliferation of cyborg bodies and identities in sites of educational practice and signal my intention to draw on theoretical frameworks provided by Deleuze and ANT to explore their pedagogical implications. I wrote (with unwarranted confidence) that my paper would "demonstrate how a becoming-cyborg teacher might deploy popular and theoretical conceptions of cyborgs as heuristics in educational work," but I had very few ideas about how I might do this.

In searching recent literature on cyborgs and education, I found "A Manifesto for Cyborg Pedagogy?" by Tim Angus, Ian Cook, and James Evans (2001), an account of teaching a university course that was explicitly grounded in ANT. I was impressed by the authors' thoughtful theorizing of cyborg pedagogy, but I was curious as to how Deleuzian (con)figurations might "add value" to their approach. That was when the ants appeared— from several directions simultaneously. In retrospect, I surmise that my frequent reading of the acronym "ANT" brought them out of the recesses of my memory into the forefront of my consciousness.

I recalled the theoretical ants in Deleuze and Guattari's (1987) recollections of writing *A Thousand Plateaus*—"we watched lines leave one plateau and proceed to another like columns of tiny ants" (22)—and in Patricia O'Riley's (2003) description of rhizomes as being "like crabgrass, ants, wolf packs, and children" (27). I recalled my son's fascination with the SimAnt computer game in the mid-1990s and the giant mutant ants from movies such as Gordon Douglas' (1951) *Them!* (1951) and Bert Gordon's (1977) *Empire of the Ants*. But the ants that clamored more insistently for my attention were those that populated some of my favorite fictions, such as H.G. Wells' (1905) *The Empire of the Ants*, Philip K. Dick's (1969/1991) "The Electric Ant," and Rudy Rucker's (1994) *The Hacker and the Ants*.

The most generative fictional ant came from Jerry Prosser's (Prosser and Geary 1992) graphic novel *Cyberantics*, which purports to be an annotated version of an illustrated children's book written by an eccentric cyberneticist as a report of his achievements in building (and setting loose) a cybernetic ant. *Cyberantics* is an ingenious and amusing *metafiction*, a story that, in Patricia Waugh's (1984) words, "draws attention to its status as an artifact in order to pose questions about the relationship between fiction and reality" (2). As a metafiction, *Cyberantics* functions as a complex system generating multiple interpretations and displays the properties that contemporary science calls chaos and complexity. Thus, it explores and illustrates, in a form accessible to children and adults alike, an important correspondence between postmodern science and literature. As Peter Stoicheff (1991) writes, "metafiction and scientific chaos [and I would add *scientific complexity*] are embraced by a larger revolution in contemporary thought that examines the similar roles of narrative, and of investigative procedure, in our 'reading' or knowledge of the world" (85). *Cyberantics* can therefore be understood as a postmodern science education text. It embeds stories of modern science, a delightful children's story, and a satire suitable for children and adults, within a complex and complicating metafiction that inhabits a conceptual space shared by much postmodernist science and post-structuralist cultural theorizing.

I realized that *Cyberantics* exemplifies what is missing from Angus et al.'s (2001) manifesto for cyborg pedagogy: Their work is *cyber* without the *antics*, that is, it lacks the art, paradox, and humor that might motivate us to imagine and invent maps of networks that *experiment* with the real rather than provide mere tracings of it.

Without *Cyberantics* I doubt that I would have coined "rhizomantic" or appreciated the interpretive possibilities of this neologism. When I wrote "rhizomantic" as "rhizomANTic" I realized that it signified concisely my suspicion that ANT cannot wholly be accommodated by rhizomatics—it fits, but sits a little awkwardly and uncomfortably. I was then able to demonstrate the extent of this fit by comparing Haraway's and actor-network theorists' approaches to writing cyborgs with each other and with the implications of Deleuze and Guattari's work.

UNDOING ANTHROPOCENTRISM IN PLACE-BASED ENVIRONMENTAL EDUCATION RESEARCH

Whereas "RhizomANTically Becoming-Cyborg" addressed issues of performing posthuman pedagogies, my academic interests in recent years have shifted toward issues of performing place-based environmental education research. This was necessitated by a change of jobs in 2006, when I was appointed as Foundation Professor and Head of the School of Outdoor and Environmental Education at La Trobe University. The philosophy underlying the school's programs questions the often taken-for-granted universalist approaches to outdoor education framed around concepts of adventure and/or character building and emphasizes instead the significance of specific contexts and locations of outdoor environmental education practices.

From a posthumanist standpoint, I am now curious to explore (and seek to resolve) an apparent contradiction in the literature of environmental education research. On the one hand, many environmental activists, philosophers, and educators view anthropocentrism as an undesirable ethical position and valorize conceptual alternatives such as "biocentrism" and/or "ecocentrism." On the other hand, most reports of environmental education research privilege an anthropocentric gaze, which assumes autonomous human subjects as starting points for knowledge production and the focus of attention for data production and analysis. This is particularly noticeable in U.S. literature, where, for example, the majority of research reports published in the *Journal of Environmental Education* up to the late 1990s were modeled on positivistic science education research. Ian Robottom and Paul Hart (1995), who reviewed environmental education research from the 1970s onward, conclude that the predominant approach could be characterized as "applied science in nature" (that is, purportedly experimental), "objectivist," "instrumentalist," and "behaviorist" (5). Although environmental education research in Australia, Canada, Europe, and South Africa (and, more recently, the United States) has deployed a variety of post-positivist approaches, these have chiefly involved interpretive and critical methodologies in which human subjects remain the key focus of attention. With some noteworthy exceptions, relatively few examples of environmental education research enact the feminist and post-structuralist methodologies that, for at least two decades in the wider discipline of education, have contested humanistic assumptions and theorized learners as situational, contextual, and discursively inscribed.

Holding the idea of "human" under erasure, I suggest that challenging hierarchical anthropocentrism (i.e., challenging the assumption of human superiority) does not prevent us from acknowledging an "irreducible anthropocentrism," that is, accepting that we necessarily experience the world with species-specific biophysical limitations *and possibilities*. However, we must also consider how an understanding of irreducible anthropocentrism might be changed by accepting that we increasingly experience the world as *posthumans*, with perhaps (eventually) *fewer* species-specific biophysical limitations and with further possibilities provided by biophysical extensions and enhancements.

Taking up Deleuze's (1994) notion that difference is generative, I suggest that conceiving our material selves as different from other environmental materials with which we interact should dispose us toward understanding posthuman/place relations as mutually constitutive. That is, posthuman/place relations are not about individual subjects autonomously forming and developing relations with the world but, rather, about realizing that these relations always already exist, and might be as much influenced by the behavior of other materials in the places we inhabit as they are by our intentional or unintentional actions. Such considerations support what Karin Hultman and Hillevi Lenz Taguchi (2010) call a *relational materialist* methodology, which, in the context of place-based environmental education research, would involve creating concepts for understanding learners as emergent in relational fields in which nonhuman materials are inevitably at play in constituting their becomings. This methodological approach is consistent with the feminist post-structuralist materialism exemplified by Haraway (1991, 2007) and Karen Barad (2003, 2011), with particular reference to the latter's elaboration of a materialist, naturalist, and posthumanist performativity.

Such an approach can be further inflected by Deleuze and Guattari's (1987) description of the Earth as "an immense Abstract Machine" (254), in which (post)humans are always in composition with other materials, and by what N. Katherine Hayles (2012) has recently termed technogenesis, that is, "the idea that human and technics have coevolved together" (24). Hayles focuses in particular on digital technologies and argues that a human individual's interactions with digital media are not only cognitive but also "have bodily effects on the physical level" (15). For Hayles, embodiment "takes the form of extended cognition, in which human agency and thought are enmeshed within larger networks that extend beyond the desktop computer into the environment" (15). In Hayles's view, "all cognition is embodied, which is to say that for humans, it exists throughout the body, not only in the neocortex. Moreover, it extends beyond the body's boundaries in ways that challenge our ability to say where or even if cognitive networks end" (31).

Elsewhere, Hayles (2005) argues that the complex interactions shaping our ideas of "human nature" include material culture:

> Anthropologists have long recognized that the construction of artifacts and living spaces materially affects human evolution. Changes in the human skeleton that permitted upright walking co-evolved, anthropologists believe, with the ability to transport objects, which in turn led to the development of technology. We need not refer to something as contemporary and exotic as genetic engineering to realize that for millennia, a two-cycle phenomenon has been at work: humans create objects, which in turn help to shape humans. This ancient evolutionary process has taken a new turn with the invention of intelligent machines. (131–132)

Hayles (2012) introduces the concept of technogenesis in a section titled "How We Read: Close, Hyper, Machine" (68) in which she distinguishes between close reading, requiring deep attention, that characterizes much academic research, and fast or hyper-reading that relies on sporadic sampling. Hayles argues that these different types of cognition are embodied "conscious, unconscious, and nonconscious processes" (68) and cites recent neurological studies that demonstrate measurable differences between the brain functions of someone close reading and performing a Google search (76–78). The embodied neural plasticity that links digital media with various types of reading and attention, as demonstrated by neurological and cognitive research, exemplifies for Hayles a mechanism of technogenesis whereby "epigenetic changes in human biology can be accelerated by changes in the environment that make them even more adaptive, which leads to further epigenetic changes" (24). Although the idea of an interrelationship between human evolution and human-produced technologies is not new, Hayles's concept of a technogenesis driven by digital media is more complex than neo-Darwinian understandings that view the environment as largely static, with organisms changing to accommodate to it across lengthy periods of time. In Hayles's view, both humans and digital technologies change across much shorter time scales because of neural plasticity at various levels, including unconscious perceptions.

Hayles (2012) offers persuasive evidence that refutes the claims of anti-digital media journalists, such as Nicholas Carr (2010), that hyperlinked reading causes the degradation of comprehension and suggests that the "condescending view of media . . . forecloses an important resource for contemporary self-fashioning, for using [neural] plasticity both to subvert and redirect the dominant order" (97). She adds:

> It is far too simplistic to say that hyper attention represents a cognitive deficit or a decline in cognitive ability among young people . . . On the contrary, hyper attention can be seen as a positive adaptation that makes young people better suited to live in information-intensive environments. (112)

Hayles (2012) prompts me to consider the implications of her accounts of how we read and think for place-based environmental education research. The concepts of close and hyper-reading do not only apply to print and electronic media, but also to our "reading" of landscapes and activities located in them. Walking in a rainforest can be as "information-intensive" as searching the Internet, but I know of no studies of the brain functions of people reading and attending to such environments in different ways that might be the equivalents of the neurological and cognitive studies of close and hyper-reading. I can envisage considerable conceptual, methodological, and technical difficulties in conducting such research in outdoor environments, but I suggest that the underlying question of how a propensity for hyper-reading affects environmental interpretation is nevertheless worthy of exploration.

INCONCLUSION

I share Susanne Kappeler's (1986) antipathy to the conventional ways of concluding an academic essay: "I do not really wish to conclude and sum up, rounding off the argument so as to dump it in a nutshell on the reader. A lot more could be said about any of the topics I have touched upon" (212).

All I wish to "dump . . . on the reader" is a heartfelt phildickian request to question and critique received understandings of reality and humanity, which I hope I have exemplified to some extent in the autobiographical vignettes recounted above.

NOTES

1. *Urban Dictionary*, http://www.urbandictionary.com/define.php?term=phildickian (accessed April 4, 2011).
2. I am particularly grateful for Weaver's overgenerous characterization of me as "the Philip K. Dick . . . of curriculum studies" but query on historical grounds his reference to Robocop. Arguably, the first cyborg in film appeared in Eugène Lourié's (1958) *The Colossus of New York*. Cybermen appeared

in the television series *Dr. Who* (1966), but I suspect that the first cyborg in film to capture the public imagination was Darth Vader in George Lucas' *Star Wars* (1977). For the record, and despite the gender difference, the cinematic cyborg with whom I prefer to identify is Major Motoko Kusanagi from Mamouri Oshii's animé movie *The Ghost in the Shell* (1995), a law-enforcement officer who quotes feminist philosophers and berates any of her male colleagues who dare to utter misogynistic remarks.

3. As Donna Haraway (1989) explains, SF designates "a complex emerging narrative field in which the boundaries between science fiction (conventionally, sf) and fantasy became highly permeable in confusing ways, commercially and linguistically"; SF also signifies "an increasingly heterodox array of writing, reading, and marketing practices indicated by a proliferation of 'sf' phrases: speculative fiction, science fiction, science fantasy, speculative futures, speculative fabulation" (5).

4. Following Haraway(1994), I find diffraction a more generative optical metaphor than reflection: "My favorite optical metaphor is diffraction—the noninnocent, complexly erotic practice of making a difference in the world, rather than displacing the same elsewhere" (63).

5. For example, in a 1950 interview, the abstract expressionist Jackson Pollock was asked: "'Then you don't actually have a preconceived image of a canvas in your mind?' He replied: 'Well, not exactly—no—because it hasn't been created, you see. Something new—it's quite different from working, say, from a still life where you set up objects and work directly from them'" (quoted in Pinar 1994, 7). Richardson (2001) makes a parallel point about writing as research: "I was taught . . . not to write until I knew what I wanted to say, until my points were organized and outlined. No surprise, this static writing model coheres with mechanistic scientism, quantitative research, and entombed scholarship" (35).

6. I use the terms "popular" and "academic" to register my perceptions of difference across sites of cultural production, not to inscribe a binary distinction.

7. Rosi Braidotti (2000, 170) argues that "the notion of 'figurations'—in contrast to the representational function of 'metaphors'—emerges as crucial to Deleuze's notion of a conceptually charged use of the imagination."

8. Drawing attention to the ANT in semantics is gratuitous, but if I don't someone else will.

9. See http://www.lancs.ac.uk/fass/centres/css/ant/antres.htm (accessed April 10, 2008).

10. In regard to the use of full names in the reference list, I depart from the *Publication Manual of the American Psychological Association* to facilitate reading the gender politics of the sources I draw on for this chapter. I also believe that it is discourteous to authors to arbitrarily truncate the ways in which they prefer to identify themselves.

|REFERENCES[10]

Angus, Tim, Cook, Ian, and Evans, James. (2001). "A Manifesto for Cyborg Pedagogy?" *International Research in Geographical and Environmental Education* 10 (2): 195–201.

Barad, Karen. (2003). "Posthumanist Performativity: Toward an Understanding of How Matter Comes to Matter." *Signs: Journal of Women in Culture and Society* 28 (3): 801–831.

Barad, Karen. (2011). "Nature's Queer Performativity." *Qui Parle* 19 (2): 121–158.

Braidotti, Rosi. (2000). "Teratologies." In *Deleuze and Feminist Theory*, ed. Ian Buchanan and Claire Colebrook, 156–172. Edinburgh: Edinburgh University Press.

Carr, Nicholas G. (2010). *The Shallows: What the Internet Is Doing to Our Brains*. New York: W.W. Norton and Company.

Clarke, Arthur C. (1953). *Childhood's End*. New York: Ballantine.

Deleuze, Gilles. (1994). *Difference and Repetition*. Trans. Paul Patton. New York: Columbia University Press.

Deleuze, Gilles, and Guattari, Félix. (1987). *A Thousand Plateaus: Capitalism and Schizophrenia*. Trans. Brian Massumi. Minneapolis: University of Minnesota Press.

Deleuze, Gilles, and Guattari, Félix. (1994). *What Is Philosophy?* Trans. Graham Burchell and Hugh Tomlinson. London: Verso.

Dick, Philip K. (1969/1991). *We Can Remember It for You Wholesale: Volume 5 of the Collected Stories of Philip K. Dick*. London: Grafton.

Douglas, Gordon (Director). (1954). *Them!* USA: Warner Bros.

Eco, Umberto. (1984). *Postscript to* The Name of the Rose. Trans. William Weaver. New York: Harcourt, Brace and Jovanovich.

Gordon, Bert I. (Director). (1977). *Empire of the Ants*. USA: American International Pictures

Gough, Annette. (2003). "Embodying a Mine Site: Enacting Cyborg Curriculum?" *Journal of Curriculum Theorizing* 19 (4): 33–47.

Gough, Noel. (1987). "Futures in Curriculum: The Anticipatory Generation of Alternatives." *Melbourne Studies in Education* 29 (1): 23–34.

Gough, Noel. (1991). "An Accidental Astronaut: Learning with Science Fiction." In *Reflections from the Heart of Educational Inquiry: Understanding Curriculum and Teaching through the Arts*, ed. George Willis and William H. Schubert, 312–320. Albany: State University of New York Press.

Gough, Noel. (1993). *Laboratories in Fiction: Science Education and Popular Media*. Geelong: Deakin University.

Gough, Noel. (1994). "Imagining an Erroneous Order: Understanding Curriculum as Phenomenological and Deconstructed Text." *Journal of Curriculum Studies* 26 (5): 553–568.

Gough, Noel. (1995). "Manifesting Cyborgs in Curriculum Inquiry." *Melbourne Studies in Education* 36 (1): 71–83.

Gough, Noel. (2000). "Interrogating Silence: Environmental Education Research as Postcolonialist Textwork." *Australian Journal of Environmental Education* 15/16:113–120.

Gough, Noel. (2002). "Thinking/Acting Locally/Globally: Western Science and Environmental Education in a Global Knowledge Economy." *International Journal of Science Education* 24 (11): 1217–1237.

Gough, Noel. (2004). "RhizomANTically Becoming-Cyborg: Performing Posthuman Pedagogies." *Educational Philosophy and Theory* 36 (3): 253–265.

Gough, Noel. (2007). "Changing Planes: Rhizosemiotic Play in Transnational Curriculum Inquiry." *Studies in Philosophy and Education* 26 (3): 279–294.

Gough, Noel. (2008). "Narrative Experiments and Imaginative Inquiry." *South African Journal of Education* 28 (3): 335–349.

Grumet, Madeleine R. (1981). "Restitution and Reconstruction of Educational Experience: An Autobiographical Method for Curriculum Theory." In *Rethinking Curriculum Studies: A Radical Approach*, ed. Martin Lawn and Len Barton, 115–130. London: Croom Helm.

Haraway, Donna J. (1985). "A Manifesto for Cyborgs: Science, Technology and Socialist Feminism in the 1980s." *Socialist Review* 15 (2): 65–107.

Haraway, Donna J. (1989). *Primate Visions: Gender, Race, and Nature in the World of Modern Science*. New York: Routledge.
Haraway, Donna J. (1991). *Simians, Cyborgs, and Women: The Reinvention of Nature*. New York: Routledge.
Haraway, Donna J. (1994). "A Game of Cat's Cradle: Science Studies, Feminist Theory, Cultural Studies." *Configurations: A Journal of Literature, Science, and Technology* 2 (1): 59–71.
Haraway, Donna J. (1997). *Modest_Witness@Second_Millennium.FemaleMan©_Meets_OncoMouse™: Feminism and Technoscience*. New York: Routledge.
Haraway, Donna J. (2007). *When Species Meet*. Minneapolis: University of Minnesota Press.
Hayles, N. Katherine. (2005). "Computing the Human." *Theory, Culture and Society* 22 (1): 131–151.
Hayles, N. Katherine. (2012). *How We Think: Digital Media and Contemporary Technogenesis*. Chicago: University of Chicago Press.
Hultman, Karin, and Lenz Taguchi, Hillevi. (2010). "Challenging Anthropocentric Analysis of Visual Data: A Relational Materialist Methodological Approach to Educational Research." *International Journal of Qualitative Studies in Education* 23 (5): 525–542.
Kappeler, Susanne. (1986). *The Pornography of Representation*. Cambridge: Polity.
Law, John. (1999). "After ANT: Topology, Naming and Complexity." In *Actor Network Theory and After*, ed. John Law and John Hassard, 1–14. Oxford: Blackwell.
Lourié, Eugène (Director). (1958). *The Colossus of New York*: Paramount Pictures.
Lucas, George (Director). (1977). *Star Wars*. USA: 20th Century Fox.
O'Riley, Patricia A. (2003). *Technology, Culture, and Socioeconomics: A Rhizoanalysis of Educational Discourses*. New York: Peter Lang.
Oshii, Mamouri (Director). (1995). *Ghost in the Shell*. Japan: Shochiko.
Pinar, William F. (1975a). "*Currere*: Towards Reconceptualization." In *Curriculum Theorizing: The Reconceptualists*, ed. William F. Pinar, 396–414. Berkeley, CA: McCutchan.
Pinar, William F., ed. (1975b). *Curriculum Theorizing: The Reconceptualists*. Berkeley, CA: McCutchan.
Pinar, William F. (1994). *Autobiography, Politics and Sexuality: Essays in Curriculum Theory 1972–1992*. New York: Peter Lang.
Pinar, William F., and Reynolds, William M., eds. (1992). *Understanding Curriculum as Phenomenological and Deconstructed Text*. New York: Teachers College Press.
Prosser, Jerry, and Geary, Rick, eds. (1992). *Cyberantics*. New York: Dark Horse Comics.
Reid, William A. (1981). "The Deliberative Approach to the Study of the Curriculum and Its Relation to Critical Pluralism." In *Rethinking Curriculum Studies*, ed. Martin Lawn and Len Barton, 160–187. London: Croom Helm.
Richardson, Laurel. (2001). "Getting Personal: Writing-Stories." *International Journal of Qualitative Studies in Education* 14 (1): 33–38.
Robottom, Ian, and Hart, Paul. (1995). "Behaviourist E[nvironmental] E[ducation] Research: Environmentalism as Individualism." *Journal of Environmental Education* 26 (2): 5–9.
Rucker, Rudy. (1994). *The Hacker and the Ants*. New York: Avon Books.
Stoicheff, Peter. (1991). "The Chaos of Metafiction." In *Chaos and Order: Complex Dynamics in Literature and Science*, ed. N. Katherine Hayles, 85–99. Chicago: University of Chicago Press.

Waugh, Patricia. (1984). *Metafiction: The Theory and Practice of Self-Conscious Fiction*. London: Methuen.

Weaver, John A. (1999). "Synthetically Growing a Post-Human Curriculum: Noel Gough's Curriculum as a Popular Cultural Text." *Journal of Curriculum Theorizing* 15 (4): 161–169.

Weaver, John A. (2010). *Educating the Posthuman: Biosciences, Fiction, and Curriculum Studies*. Rotterdam: Sense Publishers.

Wells, H.G. (1905). *Empire of the Ants*. London: Heinemann

Willis, George, and Schubert, William H., eds. (1991). *Reflections from the Heart of Educational Inquiry: Understanding Curriculum and Teaching through the Arts*. Albany: State University of New York Press.

11 Resisting Becoming a Glomus Within Posthuman Theorizing

Mondialisation and Embodied Agency in Educational Research

Annette Gough

Un monde est précisément cela où il y a une place pour tout le monde: mais place véritable, celle qui fait qu'il y a véritablement lieu d'y être (dans ce monde). Sinon, ce n'est pas <monde>: c'est <globe> ou <glome>, c'est <terre d'exil> et <vallée de larmes>. (Nancy 2002, 42)[1]

As an environmental educator, I am very aware of the relationships between humans and their environments and the need to "consider the environment in its totality—natural and built, technological and social (economic, political, technological, cultural-historical, moral, aesthetic)" (UNESCO 1978, 27). I am also aware of the tensions between this environment-is-everything view and the United Nations Decade of Education for Sustainable Development's vision of "a world where everyone has the opportunity to benefit from education and learn the values, behavior and lifestyles required for a sustainable future and for positive societal transformation" (UNESCO 2005, 6). All environments are continually under threat from human and natural interventions such that the world is no longer necessarily a place for everyone and it is verging on becoming, in Nancy's (2002) words, a land of exile or a vale of tears, a *globe* or a *glome*.

This chapter furthers my explorations of the relationships between my practice as an environmental educator interested in embodied agency in educational research—the continuing evolution of globalization and education for sustainable development (ESD), and my posthuman state—and within this, moving beyond traditional autobiography as the writing of the self to a grafting of the self that is reconstituted through medical procedures. As Probyn (1993, 27–28) argues, "in conceiving of experience as incorporated within a mode of theorizing and of speaking within theory, we are also brought to consider the ways in which its effects can be 'struggled' over." My exploration is particularly guided by Foucault's (1984b, 83) genealogy, situated within the articulation of the body and history, where "the body is the inscribed surface of events (traced by language and dissolved by ideas), the locus of a dissected self (adopting the illusion of substantial unity), and a volume in perpetual disintegration," and the task of genealogy is to expose both "a body totally imprinted by history and the process of history's destruction of the body."

A starting point for this chapter is John Weaver's (2010, 31) assertion that "each person who crosses the modern boundaries of human and machine and enters into the artificially natural realm of the posthuman has their own journey story to tell." My cyborg (posthuman) stories (see Gough 2003, 2004, 2005) are ones of resistance, as Weaver (2010, 31) rightly recognizes when he classifies me as "a reluctant posthuman theorist," yet they are also conversations with the posthuman that are both theoretical and a material reality.

In this earlier writing I focused on my work as an environmental educator and how the blurring of the binary boundaries between human and animal, human/animal and machine in becoming a cyborg/posthuman, enabled me to trouble "the relationship between the body, medical technology, and the environments that (re)shape one's identity" (Weaver 2010. 31). This chapter continues my conversations with the posthuman at both theoretical and material levels, and in an environmental education context. It incorporates other theoretical and policy framings that have emerged in the decade since I started writing my cyborg curriculum stories as well as my more recent experiences of being even more closely grafted to a machine, furthers discussions about autobiography and writing the body of the researcher into educational research by focusing on theorizing poverty and aging in a world that is increasingly becoming not for everyone, and explores what this means for my practice as an environmental educator and for environmental education.

Thus, a second starting point for this chapter is the notion of *glomus*, which Weaver (2010, 1) quotes from Jean-Luc Nancy (2007, 34) on the first page of his landmark book on educating the posthuman:

In such a glomus, we see the conjunction of an indefinite growth of techno-science, or a correlative exponential growth of populations, of a worsening of inequalities of all sorts within these populations—economic, biological, and cultural—and of a dissipation of the certainties, images, and identities of what the world was with its parts and humanity with its characteristics.[2]

GLOMUS TO GLOBALIZATION

The sense of *glome* to which Nancy refers is the old word "glome" or "glomus," such as in ag*glom*eration, with its senses of con*glom*eration: "a piling up, with the sense of accumulation that, on the one hand, simply concentrates . . . the well-being that used to be urban or civil, while on the other hand, proliferates what bears the quite simple and unmerciful name of misery" (Nancy 2007, 33). According to Nancy (2007, 33–34), this "agglomeration invades and erodes what used to be thought of *globe* which is nothing more now that its double, *glomus*." This relationship between *glome* and *globe* opens up the opportunity for Nancy to articulate the transition from *globe* to *globalization* (and *monde* to *mondialisation*). For Nancy:

> globalization not only has modified the world, it has essentially changed the way we relate to the world, our being in that world and, on a yet more fundamental level, our being as such. We can no longer consider ourselves as standing outside the world, i.e. as *subject* to whom the world is an *object*. Globalization has made clear that our very relation to the world is more basic than the autonomous subjects we suppose we are. (De Kesel n.d., 1)

Nancy then argues that, since our "world" has become a "globe," we need to make a decision to reinvent or (re-)create the world by deciding to deconstruct the logic of the double bind in our present globalization discourse. De Kesel (n.d., 16) interprets this process as a work in progress:

> Our world is the deconstruction, i.e. the passage and the transition from the globe (to be deconstructed) to the "world" (as what is supposed to be the result of this deconstruction) . . . The "*mondialisation*" will remain within the transition towards this beyond. It will remain in the act of creation that it is. The "*mondialisation*" will force us to redefine our world as being this very transition. And to create such a world, we have to assume ourselves as being the *Dasein* of that transition. In the case of globalization, we have to be the place (*Dasein*) where the event of the transition from "globe" to "world" happens, occurs, takes place. We therefore have to assume our own being as transition, as an "in between" as such.

I will now use this outline of Nancy's argument for creating the world, *mondialisation*, as a replacement for globalization as a framework for analyzing the international documents around the United Nations Decade of Education for Sustainable Development that have appeared since I last wrote in a posthuman space. These then inform my discussion of writing the body of the environmental educator into working in this area within a context of becoming more posthuman.

CHANGING ENVIRONMENTAL EDUCATION DISCOURSES

Numerous reports over the past two-plus decades from international and national government bodies (see, for example, Beeton et al. 2006; Garnaut

2008; Stern 2007; United Nations 1993, 2002, 2012; World Commission on Environment and Development 1987) agree that a holistic approach toward sustainable development—"development that meets the needs of the present without compromising the ability of future generations to meet their own needs" (World Commission on Environment and Development 1987, 8.)—is needed. Such sustainable development encompasses the interconnectedness of social, economic, and environmental issues, rather than just focusing on environmental protection.

These reports also acknowledge the importance of education at all levels in achieving a sustainable future:

> Education is critical for promoting sustainable development and improving the capacity of the people to address environment and development issues . . . It is also critical for achieving environmental and ethical awareness, values and attitudes, skills and behaviour consistent with sustainable development, and for effective public participation in decision-making. (United Nations 1993, para. 36.3)

This education for sustainability (or sustainable development) is the means by which schools and communities can (and should) work toward creating a sustainable future.

The origins of the current ESD movement can be traced back to the 1972 United Nations Conference on the Human Environment held in Stockholm and its Declaration, which proclaims: "to defend and improve the environment for present and future generations has become an imperative goal for mankind" (UNESCO 1978, 24). Concerns about the natural environment as well as the human environment continued in the Belgrade Charter Framework for Environmental Education (UNESCO 1975), which includes the statements that:

> It is absolutely vital that the world's citizens insist upon measures that will support the kind of economic growth which will not have harmful repercussions on people—that will not in any way diminish their environment and their living conditions . . .
> Millions of individuals will themselves need to adjust their own priorities and assume a "personal and individualised global ethic"—and reflect in all of their behaviour a commitment to the improvement of the quality of the environment and of life for all the world's people . . .
> The reform of educational processes and systems is central to the building of this new development ethic and world economic order . . .
> This new environmental education must be broad based and strongly related to the basic principles outlined in the United Nations Declaration on the *New Economic Order.*

The intention of this statement, in its concern for "the improvement of the quality of the environment and of life for all the world's people," is quite congruent with Nancy's (2007) concerns about the invasion and erosion of *globe* and it becoming a *glomus*.

Perhaps the most important international meeting regarding environmental education was the Intergovernmental Conference on Environmental Education held in Tbilisi (USSR) in 1977 (UNESCO 1978). The goals and objectives of environmental education recommended at this conference (UNESCO 1978, 26–27) continued to be endorsed at subsequent UNESCO and UN meetings. For example, the report of the 1987 UNESCO Moscow International Congress on Environmental Education and Training states that the "Recommendations of the Tbilisi Conference (1977) on environmental education goals, objectives and guiding principles are to be considered as providing the basic framework for environmental education at all levels, inside or outside the school system" (UNESCO-UNEP 1988, 6). Similarly, the education chapter of *Agenda 21*, the strategy plan from UNCED, states that "the Declaration and Recommendations of the Tbilisi Intergovernmental Conference on Environmental Education organized by UNESCO and UNEP and held in 1977, have provided the fundamental principles for the proposals in this document" (United Nation 1993, para. 36.1). The goals from the Tbilisi conference (UNESCO 1978, 26) to which these documents refer are:

1. The goals of environmental education are:
    (a) to foster clear awareness of, and concern about, economic, social, political and ecological interdependence in urban and rural areas;
    (b) to provide every person with opportunities to acquire the knowledge, values, attitudes, commitment and skills needed to protect and improve the environment;
    (c) to create new patterns of behaviour of individuals, groups and society as a whole towards the environment.

As with the Belgrade Charter statement noted above, the focus here is on the total environment and its improvement and protection as well as not having "harmful repercussions on people."

There was a transition in terminology between the Belgrade Charter (UNESCO 1975) and the Tbilisi Declaration (UNESCO 1978) and later reports in that "environmental education" was increasingly being replaced by ESD in both *Agenda 21*, the report of the 1992 Earth Summit held in Rio de Janeiro (UNCED 1992) and the report of the 2002 United Nations World Summit on Sustainable Development held in Johannesburg (United Nations 2002). This World Summit declared education as critical for promoting sustainable development. However, the vision from *Agenda 21* had broadened from focusing "the role of education in pursuing the kind of development that would respect and nurture the natural environment" to encompass "social justice and the fight against poverty as key principles of development that is sustainable" (UNESCO 2004, 7), as is evident in this statement in the World Summit report (United Nations 2002, 2):

> We recognize that poverty eradication, changing consumption and
> production patterns and protecting and managing the natural resource
> base for economic and social development are overarching objectives of
> and essential requirements for sustainable development.

This statement is significant in that the environment is now seen as a "natural resource base for economic and social development," and notions of
improving the quality of the environment, contained in earlier statements,
have disappeared. This instrumentalization of nature has taken place
because of what Nancy (2007, 94) calls *ecotechnology*:

> it is clear that so-called natural life, from its production to its conser-
> vation, its needs, and its representations, whether human, animal, veg-
> etal, or viral, is henceforth inseparable from a set of conditions that are
> referred to as "technological," and which constitute what must rather
> be names *ecotechnology* where any kind of "nature" develops for us
> (and by us).

Indeed, as Boetzkes (2010, 29) argues, drawing on Nancy:

> there is no nature for us that is not thought through *ecotechnology*, be
> it a reductive biological model, the conservation paradigm, resource
> management, sustainability, global warming, hybrid cars, compact flu-
> orescent light bulbs, and wind turbines to name only a few of the many
> discourses and accompanying techniques that identify and define the
> natural realm in our relationship to it.

Silences around the intrinsic value of the environment, and even biodiversity, continued into the outcomes report of the Rio+20 United Nations
Conference on Sustainable Development (United Nations 2012) where the
thematic areas and cross-sectoral issues are summarized as:

- Poverty eradication
- Food security and nutrition and sustainable agriculture
- Energy
- Sustainable transport
- Sustainable cities
- Health and populations
- Promoting full and productive employment, decent work for all, and
  social protections.

That these are the priorities for sustainable development is consistent with
Nancy's (2007) argument that *ecotechnologies* produce a sense of nature
by their very "denaturation" and that "it is in denaturation that that something like the representations of a 'nature' can be produced" (87).

Following proposals from Japan and Sweden, and following the Johannesburg Plan of Implementation, the United Nations General Assembly, at its 57th Session in December 2002, adopted a resolution to start the Decade of Education for Sustainable Development (DESD) from January 2005. UNESCO was designated to be the lead agency for the decade and it developed an International Implementation Scheme for the DESD (UNESCO 2004, 2005).

The UNESCO scheme brought together a range of international initiatives that were already in place—in particular the Millennium Development Goals (MDG) process, the Education for All (EFA) movement, and the United Nations Literacy Decade (UNLD)—with ESD.

> All of these global initiatives aim to achieve an improvement in the quality of life, particularly for the most deprived and marginalised, fulfillment of human rights including gender equality, poverty reduction, democracy and active citizenship. If the MDGs provide a set of tangible and measurable development goals within which education is a significant input and indicator; if EFA focuses on ways of providing educational opportunities to everyone, and if the UNLD concentrates on promoting the key learning tool for all forms of structured learning, DESD is more concerned than the other three initiatives with the content and purpose of education. Conceiving and designing ESD challenges all forms of educational provision to adopt practices and approaches which foster the values of sustainable development. (United Nations University 2006)

Somewhere between the environmental education statements from Belgrade (UNESCO 1975) and Tbilisi (UNESCO 1978) and the ESD statements from Johannesburg (United Nations, 2002) and about the decade (UNESCO 2004, 2005), a concern for the environment disappeared and the total focus became the human condition, or what Nancy (2007, 87) calls *denaturation*.

During the decade, there were two reviews (Wals 2009; Wals and Nolan 2012) of progress that recognize that ESD is being interpreted in many different ways in different contexts and that ESD has replaced environmental education in some instances in formal education. However, in the first review it is also noted that "many countries have a tradition in addressing the environmental dimension of sustainability and are quite comfortable in doing so, this is less the case when it comes to the social, economic and cultural dimensions" (Wals 2009, 71). In the next review, Wals and Nolan (2012, 65) found that "given the world's increasing concern with SD issues, ESD appears well positioned to play a synergizing role among a wide variety of sub-fields of education. These include environmental education, global citizenship education and, more recently, consumer education, climate change education and disaster risk reduction." This latter statement is prescient in that UNESCO, as part of the UNESCO secretary-general's Global Education First Initiative that was launched in 2012 (UNESCO 2013a, annex 2), is already investigating global citizenship education as an emerging perspective (UNESCO 2013a, 3) that encompasses sustainability:

> Global citizenship education aims to empower learners to engage and assume active roles both locally and globally to face and resolve global challenges and ultimately to become proactive contributors to a more just, peaceful, tolerant, inclusive, secure and sustainable world.

The January 2014 session of the UNESCO executive board (UNESCO 2014) endorsed a Proposal for a Global Action Programme on Education for Sustainable Development (UNESCO 2013b) that will be the successor program to the Decade of Education for Sustainable Development post 2014, subject to its approval at the sixty-ninth session of the UN General Assembly. The proposed action program acknowledges the need to promote global citizenship and builds on the outcome document of the United Nations Conference on Sustainable Development (Rio+20) (United Nations 2012), where member states agreed "to promote education for sustainable development and to integrate sustainable development more actively into education beyond the United Nations Decade of Education for Sustainable Development" (UNESCO 2013b, annex 1). The first principle guiding the action program is that:

> ESD allows every human being to acquire the knowledge, skills, values and attitudes that empower them to contribute to sustainable development and take informed decisions and responsible actions for environmental integrity, economic viability, and a just society for present and future generations. (UNESCO 2013b, annex 2)

This principle reflects the changes in orientation between environmental education and ESD when it is compared with one of the goals for environmental education stated in the Tbilisi Declaration (and noted earlier): "to provide every person with opportunities to acquire the knowledge, values, attitudes, commitment and skills needed to protect and improve the environment" (UNESCO 1978, 26). This goal at least acknowledges the need to protect and improve the environment and not just focus on human society. Some environmental education researchers have described this change from environmental education as consistent with globalization, where they see the concept of SD as acting "both as a product and as an agent of a globalization process embedded in neo-liberal economics" (Sauvé, Brunelle, and Berryman 2005, 280). Jickling and Wals (2008, 2) take this further when they argue:

> Globalizing ideologies and the corresponding material effects are also having an impact on education. The powerful wave of neo-liberalism

rolling over the planet, with pleas for "market solutions" to educational problems and universal quality-assurance schemes, are homogenizing the educational landscape.

This is not the place to continue a discussion of neoliberal globalization and ESD, but I believe that it is important to note that there is a critique of the neoliberal agenda of sustainable development and the cooption of education (particularly ESD) into this is neither recent nor welcomed by many researchers, and this complements my concerns, and Nancy's.

EMBODIED AGENCY AND THE POSTHUMAN ENVIRONMENTAL EDUCATOR

Embodiment, embodied writing, and embodied subjects have particular connections with posthumanism. Stefan Herbrechter (2103), for example, discusses embodiment in his analysis of the posthuman condition, and N. Katherine Hayles (1999, 24) argues that literature and science "are a way of understanding ourselves as embodied creatures living within and through embodied worlds and embodied words." Rosi Braidotti (2002) similarly argues, "the embodied subject is thus a process of intersecting forces (affects) and spatio-temporal variables connections" (21), and "embodied accounts illuminate and transform our knowledge of ourselves and of the world" (12). At this time she was, like me, writing of cyborg subjectivity, where a cyborg is not a unitary subject position but "an embodied and socially embedded human subject that is structurally inter-connected to technological elements or *appatari*" (Braidotti 2002, 17). In her more recent writings, Braidotti (2013) notes that "discourses and representations of the non-human, the inhuman, the anti-human, the inhumane and the posthuman proliferate and overlap in our globalized, technologically mediated societies" (2) and argues for "post-anthropocentric posthumanism" that focuses "entirely on the normatively neutral relational structures of both subject formation and of possible ethical relations" (92).

Just as Nancy (2002, 2007) argues for *mondialisation* to resist the agglomeration that has invaded previous conceptions of the world and made it a *glome* and reinvented or (re-)created the world, recognizing that we will always be in transition, Braidotti (2013, 93) argues that "we need to become the sort of subjects who actively desire to reinvent subjectivity as a set of mutant values and to draw our pleasure from that, not from the perpetuation of familiar regimes."

Beyond posthumanist theorizing there is growing recognition that there are no binaries—such as mind–body, human–nature, nature–culture, or human–machine—but blurred boundaries (Braidotti 2002). For example, Rosemarie Anderson (2001, 96) writes:

In our times, we are preoccupied with the separateness and distinctiveness of our physical bodies from the world. What madness is this? Even at a material level we are mostly made of water and trace minerals. The elements of the earth make for embodiment, otherwise we would not be here at all. *Our bodies are utterly embedded in the world.*

Anderson's statement, that "we are mostly made of water and trace minerals," became even more true for me in May 2012 when I underwent a total replacement of one of my knees because of osteoarthritic and cartilage degeneration that was making mobility difficult. This new event provided another opportunity for me to reflect on "the artificially natural realm of the posthuman" (Weaver 2010, 31) that I had overtly entered, and to explore autobiography and identity in the context of my educational research. The new knee makes me even more a subject of technoscience and more posthuman, and provides an opportunity for me to interpret this experience through "the possibilities of theorizing within stories instead of about them" (Bochner 2001, 141) by elaborating "the theoretical significance of approaching identity as a performative struggle over the meanings of experiences as discourses navigate the body and the body anchors discourse" (Langellier 2001, 147). In so doing, I recognize that I am one again taking up Stanley's (2000, 6) challenge that, "as self-styled 'intellectuals,' we should take risks in confronting and discussing the things that matter in life, even though much of academia will see us as departing from the standards of 'scientism' . . . from its notions of rigor, detachment, rationality, objectivity," and I am engaging in post-structuralist educational research where embodied subjects are nonunitary, multiple, and complex.

My new knee brought me into solid confrontation with Nancy's *glomus* as discussed by Weaver (2010, 5): "The glomus is the privileging of the artificial body over the natural body. The artificial body represents accumulation of wealth, access to state of the art medicine, and disposable income to stave off aging, live longer, and avoid genetically influenced diseases." That I could have my knee replaced when I wanted, where I wanted, and by my preferred doctor was only because I have the "disposable income to stave off aging." Although, to me, my mobility issues were significant, in many ways they were a "first world problem" compared with the major survival issues of people in other parts of the world and the other inequalities they face. Instead of an embodied mine site post–breast cancer surgery (Gough 2003, 2004, 2005), I now feel that I embody the products from that mine site (which in some ways I do given the content of the materials in the replacement knee) and that I am more aware of my relative wealth and privilege in being able to have a new knee. Even though the scar is mostly hidden, it is evidence of my ability to indulge my own health issues and resolve them relatively simply (though medico friends tell me I was lucky to not experience any infection or other issues).

My new knee has made me much more aware of the inequalities in society and the importance of "social justice and the fight against poverty as key principles of development that is sustainable" (UNESCO 2004, 7) but also that this should not be at the expense of protecting, respecting, and nurturing the natural environment. For example, at the moment in Australia we have two World Heritage areas under threat by actions of the recently elected conservative Australian government. The Great Barrier Reef is being threatened by the recently approved dumping of dredged materials for a port expansion in the Reef's waters, and there is a current proposal to excise seventy-four thousand hectares from the boundaries of the Tasmanian World Heritage Wilderness Area, even though the forestry industry does not want this action. And all of this comes from a government where the leader, Prime Minister Tony Abbott, has been named "world's biggest climate grinch in 2013" (Phillips 2013), and he continues with inhuman responses to asylum seekers arriving in boats off Australia (AFP 2014), which are major problems for Australia internationally. Yet these actions are just the tip of the iceberg of the human/environment confrontations going on around the *glome*. The thematic areas and cross-sectoral issues listed in the Rio+20 Outcomes document (United Nations 2012) could well have been written from Nancy's (2002, 2007) analysis of globalization—and these, and the environment itself, do need to be addressed if we are do re-create a world for everyone.

CONCLUSION

At times globalization seems already here and all encompassing, and one could almost accept Ulrich Beck's (2006) argument that people throughout the world have all already become cosmopolitans by default because of an inescapably global form of exposure and witnessing. However, when one looks at the themes for sustainable development (United Nations 2012), it seems that there is a significant proportion of the human population of the planet that are affected by globalization but do not necessarily recognize it as such. That the environment as a distinct entity, not a "natural resource base for economic and social development" (United Nations 2002, 2), has been silenced by both globalization (and cosmopolitization) is a concern that can be addressed through Nancy's (2002, 2007) *mondialisation*, though even this is always in transition.

As an environmental educator, I believe it is important to resist the globalization that has changed the world to a *glome* and reassert a world for everyone where the environment is more than a natural resource base. It is also important for humans to work collectively in actions at global and local levels to address the "challenges such as sustainable development, including climate change, [that] are demonstrating the need for cooperation and collaboration beyond land, air, and water boundaries" (UNESCO 2013a, 2), as well as the worsening inequalities within the exponentially growing human populations and the accompanying dissipation of humanity and its characteristics (Nancy 2007). Understanding the world through posthuman theory that is based on "an assumption about the vital, self-organizing and yet non-naturalistic structure of living matter itself" (Braidotti 2013, 2), a nature-culture continuum, is a great place to start. As Foucault (1984a, 50) argues:

> The critical ontology of ourselves has to be considered not, certainly, as a theory, a doctrine, nor even as a permanent body of knowledge that is accumulating; it has to be conceived as an attitude, an ethos, a philosophical life in which the critique of what we are is at one and the same time the historical analysis of the limits that are imposed on us and an experiment with the possibility of going beyond them.

I started this chapter with a quote from Jean-Luc Nancy that framed my resistance to becoming a glomus. I would like to end with a quote and the Japanese kanji for life as used by Ruth Ozeki in her recent novel, *A Tale for the Time Being*. This Zen notion of the interlinking of time and being captures the posthuman condition and why we need to resist the silencing of the environment in sustainable development discourses: "Time itself is being . . . and all being is time . . . In essence, everything in the entire universe is intimately linked with each other as moments in time, continuous and separate" (Ozeki 2013, 30).

ACKNOWLEDGEMENT

I would like to thank John Weaver for drawing the work of Jean-Luc Nancy to my attention, as it has been so generative for my writing, and my son, Simon, for bringing a Japanese sensibility to our family's life in recent years. I would also like to acknowledge the significant role that my life partner, Noel Gough, has had in the evolution of my writing in this area—I could not have done it without him, but any errors are still mine.

NOTES

1. "A world is precisely that in which there is room for everyone, but a genuine place, one in which things can genuinely *take place* (in this world). Otherwise, this is not a 'world': It is a 'globe' or a 'glome,' it is a 'land of exile' and a 'vale of tears'" (translation as in Nancy 2007, 42).

2. "Dans ce *glomus* se joue la conjunction d'une croissance indéfinie de la techno-science, d'une croissance corrélative exponentielle de la population, d'une aggravation en elle des inégalitiés de tous les orders—économique, biologique, culturel—et d'une dissipation égarée des certitudes, des images et des identitiés de ce qui fut le monde" (Nancy 2002, 14–15).

REFERENCES

AFP. (2014). "Operation to Stop Boats Like a War: Tony Abbott." *The Australian*, January 10. Retrieved January 10, 2014, from www.theaustralian.com. au/national-affairs/policy/operation-to-stop-boats-like-a-war-tony-abbott/story-fn9hm1gu-1226798801617.

Anderson, R. (2001). "Embodied Writing and Reflections on Embodiment." *Journal of Transpersonal Psychology* 33 (2): 83–98.

Beck, U. (2006). *Cosmopolitan Vision.* Cambridge: Polity.

Beeton, R.J.S., Buckley, K.I., Jones, G.J., Morgan, D., Reichelt, R.E., and Trewin, D. (2006). *Australia State of the Environment 2006. Independent Report to the Australian Government Minister for the Environment and Heritage.* Canberra: Department of the Environment and Heritage.

Bochner, A.P. (2001). "Narrative's Virtues." *Qualitative Inquiry* 7 (2): 131–157.

Boetzkes, A. (2010). "Waste and the Sublime Landscape." *Canadian Art Review* 35 (1): 22–31.

Braidotti, R. (2002). *Metamorphoses: Towards a Materialist Theory of Becoming.* Cambridge: Polity.

Braidotti, R. (2013). *The Posthuman.* Cambridge: Polity.

De Kesel, M. (n.d.). "The Question of the World: Some Remarks on Jean-Luc Nancy's Reflection on Globalization." Retrieved December 4, 2013, from http://home.scarlet.be/~mk347385/bestanden/The%20Question%20of%20the%20World.pdf.

Foucault, M. (1984a). *The Care of the Self. The History of Sexuality, Vol. Three.* Trans. Robert Hurley. New York: Vintage Books.

Foucault, M. (1984b). "Nietzsche, Genealogy, History." In *The Foucault Reader*, ed. P. Rabinow, 76–100. London: Peregrine (Penguin).

Garnaut, R. (2008). *The Garnaut Climate Change Review: Final Report.* Port Melbourne: Cambridge University Press.

Gough, A. (2003). "Embodying a Mine Site: Enacting Cyborg Curriculum." *Journal of Curriculum Theorizing* 19:33–47.

Gough, A. (2004). "Blurring Boundaries: Embodying Cyborg Subjectivity and Methodology." In *Educational Research: Difference and Diversity*, ed. H. Piper and I. Stronach, 113–127. Aldershot: Ashgate.

Gough, A. (2005). "Body/Mine: A Chaos Narrative of Cyborg Subjectivities and Liminal Experiences." *Women's Studies* 34 (3–4): 249–264.

Hayles, K. (1999). *How We Became Posthuman: Virtual Bodies in Cybernetics, Literature and Informatics.* Chicago: University of Chicago Press.

Herbrechter, S. (2013). *Posthumanism: A Critical Analysis.* London: Bloomsbury Academic.

Jickling, B., and Wals, A. (2008). "Globalization and Environmental Education: Looking Beyond Sustainable Development." *Journal of Curriculum Studies* 40 (1): 1–21.

Langellier, K.M. (2001). "'You're Marked' Breast Cancer, Tattoo, and the Narrative Performance of Identity." In *Narrative and Identity: Studies in Autobiography, Self and Culture*, ed. J. Brockmeier and D. Carbaugh, 145–184. Amsterdam: John Benjamins.

Nancy, J-L. (2002). *La creation du monde ou la mondialisation*. Paris: Galilée.

Nancy, J-L. (2007). *The Creation of the World or Globalization*. Trans. Francois Raffoul and David Pettigrew. Albany: State University of New York Press.

Ozeki, R. (2013). *A Tale for the Time Being*. Melbourne: Text Publishing Company.

Phillips, A. (2013). "Tony Abbott Named World's Biggest Climate Grinch in 2013." Retrieved February 1, 2014, from http://reneweconomy.com.au/2013/tony-abbott-named-worlds-biggest-climate-grinch-in-2013-95663.

Probyn, E. (1993). *Sexing the Self: Gendered Positions in Cultural Studies*. London: Routledge.

Sauvé, L., Brunelle, R., and Berryman, T. (2005). "Influence of the Globalized and Globalizing Sustainable Development Framework on National Policies Related to Environmental Education." *Policy Futures in Education* 3 (3): 271–283.

Stanley, L. (2000). "Children of Our Time: Politics, Ethics and Feminist Research Processes." In *Feminism and Educational Research Methodologies*, ed. Heather Hodkinson, 5–35. Manchester: Manchester Metropolitan University.

Stern, N. (2007). *The Economics of Climate Change: The Stern Review*. Cambridge: Cambridge University Press.

UNESCO. (1975). *The Belgrade Charter: A Global Framework for Environmental Education*. Retrieved July 21, 2006, from http://unesdoc.unesco.org/images/0001/000177/017772eb.pdf.

UNESCO. (1978). *Intergovernmental Conference on Environmental Education: Tbilisi (USSR), 14–26 October 1977. Final Report*. Paris: UNESCO.

UNESCO. (2004). *United Nations Decade of Education for Sustainable Development 2005–2014. Draft International Implementation Scheme. October 2004*. Paris: UNESCO. Retrieved October 7, 2013, from portal.unesco.org/education/en/file_download.php/03f375b07798a2a55dcdc39db7aa8211Final+IIS.pdf.

UNESCO. (2005). *United Nations Decade of Education for Sustainable Development (2005–2014): International Implementation Scheme. ED/DESD/2005/PI/01*. Retrieved October 7, 2013, from http://unesdoc.unesco.org/images/0014/001486/148654e.pdf.

UNESCO. (2013a). *Global Citizenship Education: An Emerging Perspective. Outcome Document of the Technical Consultation on Global Citizenship Education*. Seoul: UNESCO and the Republic of Korea. Retrieved January 7, 2014, from http://unesdoc.unesco.org/images/0022/002241/224115E.pdf.

UNESCO. (2013b). *Proposal for a Global Action Programme on Education for Sustainable Development as Follow-Up to the United Nations Decade of Education for Sustainable Development (DESD) After 2014. Executive Board 192 EX/6*. Paris: UNESCO. Retrieved January 7, 2014, from http://unesdoc.unesco.org/images/0022/002223/222324e.pdf.

UNESCO. (2014). *Decisions adopted by the Executive Board at its 192nd Session*. Paris: UNESCO. Retrieved February 8, 2014, from http://unesdoc.unesco.org/images/0022/002238/223810e.pdf.

UNESCO-UNEP. (1988). *International Strategy for Action in the Field of Environmental Education and Training for the 1990s*. Paris: UNESCO and UNEP.

United Nations. (1993). *Agenda 21: Earth Summit: The United Nations Programme of Action from Rio*. New York: United Nations. Retrieved January 7, 2014, from http://sustainabledevelopment.un.org/content/documents/Agenda21.pdf.

United Nations. (2002). *Report of the World Summit on Sustainable Development: Johannesburg, South Africa, 26 August-4 September 2002*. Retrieved January 7, 2014, from http://www.un.org/jsummit/html/documents/summit_docs/131302_wssd_report_reissued.pdf.

United Nations. (2012) *The Future We Want: Outcomes Document Adopted at Rio + 20*. Rio de Janeiro: United Nations. Retrieved January 7, 2014, from

http://www.uncsd2012.org/content/documents/727The%20Future%20
We%20Want%2019%20June%201230pm.pdf.

United Nations University. (2006). "FAQ: Education for Sustainable Development." Retrieved July 21, 2006, from http://www.ias.unu.edu/research/esd.cfm.

Wals, A. (2009). *Review of Contexts and Structures for Education for Sustainable
Development 2009*. Paris: UNESCO. Retrieved January 7, 2014, from http://
unesdoc.unesco.org/images/0018/001849/184944e.pdf

Wals, A., and Nolan, C. (2012). *Shaping the Education of Tomorrow: 2012 Report
on the UN Decade of Education for Sustainable Development, Abridged*.
Paris: UNESCO. Retrieved January 7, 2014, from http://unesdoc.unesco.org/
images/0021/002166/216606e.pdf.

Weaver, J.A. (2010). *Educating the Posthuman: Biosciences, Fiction, and Curriculum Studies*. Rotterdam: Sense Publishers.

World Commission on Environment and Development. (1987). *Our Common
Future*. Oxford: Oxford University Press.

12 To What Future Do the Posthuman and Posthumanism (Re)Turn Us; Meanwhile How Do I Tame the Lingering Effects of Humanism?

John A. Weaver

Meanwhile. (Bogost 2012, 50)

What can tame man? (Sloterdijk 2009, 20)

We could simply let the human–animal distinction go or, at the very least, not insist on maintaining it. (Calarco 2008, 149)

In my conclusion to *Educating the Posthuman* (2010), I used Toni Morrison's imagery of Jacob's empty brick house in *A Mercy* to suggest we do not know who will count as posthuman. Morrison's narrative, to me, was a statement of disappointment that no matter how different Jacob and all his progeny were from the D'Ortegas of the world, humans were still unfit to dwell in the home fit for the cultured and civilized. Humanity after almost four hundred years is still barbaric. My subsequent work still focused on the imagery of the posthuman and Jacob's house with Robert Pogue Harrison's work as my primary concern. Harrison's home is also empty: Americans are homeless because we have lost our poetic voice. "Instead of a nation of poets," Harrison suggests, "[we] became a nation of debtors, property owners, shopkeepers, spectators, gossipers, traffickers in rumor, prejudice, and information—capitalists who in their strange uncertainty about life pursue the delusions of recovery in their appropriation of everything" (1992, 231). "When it [meaning America] loses its poets," Harrison warns, "it loses access to the meaning of dwelling. When it loses the meaning of dwelling, it loses the means to build" (238). We are not fit to inhabit a posthuman world because we are still too barbaric toward one another, selling everything for the right price. We lose our poetic voice and with it our ability to dwell in an abode, to say nothing of our ability to build one.

Can animals solve our problem in Jacob's empty home or Harrison's homeless shelter? Perhaps, but there is one major problem. They rarely are invited to the homecoming or the housewarming party. There were no animals mentioned in any detail in *A Mercy* or in Harrison's trilogy concerning the plight of humanity. Jacob rides a horse, but it's a horse with no name, no life other than being an object to ride between point A and point B. Giants, dead people, and legends of folktales make an appearance in Harrison's work but little mention of animals other than to make a point about the sorry state of humanity. In my own previous work, animals make a cameo appearance to discuss the treatment of animals in farming and health care compared with humans, but then they walk offstage. Ian Bogost gently reminds us that "posthuman approaches still preserve humanity as a primary actor" (2012, 7). How can those of us interested in the posthuman approach this issue of including non- human sentient beings in our homes? "Where there are houses," Peter Sloterdijk writes, "there are also decisions about who shall live in them" (2009, 21). Who and how these decisions are made is what I want to explore in this chapter.

While posthumanists have something to offer us, posthumanism is still trapped in humanism. On one level, when we explore Nietzsche's contribution to this discussion, we will see that humanism may still be very much needed. Yet, on another level, when we discuss the "meanwhile" and the "so on" of posthumanism, we will see posthumanists are still trapped in very humanist disciplinary boundaries, closely guarding their borders from the "meanwhile" education heathens and the "so on" barbarians rushing the university gates demanding to be recognized. My contention is that one cannot address the natures and meanings of posthumanism without acknowledging the primary places where humans are indoctrinated into anthropocentrism and where they intersect with nonhuman sentient beings and machines: educational institutions.

I start with Graham Harman's object oriented philosophy—what Bogost calls Object Oriented Ontology (OOO)—because it opens the posthumanist door to nonhuman sentient beings. Although I know of no place where Harman describes himself as posthumanist, his philosophy is a challenge to anthropocentrism (even if he neglects educational matters in his account of the "so on"). After journeying around Harman's world of objects, I (re)turn to Nietzsche and his thoughts on culture and civilization in order to put forth an argument concerning the taming of humans and nonhuman beings. In the wake of my engagements with Harman and Nietzsche, I approach the posthumanist thought of Pettman and Wolfe. Drawing attention to these posthumanists' general neglect of education, I argue that humanism, in its anthropocentric form, still lingers in posthumanist thought. It will be curriculum studies scholars' best interest to begin a dialogue with posthumanists to help us understand better the abundance of interactions within educational institutions and for the posthumanists to see their agenda of minimizing the impact of anthropocentrism and broadening the scope of who is a sentient being can never been accomplished without widening their scope to include educational institutions.

THE SECRET LIFE OF DIRT AND TAMING ANIMALITY: OBJECTED ORIENTED ONTOLOGY AND POSTHUMANISM

Graham Harman has made his reputation by challenging established philosophical thought. He wants to adopt neither a conservative analytical approach to philosophy nor acontinental philosophy as it is articulated. Instead he wants to rethink our world in a novel philosophical manner, most importantly the world of animals, sunflowers, hammers, and dirt. Harman wishes to take Heidegger's thought to places even Heidegger would be uncomfortable going. Harman wants to rethink "being" such that it is not limited to humans. He refers to all objects as tool-beings. "Contrary to the usual view," Harman notes, "tool-being does not describe objects insofar as they are handy implements employed for human purposes. Quite the contrary: readiness-to-hand (*Zuhandenheit*) refers to objects insofar as they withdraw from human view into a dark subterranean reality that never becomes present to practical action any more than it does to theoretical awareness" (2001, 1). All objects inhabit a realm in which they interact sometimes with humans, but not necessarily always, and with other objects. As this interaction takes place though, Harman notes, the essence of the object withdraws into a dark realm away from humans and other objects. When we interact with a hammer it is present in a relationship with the user but this use does not describe its usefulness or essence. These characteristics recede from the interaction.

The acknowledgment that an object has an existence of its own independent from humans and other objects undermines an anthropocentric perspective. Harman notes that one mistake Heidegger makes is assuming that an object has no meaning or essence until the human comes along and gives it meaning. He uses the example of a construction site to make his point. "Consider what happens at the construction site when no humans are in the vicinity, as at 3 A.M. on a national holiday. There are moments when Heidegger seems to think that all the objects on the site are nothing more than independent physical masses until Dasein arrives on the scene. . . . For Heidegger, it is only human beings who possess this magical antidote" (2001, 33–34). Harman rejects this notion. "The world cannot be thought of as a total empire of meaning that only humans would be able to break up into individual zones. . . . The world is not just one; it is also many. It is not made up solely of pieces that push beyond themselves and lose their identity in a cosmic meaning-contexture" (2001, 34). Every object is simultaneously in a world and within its own "specific territories that erupt in the midst of it" (2001, 34). All objects can be used in many different ways but these objects, including humans, still retreat into their own realms away from the world.

Another example Harman gives is a piece of paper and its relationship with a piece of dust or a fire. Harman notes "the paper is involved in relations with specific entities, not with the world as a whole" (2001, 34). More importantly in this interaction between paper and dust or fire "no humans need to exist in order for the paper screen to resist dust or perish by fire" (2001, 34). Nonhuman tool-beings live an existence beyond humans that we cannot control, name, or experience. "As a matter of fact," Harman insists, "tool-analysis does not rely in the least on any priority of the human standpoint. . . . Tools [and here a tool can be any object, including animals] execute their being 'for the sake of' a reference, not because people run across them, but because they are utterly determinate in their referential function" (2001, 29).

Harman is suspending his anthropocentric perspective by recognizing that a tool-being does not lose its being just and only because it interacts with a human. A hammer is not just a tool humans use, but its being retreats as it enters into this relationship between human, hammer, hammered object, and overall project. Harman suggests:

> tool-being is notable both for its invisibility and for its totality. Always in action, the tool assumes a determinate stance in the midst of reality: compressing other entities into submission, while also giving way beneath the forces they return. As such, the work of the tool forever recedes behind its radiant surface profile. The tool-being of the ready-at-hand is not simply withdrawn from view "for the most part," since by definition it is irreducible to anything that could ever be seen. . . . Wherever we might look, tool-being always lies elsewhere. (2001, 24)

For Harman a key is that "*Das Zuhandene* and *das Vorhandene* are not two different types of entities, but two irreducible faces of the same entity. The hammer is ready-to-hand in one sense and present-at-hand in another" (2001, 31). It is being used in a project within the world but it is also retreating from that project and its being is retreating into its own realm, disconnected from the hammer user and the project. The same can be said for any object, including animals. Animals have an existence all their own and there is no need for humans to give their lives meaning.

Harman's tool-being frees humans, animals, other non-sentient beings and even inanimate objects from an anthropocentric view point. It does not devalue human experience, but it does not assume that any nonhuman needs human ratification or verification in order to exist. "Yes, we are exceptional," Pettman shouts out with glee, "but we are not alone in this. Every animal, indeed every machine, is exceptional in its own way" (2011, 199). That I have to stress this makes humans sound bipolar. As Pettman announces that we are exceptional, I envision tens of billions of people from the past and present shouting with joy, proclaiming their superiority over other entities, including inanimate objects such as computers. I see them taking this assertion of exceptionality and proclaiming dominion over all others. What is it that moves humans to rationalize that our exceptionality means we can exterminate species and even to proclaim superiority over many in our own species? Our equating exceptionality with superiority is short-lived and thus begins a depressed state. As Pettman quickly notes, we human tool-beings are not alone; all tool-beings are exceptional. Yes, I can type on a computer and as far as I know dogs cannot, but I do not possess the exceptional sense of smell and hearing that dogs do. I can watch a baseball game and experience its beauty, but I do not have the sight of a hawk. A hawk is exceptional in this matter. The dog, hawk, computer, and even dirt do not need me in order to have an existence, to be a tool-being, nor do I need them. Harman frees up our thinking, dismantles anthropocentric viewpoints, and opens a different world for us. Harman creates a new aesthetic in which we can experience a new way of being in the world.

Just as Harman creates a new aesthetic, Nietzsche teaches us what this new aesthetic should be. A Nietzschean aesthetic surges from the animal and is the source of creativity and imagination. The animal aesthetic is part of a continual tension between competing forces: between humanity and animality, memory and forgetting, culture and civilization, taming animality and unbridling the untamed. This is not a free market competition where a winner is expected to emerge and the losers just fade away like a VHS video, an Atari game, or a 45 record; it is a never-ending struggle. If humanity, memory, and civilization were to win out and our human animality, forgetfulness, culture, and untamedness were to be controlled, then our creativity and imagination would stagnate; our society would decline. Of course, this has long since happened.

Human animality is our culture. As Vanessa Lemm suggests, "what distinguishes the human animal from other animals is its culture" (2009, 1). This culture emerges from our animal nature to forget rather than our human tendency to remember. Through human memory and animal forgetfulness, our cultivation begins. Lemm again: "Whereas civilization distinguishes itself as the forgetting of the animal and of animal forgetfulness, culture distinguishes itself as the memory of the animal and of animals forgetfulness" (2009, 10–11). The human remembers and by its memory creates a civilization that forgets its animality, its creative animal instincts. Culture works in the opposite direction, remembering its animal origins, thereby invoking a forgetfulness that animals invoke as they survive another day. It is this forgetfulness that allows humans to create life. Memory, on the other hand, fosters a ressentiment. "Those who have recovered the forgetfulness of the animal," Lemm believes, "are those who do not dwell on the past. They feel no resentment for the past because they are powerful enough to form and transform past suffering into future life" (2009, 69). Memory sticks us to the past, a past that tames our animal creativity, denying us an opportunity to invent life in abundance. Forgetting, on the other hand, demands we create anew. Memory links humans to nihilism as the past becomes a history set in stone with no meaning for us today. Forgetfulness, however, values the past because with each individual in order to live a life must confront the past and construct a meaning of history. This interplay between the human, their animality, and forgetfulness creates a culture full of life that "emerges and overflows, indifferent to rationality and morality of its forms, and hence, powerful in its generosity and creativity" (2009, 13).

Culture in a Nietzschean sense then is constantly seeking to find ways to overcome civilization and its stagnate ways, its taming tendencies. Culture is finding in the "human being . . . the possibility of infinite self-overcomings" (Lemm 2009, 23) while civilization seeks out the infinite to place in concrete the finite. Culture educates "the human animal so as to 'twist free' a 'second nature', a 'more natural nature that betrays the features of its irreducible singularity" (Lemm 2009, 24). Education for civilization is the construction of morality and rationality. This force for civilization tames the spirit, "reduces expenditures, narrows perspectives, and limits horizons" (Lemm 2009, 55). The primary force for this reduction, narrowing, and limiting is formal education. Primary and secondary education disciplines the student into a state of mediocrity and higher education refines this narrow thinking into refined mediocre taste.

We avoid the taming traps of civilization not by eliminating it for eliminating the forces of civilization would also eliminate the infiniteness of culture. Instead, we work the creative tension between culture and civilization. Where civilization seeks to install a morality or a rationality, culture seeks not to eliminate that morality or rationality but find its limits in order to create something different. As civilization seeks to tame the animality of humans, culture creates from it by letting human animality to roam the mind, body, and world so it can create life. Civilization seeks to tame this life, and often this taming is founded in a tradition of humanism. Enter Peter Sloterdijk.

Where Nietzsche and his surrogate Vanessa Lemm use the word "education" to describe both the potential of culture and the limits of civilization, Sloterdijk uses "humanism" to discuss the taming forces of civilization. He describes humanism as a "telecommunication in the medium of print to underwrite friendship" that has lasted for twenty-five hundred years. He suggests that "books" embodying humanism "are thick letters to friends" (2009, 12). This friendship, though, is very special. It is a friendship limited to those who are literate, and for the early communicators of friendship there were very few in the circle. Even with a select few in the group, there are rules. "It is one of the rules of the game" Sloterdijk admits, "of literate culture that the senders cannot know their eventual recipients" (2009, 12). The first humanists wrote long love letters to friends whom they did not know but had to belong to "the cult of the literate" (2009, 13). This cult though grew even bigger as humanism connected itself to nationalism. The letters of friendship by the 1800s "were turned, through booksellers and higher education, into effective forces for nation building. What are modern nations except the effective fictions of literate publics," Sloterdijk asks, "who have become a like-minded collective of friends through reading the same books? Universal obligatory military service for young men and the universal obligation to read the classics for young people of both genders were characteristics of the classical bourgeois state" (13–14).

This friendship of the literate and of nationals has morphed today into "a media question, if we understand by media the means of communion and communication by which human beings attain to that which they can and will become" (Sloterdijk 2009, 16). Film, radio, television, the internet, cell phones, and now Facebook all have become part of the long letters people write to other friends. My BFF is no longer a literate elite, a national, or fellow marine, it is an Englishman who mimed his way onto the silver screen and our consciousness, a wooden man named Charlie McCarthy, or a shadowy person who knew all, a modern family, a binary code, or an old long-lost friend found again on a social website. Whatever humanism morphs into, Sloterdijk believes "humanism as a word and a movement always has a goal, a purpose, a rationale: it is the commitment to save men from barbarism . . . the taming of men. And its hidden thesis is: reading the right books calms the inner beast" (2009, 15).

With this taming comes domesticity. We are housed and with our housing we are separated from other animals. What concerns Sloterdijk the most is the domestication and breeding of the human animal is ushering in a new era marked by genetic engineering. With the rise of biological alterations, we have the rejoining of the humanities and sciences once again or, as Sloterdijk says, "reading and breeding have more to do with each other than cultural historians are able or willing to admit" (2009, 23). This recombination of humanism creates the (re)appearance of a different set of issues. The reading and breeding of humanism creates alarming opportunities to create humans who are "objects, not agents, of selection" (Sloterdijk 2009, 23). A "self-taming" Sloterdijk calls it (24). With this unique ability, "humans are self-fencing, self-shepherding creatures. Wherever they live, they create parks around themselves" (25). The key to self-fencing and self-shepherding is to know there are two arts, according to Sloterdijk: "herding the horned and herding the hornless; and obviously one will find the true shepherd of men only by excluding the shepherds of horned animals" (25). This new era of humanism comes with a map that is both genetic and political. The shepherds of humans will be herders of the "right" letter writers. It means non-Westerners need not apply, the poor who are reduced to gun-toting gangbangers are disqualified, as are illegals unless "they" have some skill "we" can utilize, and queers unless of course there is some breeding technique to change them or keep them in the fence/ closet. The horned critters have their own shepherds and we can find them in our homes, in zoos, preserves, and maybe in the wild, but clearly they are found in different fields away from the hornless. There is one key dimension in Sloterdijk's metaphor of human and animal difference. With the recombination of reading and breeding, horned creatures are not just nonhuman sentient beings. Horned creatures are becoming also those humans that do not have much value to an economically grotesque society. Disabled citizens of the world, the poor, women in fundamentalist-controlled areas such as Iran, Afghanistan, Pakistan, Indiana, and Texas are all horned creatures to the humanist today.

Sloterdijk leaves us with some important insights and serious warnings about the taming tendencies of a humanist society. Can we conclude that posthumanism is the route to follow in avoiding the taming forces of humanism? Does posthumanism reshape our home? One thing we can say for sure is that the rise of posthumanism cannot, in a Nietzschean sense, mean the fall and extinction of humanism. If this were the case, then posthumanism would merely be a new civilization, just as life-threatening as humanism. It is to these questions I wish to now turn.

OF FLESHY POSTHUMANISM AND FACTORY FARMING

Cary Wolfe, one of the central thinkers of posthumanism, acknowledges that posthumanism is a reaction to many developments loosely called humanism. First, posthumanism responds to the rise and development of modern man or the notion that human beings are the reason for the existence of the Earth, the meaning of life on Earth, and as a result of these first two dimensions justification for the dominance of man over all on Earth. Animals and all objects on Earth are not born with alienable rights but are granted rights by the rational thinking and benevolent voice of God on Earth: human beings. Humanism is also the rise of disciplinarity. Disciplinarity existed before and continues to exist after modern man emerged. Modernity marks an intensity of disciplined subjects who focus on specialized knowledge in order to tap into generalizable and universal laws concerning not only the human condition, but all that might surround man. At the same time modern man is emerging, so does, as Foucault established, modern disciplinary knowledge such as biology, economics, and linguistics; all proclaim to point toward human superiority.

As important as these characteristics of humanism may be, Wolfe is after something bigger to mark a difference between humanism and posthumanism. Posthumanism is a new ground for thought, and this new territory can be found in the work of Jacques Derrida and Nikolas Luhmann or second-generation cybernetics. Wolfe acknowledges that while both can be viewed as growing out of structuralism, Derrida is often seen as post-structural and cybernetics the epitome of structuralism. However, Wolfe believes they are both pointing in the same direction. "To put this schematically," Wolfe submits to his readers, "Derrida and Luhmann approach many of the same questions and articulate many of the same formal dynamics of meaning . . .

but they do so from diametrically opposed directions . . . the starting point for systems theory is the question of what makes order possible and how highly organized complexity, which is highly improbable, come into being at all. Deconstruction, on the other hand, begins with taken-for-granted intransigent structures . . . and then asks how the subversion of those structures by their own elements can be revealed" (2010, 13–14). Both theories—through principles of iterability, textuality, and writing—undermine fundamental principles of humanism and acknowledge the existence of a new reality: "that the human occupies a new place in the universe, a universe now populated by what I am prepared to call nonhuman subjects. And this is why, to me, posthumanism means not the triumphal surpassing or unmasking of something but an increase vigilance, responsibility, and humility that accompany living in a world so newly, and differently, inhabited" (2010, 47).

What Derrida and Luhmann have in common is an "openness to closure" that is "the very thing that separates us from the world connects us to the world" (Wolfe 2010, xxi). This openness to closure is found both in Derrida's principle of iterability or the ability of any text to be removed from its original context or adapt to newer meanings as it is placed in a new context. Think here not only of citation of textual passages, but also how stem cell regeneration or gene therapy works. These are all examples of life-affirming and life-creating forms of iterability. For second-generation cybernetics, the principle of iterability works through what they call "autopoiesis." Autopoiesis is a self-contained system that continually protects itself from its environment but is also open to its environment. It maintains and transforms its meaning or essence according to how it interacts with its environment. It creates and maintains life depending on how well it simultaneously protects itself and lives within an environment, an environment that can change depending on the circumstances just as the meaning of a text can change depending on the reading or a DNA strand can change depending on other sequences or environmental triggers. Both iterability and autopoiesis have in common a focus on meaning, and it is here that posthumanism emerges. These principles serve not only what Wolfe calls the psychic, but also the "social systems." It is an act of anthropocentrism to privilege the individual over the social systems. The psychic and the social systems both serve "as the environment for the other." "It is therefore false (or more gently, it is falsely chosen anthropocentrism) to assign the psychic . . . ontological priority over the social" (Wolfe 2010, 20). It is meaning making or the potential to make meaning that counts in this interaction between the psychic and social system, but just as individuals are making meaning from a system in order to maintain its autopoietic self, so is the system. Because *both* are making meaning both change, opening each up to the introduction of new environments. Therefore, the psychic in these environments can never be defined exclusively as human: The nonhuman has to be accounted for, as well.

Wolfe's new ground for thought places humanism in question and raises other questions. If nonhuman sentient beings and inorganic objects are no longer just there for our whim as lords over our dominion, then we not only see our relationship in social systems in new light, but our roles change. What changes is our ego, our anthropocentric view, what Dominic Pettman calls our exceptionalism. It is important to note that this blow to our ego and lesson in humility does not mean somehow human perspectives are now negated or null and void as if the superior court of nature has now finally spoken. "It is not a matter," Pettman consoles us, talking us down from the ledge, "of transcending our humanity, or of successfully becoming something else but of trying the best we can to acknowledge our persistent errors" in proclaiming our "exceptionalism" (2011, 198). What we can do is broaden our notion of exceptionalism. The tension in this play of exceptionality is to acknowledge different exceptionalities and become vigilantly aware of the easiness of allowing human exceptionalism to define all other views. It is easy to let anthropocentrism dictate our perspective of the world and erase other perspectives. To acknowledge our errors, our laziness to assume human exceptionality over all other exceptionalities is to forget our autopoietic environments. At the same time, to honor the exceptionalities of others is "to recognize the profound agency or presence of nonhuman existents" and acknowledge "all those 'betrayals of repressed human possibilities, of other powers of reason, of a more comprehensive logic of argument, of a more demanding responsibility concerning the power of questioning and response" (Pettman 2011, 202).

How anthropocentrism is approached and how the tension between humanism and posthumanism develops is highlighted below. At any given moment in the last couple of decades, one could pick up a newspaper, find an Internet article, or hear from a politician or interest group that thirty, thirty-five, or even forty million people in the United States are without health insurance. Compare this with the ASPCA's recent numbers: People with companion animals in the United States alone spent thirteen billion dollars on insurance, up 40 percent since 2006. The tension here between the care of millions of humans and the basic coverage of millions of animals in the United States requires us to seriously consider the *political* relations among humans, animals, institutions, and objects.

What can we say about the priorities of a country when some humans cannot get access to basic health care needs while animals can? Is this the price of posthumanism? Is posthumanism a new era in which animals enjoy more protections from life than many humans? Let's place this matter into an interspecies perspective. Every year dogs and cats are rescued and adopted from homelessness or an abusive environment, yet, according to Wolfe, "80 percent of the antibiotics used in the United States go to livestock on factory farms" and every year because of sub-specie living conditions millions of livestock are killed. In fact, "millions of chickens, turkeys, and ducks [were] killed worldwide—80 million alone in Southeast

Asia, 19 million more in Canada—to combat H5N1 avian influenza in the
Spring of 2004" (2013, 49). These disparities and their side effects, such as
the spreading of diseases from animals to humans or the passing of antibiotics, steroids, or hormones moving from the meat, milk, or blood of the
animal into the human system, have interspecies consequences. How are
we to interpret these disparities? Should we deny health care to animals
until all humans are covered? This is the sort of question posthumanist
politics must face.

MEANWHILE: AN EPILOGUE

Meanwhile, humanism continues to live and it lives in the oddest of places.
I have suggested that we look to OOO. Ian Bogost (2011) suggests that we
can use lists to stress the point that all objects maintain a being, an ontology
that always escapes unconcealment, especially the unconcealment humans
project onto the clearing and the open. What I find interesting about OOO
besides what I outlined above is what gets named in these lists and what is
relegated to the "so on" or the "meanwhile." Bogost proclaims the power
of "meanwhile" as he uses "the secret lives of meals," in particular, a photograph by Stephen Shore from 1977 of a Big Mac, fries, and a shake. This
photo reveals that objects are units. The "pickle dangles across the meat
patty, salt scuttles from fry, ice milk clings to the inside of plastic straw"
(Bogost 2012, 50). These interactions "tell us nothing about the perception
of milk on plastic, seed on bun. It simply catalogs [. . .] exemplifying the
ways that human intervention can never entirely contain the mysterious
alien worlds of objects. . . . Meanwhile," Bogost proclaims, "is a powerful
ontographical tool. The unit is both a system and a set" (50). Objects in
a McDonald's meal are just one example Bogost uses to show how OOO
works. I could go on and on or I could write after every list "and so on and
so on." A reader can find sunflowers, dust, cinderblocks, butterfat crystals,
gas bubbles, "weather patterns, resources, diseases . . . microbes . . . modes
of transportation, and so on" (Bryant 2011, 23–24). What you will not
find in any of these lists that are used to prove the significance of OOO is
anything associated with primary and secondary schooling. If there is a
reference to schooling, it is a reference to the university.
    What this relegation of all aspects of schooling represents is the stubborn
remnant of humanism lodged right in the middle of OOO and posthumanism. This is one reason why posthumanism cannot do without humanism
and needs it fundamentally. In this case, it is not because there is a need
for a tension between the creative forces of culture and the sediments of
civilization. It is because posthumanism still represents an attempt to guard
disciplinary boundaries in academia. As globalization, instrumentalism,
and pure and simple greed have reshaped the meaning and purpose of the
humanities within not only society, but also the universities, humanities

scholars are still clinging on to traditional boundaries to maintain a sense of intellectual force. In a way what is being proclaimed within these lists and the use of the words "meanwhile" and "so on" is a declaration that says "the world may be changing and may not value the humanities, but at least we are not those education people who do rubrics, lesson plans, learning objectives, and other nonsensical busywork. We in the humanities are scholars; ours is a vocation not a skill or an occupation." Of course, at one level who could argue with the humanities scholars for ignoring education? Their work is insightful and cutting-edge and many in education are not scholars; they are just utility conduits who are disconnected from deep theory and worldly concerns beyond passing tests and preparing for a workforce. But what this border guarding misses is the many ways OOO, iterability, and Systems Theory thrive in schools. Besides students, teachers, parents, janitors, and administrators, there are chairs, guinea pigs, cockroaches in too many schools, snakes, animal cadavers in the biology classroom, tables, tiles, lights, processed food, sodas, junk food of all kinds, basketball nets, paint, crayons, and so on. In schools is where the forces of creative culture and taming forces of civilization meet head-on. And posthumanists are missing this reality, this world of humans and nonhumans interacting every day. They are missing the sites where the tensions of posthumanism and humanism play out. This is one of the reasons why the taming forces are still thriving in the United States because there is not much competition challenging the humanist assumptions schools enforce to tame the creative and imaginative spirits of young people, teachers, administrators, parents, janitors, and cafeteria staff. What the humanist posthumanists in the humanities need is anthropology, another traditional humanist discipline. They need to take anthropological tours of any primary or secondary school, and they will immediately see what their lists are missing, what their ontology lacks, what being escapes their gaze.

REFERENCES

Bogost, I. (2012). *Alien Phenomenology: Or What It's Like to Be a Thing*. Minneapolis: University of Minnesota Press.

Bryant, L. (2011). *The Democracy of Objects*. Ann Arbor: Open Humanities Press.

Calarco, M. (2008). *Zoographies: The Question of the Animal from Heidegger to Derrida*. New York: Columbia University Press.

Harman, G. (2001). *Tool-Being: Heidegger and the Metaphysics of Objects*. Chicago: Open Court.

Harrison, R.P. (1992). *Forests: The Shadow of Civilization*. Chicago: University of Chicago Press.

Lemm, V. (2009). *Nietzsche's Animal Philosophy: Culture, Politics, and the Animality of the Human Being*. New York: Fordham University Press.

Pettman, D. (2011). *Human Error: Species-Being and Media Machines*. Minneapolis: University of Minnesota.

Sloterdijk, P. (2009). "Rules for the Human Zoo: A Response to the *Letter on Humanism*." *Environment and Planning D: Society and Space* 27:12–28.

Weaver, J. (2010). *Educating the Posthuman.* Rotterdam, Netherlands: Sense Publishing.

Wolfe, C. (2010). *What Is Posthumanism?* Minneapolis: University of Minnesota Press.

Wolfe, C. (2013). *Before the Law: Humans and other Animals in a Biopolitical Frame.* Chicago: University of Chicago Press.

Contributors

Annette Gough is a research professor in the School of Education at RMIT University, Melbourne, Australia. She has previously held senior appointments at RMIT University and Deakin University and has been a visiting professor at universities in Canada, South Africa, and Hong Kong. Her research interests span environmental, sustainability and science education, research methodologies, and gender studies, and she has completed research projects for national and state governments as well as working with UNESCO, UNEP, and UNESCO-UNEVOC on several research and development projects.

Noel Gough is foundation professor of outdoor and environmental education at La Trobe University, Victoria, Australia. Previously, he held senior academic appointments at the University of Canberra and Deakin University, and has held visiting fellowships at universities in Canada, South Africa, and the UK. His scholarship focuses on research methodology and curriculum studies, with particular reference to environmental education, science education, internationalization, and globalization. In 1997, he received the inaugural Australian Museum Eureka Prize for Environmental Education Research. He is the author or editor of five books, including *Curriculum Visions* (2002) and *Internationalisation and Globalisation in Mathematics and Science Education* (2007), and has published more than one hundred book chapters and journal articles. He is the founding editor of *Transnational Curriculum Inquiry*, and a member of the editorial boards of eleven other international research journals. He is also a past president (2008) of the Australian Association for Research in Education.

jan jagodzinski is a professor in the Department of Secondary Education, University of Alberta in Edmonton, Alberta, Canada. He is a founding member of the *Caucus on Social Theory in Art Education*; past editor of the *Journal of Social Theory in Art Education*; co-series editor, with Mark Bracher, of *Pedagogy, Psychoanalysis, Transformation* (Palgrave Press); as well as an editorial board member for *Psychoanalysis, Culture*

& Society and ten other journals. Book credits include *The Anamorphic I/i* (1996); *Postmodern Dilemmas: Outrageous Essays in Art&Art Education* (1997); *Pun(k) Deconstruction: Experifigural Writings in Art&Art Education* (1997); editor of *Pedagogical Desire: Transference, Seduction and the Question of Ethics* (2002); *Youth Fantasies: The Perverse Landscape of the Media* (2004); *Musical Fantasies: A Lacanian Approach* (2005); *Television and Youth: Televised Paranoia* (2008); *The Deconstruction of the Oral Eye: Art and Its Education in an Era of Designer Capitalism* (2010); *Misreading Postmodern Antigone: Marco Bellocchio's Devil in the Flesh (Diavolo in Corpo)* (2011); *Psychoanalyzing Cinema: A Productive Encounter of Lacan, Deleuze, and Zizek* (2012); and *Arts Based Research: A Critique and Proposal* (with Jason Wallin, 2013).

Alyce Miller is an award-winning fiction writer and essayist who teaches in the English department at Indiana University in Bloomington. She is also an attorney, practicing pro bono in family law and animal rights law. She has published three books of fiction and more than two hundred stories, essays, poems, articles, and book chapters in national journals and magazines. Awards include the Flannery O'Connor Award for Short Fiction, the Mary McCarthy Prize for Short Fiction, the Lawrence Prize, the Kenyon Review Award for Literary Excellence in Fiction, and various honorable mentions in Best American Short Stories, Best American Essays, Pushcart Prize Stories, and O'Henry Prize Stories. A nonfiction book is forthcoming from Reaktion Books' Animal Series. She is on the editorial boards of *HumAnimalia* and *Journal for Critical Animal Studies*.

Marla Morris is professor of education at Georgia Southern University. She is the author of *Curriculum and the Holocaust: Competing Sites of Memory and Representation* (2001); *Jewish Intellectuals and the University* (2006); *Teaching through the Ill Body* (2007); and *Scholars, Musicians and the Crisis of Psyche* (2008).

Helena Pedersen is associate professor of education at the Department of Child and Youth Studies, Stockholm University. Her primary research interests include critical animal studies, critical theory, educational philosophy, and posthumanism. She is author of *Animals in Schools: Processes and Strategies in Human-Animal Education* (2010), which received the Critical Animal Studies Book of the Year Award in 2010. Pedersen has published in journals such as *International Journal of Qualitative Studies in Education*; *Emotion, Space and Society*; *Studies in Philosophy and Education*; *Culture, Theory and Critique*; and *Culture and Organization*, and she is currently finalizing her research project on animal science education and critical posthumanist theory.

Pedersen is coeditor of the Critical Animal Studies book series (Rodopi) and serves on the editorial board of *Other Education: The Journal of Educational Alternatives*. Together with Tobias Linné and Amelie Björck, she coordinates the research theme "Exploring 'the Animal Turn': Changing Perspectives on Human–Animal Relations in Science, Society and Culture," funded by the Pufendorf Institute for Advanced Studies at Lund University 2013–2014.

Brad Petitfils earned his PhD in curriculum theory from Louisiana State University. He was initially inspired by the work of Jean Baudrillard, and has since developed research interests in the fields of hyperreality and posthumanism and how those theories affect undergraduate education and the development of adolescents and young adults. He is currently the director of Campus Planning and Assessment at Loyola University in New Orleans, but his real passion is teaching. He is an instructor in both the Department of Psychological Sciences and the Teaching Certification sequence, and is codirector of Loyola's summer abroad program in Paris, France. His first book, *Parallels & Responses to Curricular Innovation: The Possibilities of Posthumanistic Education*, is currently under contract with Routledge and is scheduled for publication in 2015.

Nikki Rotas is a PhD candidate at the Ontario Institute for Studies in Education at the University of Toronto. She specializes in curriculum studies and teacher development in the Department of Curriculum, Teaching and Learning. Nikki's research interests pertain to ecology, embodiment, and relational learning processes and artistic practices. Her doctoral research focuses on school gardens and student ecological intra-activity within urban settings. She is currently working as a research assistant on two Social Sciences and Humanities Research Council (SSHRC) grants on relational and interventionist art practices.

Nathan Snaza teaches modern fiction, feminist and queer theory, and educational foundations at the University of Richmond, where he is director of the Bridge to Success program. His writings have appeared journals such as *Journal of Curriculum and Pedagogy*, *Educational Researcher*, *Angelaki*, and *Journal for Critical Animal Studies*, as well as in several edited collections. His present research considers the institutionalization of disciplines, especially those involving the study and teaching of language, across humanist history in an effort to imagine posthumanist ways of thinking about education, language, politics, and community that exceed anthropocentrism. A book project based on this research, tentatively titled *AnimaLiterature*, is in its early stages.

Stephanie Springgay is an associate professor in the Department of Curriculum, Teaching, and Learning at the Ontario Institute for Studies in

Education, University of Toronto. Her research focuses on the intersections between contemporary art and pedagogy, with a particular interest in theories of movement and affect. Her most recent research-creation projects are documented at www.thepedagogicalimpulse.com and www. artistsoupkitchen.com. She has published widely in academic journals and is the coeditor of the book *M/othering a Bodied Curriculum: Theories and Practices of Relational Teaching* (with Debra Freedman, 2012); coeditor of *Curriculum and the Cultural Body* (with Debra Freedman, 2007); and author of *Body Knowledge and Curriculum: Pedagogies of Touch in Youth and Visual Culture* (2008).

Jason Wallin is associate professor of Media and Youth Culture Studies in Curriculum at the Faculty of Education at the University of Alberta, Canada, where he teaches courses in visual art, popular culture, and cultural curriculum theory. Jason is author of *A Deleuzian Approach to Curriculum: Essays on a Pedagogical Life* (2010); coauthor of *Arts-Based Research: A Critique and Proposal* (with jan jagodzinski, 2013); coeditor of *Educational, Psychological, and Behavioral Considerations in Niche Online Communities* (with Vivek Venkatesh, Juan Carlos Castro, and Jason Lewis, 2013); and coeditor of *Deleuze, Guattari, Politics and Education* (with Matt Carlin, 2014). Jason is assistant editor for the *Journal of Curriculum and Pedagogy* (Routledge) and reviews editor for *Deleuze Studies* (Edinburgh University Press).

John A. Weaver is professor of curriculum studies at Georgia Southern University. He is the author of *Educating the Posthuman* (2010); *Popular Culture: A Primer* (2004–2008); and *Rethinking Academic Politics in Germany and the United States* (2000); and editor of four other books, including *(Post) Modern Science (Education)* (with Peter Appelbaum and Marla Morris, 2001). His next book project is tentatively titled *God, Darwin, Homophobes, and an Invisible Hand*, dealing with religion, economics, and science.

Index